FV_

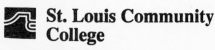

Comedy/
Cinema/Theory

Comedy/ Cinema/Theory

Edited by
Andrew Horton

University of California Press
Berkeley / Los Angeles / Oxford

University of California Press
Berkeley and Los Angeles, California

University of California Press, Ltd.
Oxford, England

Library of Congress Cataloging-in-Publication Data

Comedy/cinema/theory / edited by Andrew Horton.
    p.   cm.
    Includes bibliographical references and index.
    ISBN 0-520-06997-8 (alk. paper). — ISBN 0-520-07040-2 (pbk. :
alk. paper)
    1. Comedy films—History and criticism. 2. Comic, The.
I. Horton, Andrew.
PN1995.9.C55C65 1991
791.43'617—dc20   90-42213
                                                          CIP

Printed in the United States of America

9 8 7 6 5 4 3 2 1

The paper used in this publication meets the minimum requirements of American National Standard
for Information Sciences—Permanence of Paper for
Printed Library Materials, ANSI Z39.48-1984. ♾ ™

Stills by courtesy of Avala Film, Columbia Pictures,
the Museum of Modern Art, Paramount Pictures,
Samuel Goldwyn Company, Slovenska Filmova Tvorba,
Warner Brothers, and the authors.

Contents

Comic Occasions

Acknowledgments

To Odette who has laughed with me so often in cinemas around the world.

To the National Endowment for the Humanities for a yearlong College Faculty Fellowship (1977–1978) to participate in a seminar on comedy, to the University of New Orleans for various summer research grants, to Bill Nichols who encouraged this project from the beginning, and to various friends and colleagues in film studies, including John Belton, Fredric Jameson (who had contemplated an essay on Jacques Tati and the image of the clown in postindustrial capitalism!), Dan Georgakas, Douglas Gomery, Srdjan Karanovic, and Jacek Fuksiewicz, who have read different versions of proposals and chapters and made useful comments.

To all of the contributors. They have patiently supported the project through its evolution with good humor and cheer, especially Lucy Fischer, who initially helped me to focus the concept of this work.

To Ernest Callenbach, my editor, who deserves an Aristophanic Award for his large-hearted and clear-sighted guidance of the anthology through the numerous stages at the University of California Press.

And to all of those comics who have made me laugh, ranging from Buster Keaton and Luis Buñuel through to Preston Sturges, Woody Allen, the Coen Brothers (*Raising Arizona*), and Gyorgy Szomjas of Hungary.

Introduction

Andrew Horton

> Let the wise and philosophic
> choose me for my wisdom's sake.
> Those who joy in mirth and laughter
> choose me for the jests I make.
>
> Aristophanes, *Assemblywomen*

> *Nobody's perfect.*
> Joe E. Brown, the closing line of *Some Like It
> Hot,* upon learning that his bride-to-be (Jack
> Lemmon) is a man

Beginnings: The Unbearable Lightness of Comic Film Theory

Matters comic have recently begun to receive systematic and theoretical attention (see Selected Bibliography). But a few years ago only one broad survey, the late Gerald Mast's *The Comic Mind*, had been devoted to the subject of film comedy. His study wisely recognized the danger of the "swamp of abstract debate on the nature of comedy and the comic" and provided us with some broadly useful concepts about film comedy, especially in terms of the "comic climate" that cues viewers to expect comedy "even if we do not know what Comedy is" (9).

Nevertheless, his analysis of comedy in terms of eight comic *structures* and what he calls "comic thought" appears incomplete and restrictive in light both of theoretical work available in film, literary, and dramatic studies and of theoretical perspectives that have proven fruitful since 1979. Jerry Palmer (20–21) has recently detailed these main shortcomings. The difficulty in trying to locate the comic in plot structures, as Palmer rightly identifies, is that "the plot structures either are not specifically funny, not specific to comedy in any sense of the word, or they are not in fact plot structures, but refer to the minimum unit of comic plot, the individual joke or gag" (28).

No plot is inherently funny. Put another way, as we shall see, any plot is potentially comic, melodramatic, or tragic, or perhaps all three at once. Sophocles' *Oedipus Rex,* for instance, is constructed on what Mast identifies as comic structures 3 and 4: the reductio ad absurdum in which a sin-

1

gle mistake produces utter chaos and an investigation of the workings of a particular society that compares the responses of one social group or class with those of another. And yet apart from the tragic irony that Oedipus does not know who he is, and the use of "jokes" within several scenes based on the audience's superior knowledge, everyone agrees the play is not a comedy.

No totalizing theory of comedy has proved successful. The vastness of the territory, which includes the nature of laughter, humor, the comic, satire, parody, farce, burlesque, the grotesque, the lyrical, romance, metacomedy, and wit, precludes facile generalizations. As Harry Levin has recently written, "If there were any single generalization that could be applied with equal relevance to Chaucer, Mark Twain, Evelyn Waugh, Milan Kundera, Milesian tales, Jewish jokes, banana peels, mechanical toys, content analysis, laugh counts, broadcasts, cartoons, monkeys, hyenas, and tickling it would be much too sweeping for any plane but that of pointless platitude" (6).

Furthermore, there is a historical bias against a close and serious consideration of comedy. That comic films seldom win Academy Awards even though comedy reigns at the box office (six out of the top ten selling films in 1988) is only the latest example in a long history of criticism that has viewed comedy as inferior to other genres in Western culture. Since Aristotle designated comedy "an artistic imitation of men of an inferior moral bent" (12), it has escaped the close schematization that the epic and tragedy have undergone in Western literary theory.

And let us not forget one simple reason comedy has escaped close scrutiny: the comic is enjoyable. Why risk destroying pleasure? This is particularly true when a closer examination may well reveal a much darker subtext/context. As one critic notes of happy endings in Aristophanes' comedies, for instance, "If the only way to achieve this happy ending is to invert the order of the world, then there is something seriously wrong with world order as it stands" (McLeish, 76).

But it is just such a double awareness that this collection aims to provide. Such fresh perspectives can lead to increased pleasure and, yes, to even further laughter.

Comedy/Cinema/Theory wishes to broaden the theoretical and critical horizons regarding the study of film comedy. These chapters are not encyclopedic. Nor are they focused only on film comedy, for issues related to comic theory often apply equally to literature or drama or other expressions of the comic. Also many familiar comic films and personas are absent from these discussions. And some of the chapters have been commissioned because they go beyond the accepted comic canon: the inclusion of Alfred Hitchcock (Dana Polan, "The Light Side of Genius"), the Three

Stooges (Peter Brunette, "The Three Stooges and the (Anti-)Narrative of Violence"), and Jerry Lewis (Scott Bukatman, "Paralysis in Motion").

Furthermore the collection is divided into two simple parts—those chapters that are more weighted toward theoretical issues and therefore use a variety of examples from films to support the discussion and those chapters that more clearly use theory to illuminate particular films. The majority of the chapters concern American comedy because Hollywood has traditionally exerted a dominant influence on world film comedy. André Bazin suggests just how critical a role comedy plays within American cinema itself:

> Comedy was in reality the most serious genre in Hollywood, in the sense that it reflected, through the comic mode, the deepest moral and social beliefs of American life. (35)

Rather than limit the book to merely Hollywood comedy, however, each part is "capped" with a chapter on comedy from foreign cinema to suggest how comedy can be and has been approached from very different perspectives abroad.

The Sunny Side of the Street: Comic Perspectives

I wish to provide a brief context for the chapters that follow and to suggest additional perspectives from which comedy and film comedy might usefully be observed in future studies. Because too much theoretical writing on comedy from Aristotle to Freud has been essentialist ("The comic *is* . . ."), the following remarks are meant to be nonessentialist ("The comic *can be seen as* . . .") and thus open-ended. "The point is," writes Albert Cook, "to probe its [comedy's] depths, not to chop it into portions" (31).

Consider, for instance, how often comedy and tragedy (or, in Hitchcock's view, "suspense") blend into each other. Remember that at the end of Plato's *Symposium* Aristophanes and Socrates remained awake discussing how comedy and tragedy probably had similar origins. Both developed out of ritual celebrations for Dionysus, the god of drama and wine, and both involve, through differing routes, insight into the limitations and capabilities of human potential. "The great works of comic writing [and we can add film] have extended the range of our feelings," says George McFadden (243). More than a dramatic or literary genre, comedy has been viewed in recent years as a particular *quality* (McFadden) or vision, as Robert W. Corrigan holds when he explains that "comedy celebrates his [man's] capacity to endure" (3).

Two recent studies stand out as particularly useful. David Marc in *Comic Visions* takes a contextual/cultural perspective in analyzing television comedy and suggests that contemporary American "mass culture" can be seen as a comedy, albeit laced with ironic and even tragic overtones. In speaking of Norman Mailer's protagonist Rojack in *An American Dream,* Marc notes, "The capacity to experience, even for a moment, the comic beauty of America as 'a jeweled city' before falling prey to the tragedy of the poison gases lurking beneath the surface is what allows Rojack to keep his sanity" (9). Within this context, Marc suggests that American television offers two distinct forms of comedy: stand-up comedy and situation comedy. And as he notes, "Aesthetically at odds, these two genres of mass humor form a Janus face of American culture" (12) because stand-up comedy champions individualism and at least potentially radical ideologies, whereas situation comedy favors the status quo and social consensus. In part, Marc's book is useful for film studies because it does designate a difference between the territory carved out by film and the territory mapped out by television in American culture (neither of the two television genres has become the staple of American film comedy).

Also valuable for our purposes is Palmer's semiotic reading of film and television comedy in *The Logic of the Absurd.* Semiotics allows Palmer to read the signifying systems of comedy in their artistic shapes and organic forms. Put simply, semiotics permits us to better grasp *how* comedy works. But from the start, Palmer's investigation rightfully sweeps aside several issues that have troubled those who have pondered the comic in the past. He remarks, for instance, that laughter is no guarantee of humor (30) for it may also come from nervousness in the face of danger, grief, and so on.

Palmer's close attention to how comedy is constructed and functions also leads him to see the "double" possibility of the comic as conservative or subversive or even both at once, depending on the audience and context. As Palmer notes, semiotics can explain conservative and subversive structures within a joke, but it "is not capable of telling us whether jokes about Irish stupidity contribute to racial prejudice against the Irish" (86).

For a broader point of view, we need to search beyond semiotics. Others, such as Ludwig Wittgenstein, who have written on the theory of comedy have viewed comedy not as a genre but as a special form of "games" (195). Rather than attempting to circumscribe comedy, Wittgenstein describes it as a form of gamelike activity (like language itself) in which we can discover "family resemblances," a network of similarities that can be noted and discussed. He further suggests that such a nonessentialist view allows us to "draw a boundary for a special purpose" (section 69). In a similar vein Johan Huizinga writes provocatively about humans as *Homo ludens,* and various psychiatrists have linked comedy to "creativity" in general. Child psychiatrist D. W. Winnicott goes beyond Aristotle's observation that a baby becomes "human" around the fortieth day when he or she begins to *laugh*. According to Winnicott, a child is an "individual" by age one because at that time he or she begins to separate as well as combine fantasy and "reality" through *play*, thus constructing a "personal world" (7).

Comedy, creativity, play. These boundaries suggest a combination of control and freedom, an awareness of stated or implied rules/codes, and the imagination/fantasy to manipulate them. They also point to *pleasure* as Sigmund Freud describes in his analysis of wit, jokes, and dreams (224), no matter what aims are attributed to the comic (moral or otherwise). And as psychoanalytic theory from Freud to Jacques Lacan and beyond helps us understand, much of that pleasure has to do with temporarily suspending the "rules" of adulthood and returning, albeit symbolically, to an earlier, pre-Oedipal state. Indeed, the realm of comedy is similar to and intersects with the traditional realms of carnival and festivity, time periods when the rules and regulations of a society are briefly suspended.

A. Van Gennep, Victor Turner, and others have more precisely identified this condition as "liminality": that space of freedom between the set rules of a society (Turner, 23). Comedy evokes such an in-between state. A work that is identified in any way as comic automatically predisposes its audience to enter a state of liminality where the everyday is turned upside down and where cause and effect can be triumphed over and manipulated. Comedy thus can be partially described as a playful realm of consecrated freedom.

Back to Basics

Noël Carroll's chapter, "Notes on the Sight Gag," and Peter Lehman's chapter, "Penis-size Jokes and Their Relation to Hollywood's Unconscious," suggest the minimal units of comedy: gags (visual) and jokes (verbal). Let us consider these twin basic elements of comedy more closely.

Arthur Koestler's overlooked concept of "biosociation" and comedy is useful in helping us understand the basis of film comedy. Building on Henri Bergson's mechanistic theory of the comic and Freud's analysis of jokes and the unconscious, Koestler takes an even broader view. He observes that comedy (verbal and physical) involves the joining of "two or more independent and self contained logical chains," which creates biosociation: a "flash" (release) of emotional tension upon their intersection in the reader/viewer's mind (30). This observation helps us consider the nature of the junctions among the multiple signifying chains within a film: dialogue/image/nonverbal sound/music.

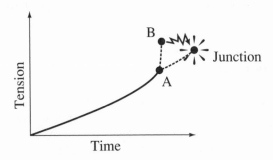

Comic biosociation

Furthermore, biosociation helps to differentiate comic from noncomic forms. No flash occurs in tragic and melodramatic structures. Rather, the narrative is constructed to involve the audience's concern (anticipation/emotion) throughout. Comedy, on the other hand, is constructed to suggest several logical chains (Koestler's phrase) that create a mixture of surprise and anticipation when they suddenly cross. Koestler diagrams various examples of such comic biosociation. The figure presented here is typical for any comic exchange (joke/gag). Elaborating on Freud's description of "economy" in humor, Koestler defines biosociation more precisely:

> One cannot tell two stories simultaneously. At "A" the narrator must leave the first association train, and let it follow its course along the dotted line as automatic expectation in the reader's mind, while he himself starts the second train at "B" and conducts it towards the crash. *This second train has to move very fast lest the first should meanwhile lose its steam, and the flash cease to be a flash.* (31)

Let us borrow from Woody Allen to see this process in practice. Woody has said in his early stand-up engagements when asked if he believes in God, "I believe that there is an intelligent spirit that controls the universe, except certain parts of New Jersey." The biosociation is the sudden flash of recognition as "A" (the theological question) and "B" ("certain parts of New Jersey") collide.

Although Palmer makes no reference to Koestler, his semiological reading of comedy is almost identical. Palmer is, however, even more precise in his study of what happens in a joke or gag. Borrowing the Greek term *peripeteia* (reversal) from discussions of tragedy, he suggests that a gag/joke results from a peripeteia, which thus evokes both surprise and anticipation when a pair of syllogisms leads to a contradictory conclusion (42). The fact that a joke or gag is concerned with two syllogisms has to do with the intersection of the *plausible* and the *implausible*.

In the Woody Allen example the syllogisms would be:

1. "Do you believe in God?" is a common theological question (major premise).
2. Allen's concluding phrase "except certain parts of New Jersey" (minor premise) appears to run contrary to any concept of an omnipotent being.
3. Conclusion: the answer is implausible because of its apparent contradiction.

And yet we are simultaneously aware of a second set of possibilities:

1. New Jersey is viewed as something of an industrial and cultural wasteland, particularly by staunch New Yorkers.
2. An intelligent spirit, particularly one housed in a New Yorker's body, might indeed choose not to associate with New Jersey.
3. Therefore the answer has an element of plausibility.

Therefore, as both Koestler and Palmer suggest, an understanding of the "double vision" of jokes and gags is inseparable from an appreciation of the structure and effect of humor and comedy in general. Palmer states that "when the spectator decodes a gag (syntagm), he does so by seeking a paradigm or paradigms that 'make sense' of the syntagm" (110). It is this flash of awareness in Koestler's terms, or the appreciation of the simultaneously plausible and implausible syllogisms in Palmer's view, that helps explain how by trying to "make sense" we are suddenly thrown into a third level of insight.

Comedy and the Deconstructive Spirit

I have previously stated in my review of Gerald Mast's study that no narrative is inherently comic. But I am now in a position to suggest that comedies are interlocking sequences of jokes and gags that place narrative in the foreground, in which case the comedy leans in varying degrees toward some dimension of the noncomic (realism, romance, fantasy), or that use narrative as only a loose excuse for holding together moments of comic business (as in a Marx Brothers' film).

The work of Jacques Derrida can take us even further in a study of film comedy and narrative. Derrida clearly views his critical activity as an outgrowth of many who have gone before him including Georg Hegel, Edmund Husserl, Friedrich Nietzsche, Martin Heidegger, Jean-Paul Sartre, and Maurice Merleau-Ponty. At its base, Derrida's activity has a subversive thrust similar to comedy's (especially the carnivalesque) subversion of norms. Jonathan Culler describes deconstruction as an attitude of *play* that exposes how a text "undermines the philosophy it asserts" (240). Derrida expresses himself even more revealingly:

> To risk meaning *nothing* is to start to *play* . . . and first to enter into the play of *différance*, which prevents any word, any concept, any major enunciation from coming to summarize and to govern from the theological presence of a *center* movement and textual spacing of differences. (14; emphasis my own)

In a sense Derrida takes Wittgenstein's concept of language as "game" (play) to its extreme. The result is an attitude that mirrors Heraclitus— "All is flux"—for our contemporary world. All hierarchies, power, and constructs are shown to contain the traces of *différance*, of their own overthrow, negation, destruction. Such an attitude toward texts suggests the need for playfulness in creators and audience and the double awareness Palmer speaks of. For deconstruction shows, as Geoffrey H. Hartman explains, "the sense of a serious, unending game, both in the writer who plays language against itself and in the reader who must uncover without losing track, the gamut of language" (1).

Let us be more specific as we consider film comedy. Derrida's writings do suggest how interwoven play is with the serious and the serious with play. To be *Homo ludens* is to be *aware:* to be alert to others and to alternatives, probabilities, possibilities, and chance (that major factor in games of every sort). Thus, play and discipline go together. Not to be aware is to be a victim, a fool, a braggart, a dictator.

Deconstructive attitudes help us to appreciate those filmmakers who use comic elements to play "against the grain" in numerous ways. Even though Jean-Luc Godard has been much analyzed, far too little attention has been paid to the *comic* dimension of his "disruptive" cinema. He has been restlessly obsessed with exploring and exposing cinematic *language,* attempting to reach what he calls "zero" in various ways. Godard has at times sounded much like Derrida when pronouncing that his films are not films but *attempts* to make films. Certainly by classical definitions Godard is not a "comic" filmmaker (no happy endings, for instance). But in the expanded sense of play and the comic as an ongoing, multifaceted critique (which, as Hartman suggests, is pleasurable), Godard can be more clearly revealed as working in the realm of comedy.

Derrida is fully aware of the irony of using language to expose language. Godard does likewise: he explores film language with film. What makes each of them *Homo ludens* is that instead of despairing that there are limitations to expression (language/film) and turning to suicide or silence, they have chosen instead to continue expressing themselves and thus to play. In such a perspective, a "happy ending" is not an important criterion for identifying the comic. Neither, strictly speaking, is the evocation of laughter (although there are some very funny moments in Godard). What emerges is the pleasure Godard takes in subverting traditional film narrative and codes of articulation, what Derrida refers to as "joyous Nietzschean affirmation."

Deconstructive theory also points to the ludic role of the viewer. Rather than being a passive member of the audience, the viewer who "plays" is actively involved. From Derrida's position, there are no observers because there are no fixed subjects or "selves" (identities), only *participants*. Such an attitude coincides with much of reader-response theory, which makes similar claims for the existence of "the text" as depending in large part on the active recreation of it in the mind of the reader/viewer (who is also in constant flux, as Heraclitus would remind us). The comic has always depended on a special relationship between creator and viewer/reader, a bond described as "a state of *conspiratorial irony*" (McLeish, 17) in Aristophanes' plays and, by implication, in all comic works. More specifically, this means that whereas tragic and melodramatic texts tend to hide their artifice in order to involve the audience emotionally, comic texts tend to acknowledge the presence of the reader/viewer (the frequent direct address of Aristophanes' characters to the audience, Chaplin's glances at the camera, or Woody Allen's opening direct-camera monologue in *Annie Hall* [1977]) and therefore reveal the texts' artifice. This self-consciousness of comedy helps establish the amount of "distance" required for the unfolding characters and events to be taken as ludic rather than tragic. Although tragedy can employ soliloquies, we rarely find an Oedipus, Willy Loman, or Citizen Kane speaking directly to the camera and thus to *us*.

Beyond simply speaking of the comic as a form of play, therefore, deconstruction points to comedy as an intensified version of language and behavior. Traditional comic theory has spoken of comedy as social and tragedy as individual. These more recent perspectives are more precise. Like language and "texts" in general, the comic is plural, unfinalized, disseminative, dependent on *context* and the intertextuality of creator, text, and contemplator. It is not, in other words, just the *content* of comedy that is significant but also its "conspiratorial" relationship with the viewer (reader). Such a conspiratorial relationship is explored by Stephen Mamber in his chapter, "In Search of Radical Metacinema," particularly in regard to parody.

Tragedy is also necessarily dialogic (a system of interrelated discourses among creator/text/contemplator). But as I have already established, tragedy (and other noncomic forms) seeks to isolate or at least reduce the number of "discourses" in order to imply a sense of "fate" and inevitability as opposed to an awareness of potentiality and "unfinalizedness" (Mikhail

Bakhtin's term). And tragedy has traditionally performed this role by effacing a direct awareness of contact between creator and contemplator.

Pre-Oedipal and Oedipal Comedy

Traditionally we think of two major divisions of comic characters: antagonists (*eirons*) and the butts of jokes and gags (*alazons*). More recently, such classical theory has been sharpened by Harry Levin, who sees these types as *playboys* (the ludicrous: those with whom we laugh) and *killjoys* (the ridiculous: those whom we laugh at). The breakdown of traditional comedy in the twentieth century and the establishment of so-called meta-comedy can be seen, in Levin's terms, in the merging of these two main comic types. Figures in the works of Samuel Beckett, Bertolt Brecht, James Joyce, and others are both ludicrous and ridiculous, playboys and killjoys simultaneously. Jerry Palmer, on the other hand, establishes four types of comic character (167–168): the everyday joke teller who has no "character"; the stand-up comic with a consistent public persona; the stereotypical character "positioned according to needs of the punch line"; and the fully drawn comic character.

Naturally, what I have said of gags and narrative holds true of character as well. As the comic character moves away from the "purity" of the simple gag or joke, other noncomic elements increasingly become involved in the makeup of the character's identity. Clearly we know none of the Keystone Kops as individuals, whereas Robin Williams in *Good Morning, Vietnam* (1987) emerges as a complex figure, part wise fool, part romantic activist caught up in a war he neither fully embraces nor rejects.

Two further distinctions help us proceed even further in determining the potential of comic characters. It is common to see a family division between Aristophanic (old) comedy and Shakespearean (new) comedy. More specifically, scholars such as Northrop Frye have seen this division as one between a social/political/intellectually pointed form of comedy (Aristophanic) and a romantic, emotional, and relational form of comedy (Shakespearean). Frye calls the latter the comedy of "the green world" (215).

In light of developments in psychoanalytic theory, however, it seems more useful to speak of Oedipal (accommodation, compromise, social integration) comedy and pre-Oedipal (wish fulfillment, dreams) comedy. Freud speaks of the comic as a sudden adult regaining of "the lost laughter of childhood" (224). If we consider children in their pre-Oedipal phase— that is, before they have confronted and resolved their Oedipal conflicts and thus integrated a sense of self with the needs of socialization with others—Aristophanes emerges as our only pure example of a form of comedy in which wish fulfillment without parental or social hindrance is clearly seen.

In most of Aristophanes' surviving comedies, a middle-aged adult goes through three stages: he or she is dissatisfied, dreams up a plan to cure that dissatisfaction, and then carries out that plan to a successful resolution. The final phase is a glorious celebration of the character's success. Lysistrata (*Lysistrata*) ends war by organizing a successful sex strike, Trygaios concludes his separate peace with Zeus (*Peace*), and Agorakrites (*Knights*) rids Athens of a pesky demagogue. A wish and a fulfillment. If, as several critics suggest, comedy in general produces pleasure and a sense of "euphoria," no comedy has been so wide open and euphoric as the brand practiced by Aristophanes. I will speak later of the festive elements of old comedy, but here let me say that Aristophanes' works present characters who dream incredible fantasies (Cloudcuckooland in *The Birds*) and, with only minor "blocking" episodes (*agons*), realize those fantasies, thus transforming all of society. Such is the stuff of stage comedy but also of childlike wish fulfillment.

If we apply this division to cinema, we see how rare this Aristophanic orientation in comic characterization has been. Most screen comedy concerns romance (new comedy) of one form or another, and romance requires personal compromise and social integration, as traditionally represented in the final marriage. Such comedy is therefore Oedipal or, as several of the chapters here that employ Lacan's terms suggest, such comedy exists in the realm of the *symbolic* (awareness of self and the beginnings of language use) as opposed to that of the *imaginary* (close bonding with the mother and no control of language).

The characters, no matter how much they have turned the everyday world upside down during the narrative, must act like "adults" to the degree of committing themselves to each other and thus to life within society. They change; society remains the same. They may have had their flings and fantasies and acted them out (*A Midsummer Night's Dream* and the rest of William Shakespeare's comedies), but in the end, order is restored, and the rules of society are maintained. From Chaplin through screwball comedy and on to Woody Allen in American film comedy, no matter how nutty or carried away the characters become, commitment to heterosexual partnerships ultimately means that some Oedipal resolution must emerge. For Chaplin, rejection rather than acceptance is most often the conclusion—thus the image of the lone Tramp in the final shot. In the sophisticated world of screwball comedy, the conclusion may project the couple's zany behavior into the future (*His Girl Friday* [1940], in which Cary Grant and Rosalind Russell must once again postpone a honeymoon to cover a hot story), while still showing that both individuals have modified their desires to be in tune with each other. And Woody Allen can at times push Oedipal comedy to the limit, as he does in *Bananas* (1971), which ends not with a traditional wedding but with Woody in bed with his wife, making love live on national television as Howard Cosell provides a "blow-by-blow" description. Even though such behavior seems to many to fall close to pre-Oedipal, we recognize that Woody and his mate are returned to a real locale—Manhattan, where the unusual is often the norm—and that if such an ending is not an Oedipal *resolution,* it is at least the beginning of a compromise!

Regarding pre-Oedipal examples, we can turn to those comic filmmakers less involved with the "emotional" realm of Oedipal comedy and more attracted to what has traditionally been labeled "farce," "slap-stick," and even "anarchistic comedy." The Keystone Kops are prime candidates, as are the Marx Brothers and much of Stan Laurel and Oliver Hardy, Bud Abbott and Lou Costello, the Three Stooges, and in more recent cinema, Mel Brooks. Even the surrealist comic-satirical films of Luis Buñuel can benefit from being considered from a pre-Oedipal perspective. For the implications of this state allow us to see that in films such as *Viridiana* (1961), *Tristana* (1970), *Discreet Charm of the Bourgeoisie* (1972), and *Phantom of Liberty* (1974), Buñuel, as a surrealist, intends to destroy *playfully* the compromises and thus the ideologies and repressions that he sees afflicting Western culture. Precisely because these comedies are less rooted in the everyday world, we can come to understand the mechanisms by which they are often more funny and more "liberating" than Oedipal comic works.

William Paul broadens our understanding of Chaplin's cinematic character by discussing a "pre-Oedipal" topic, "Charles Chaplin and the Annals of Anality." Scott Bukatman finds much of Jerry Lewis's near hysteria in Jerry's inability to fully enter the realm of the symbolic, or Oedipal. Ruth Perlmutter, on the other hand, adds to our appreciation of Woody Allen's polyphonic talent ("Woody Allen's *Zelig*") by demonstrating how the point of Zelig's chameleonlike adaptability in *Zelig* (1983) is in fact a comic parody of a Jewish-American desire for complete assimilation within American culture—a state, of course, that defeats Oedipal resolution and individuation.

Carnivalesque vs. Literary Comedy

Pre-Oedipal comedy has much in common with a spirit of carnival. Yet another set of boundaries within comedy (which thus affects the kinds of characters inhabiting the narratives) is between the comic that evolves from folk festivals and street humor, on the one hand, and from literature, on the other. In his influential study of medieval and Renaissance folk comedy, *Rabelais and His World,* Mikhail Bakhtin speaks of the liberating effects of European festive folk culture, as seen most clearly in the many festive occasions that fell under the heading of carnival. Bakhtin has aided us in more clearly realizing how "universal, democratic, and free" such carnivalesque laughter was for "the people" in preindustrial and precapitalistic cultures. Carnival, Bakhtin reminds us, was a time of sanctioned freedom when through masquerading, role reversal, games, eating, drinking, and making love, almost any behavior was permitted (short of murder and so on). "Renaissance laughter was," he writes, "one of the essential forms of the truth concerning the world as a whole, concerning history and man" (66). (That such freedom was a thousand-year-old blending of pagan and Christian elements that could lead not only to personal and social release but also to revolution has been further documented by Emmanuel Le Roy Ladurie.) Bakhtin has helped refocus our understanding of comedy through his discussion of carnival laughter by explaining both the all inclusiveness of carnival (what he terms *grotesque realism*) and the deep *ambivalence* of it. Such "laughter degrades and materializes" (20), he notes, holding that even the themes of abuse, death, and dismemberment as well as the scatological lead to "the world's revival and renewal" (7) by establishing an unfinalized state of *becoming*.

Few films deal directly with carnival, although as I discuss in my chapter, "The Mouse Who Wanted to F—k a Cow," Dusan Makavejev's films come as close to the spirit of carnival as any films ever made. But Bakhtin's critique has far-reaching consequences for our closer evaluation and appreciation of film comedy, as many of the chapters here suggest (Brunette, Fischer, Horton, Paul, Perlmutter). Of course, we can see immediately that there is much in common between pre-Oedipal and carnivalesque comedy. Aristophanes embodies as much "street" festivity as he does wish fulfillment. Building comic forms from the festive celebrations from which comedy developed, Aristophanes had the privilege of working with a living tradition of social release that we in contemporary times have almost wholly lost. But the pre-Oedipal and the Oedipal cross in carnival laughter, as we see in Shakespeare's comedies. C. L. Barber's excellent study, *Shakespeare's Festive Comedy,* convincingly depicts the living carnivalesque conventions from which Shakespeare was able to fashion his "green world" comedies.

Bakhtin's perspective enables us to see the carnivalesque backgrounds of Chaplin (vaudeville), Keaton (vaudeville acrobat), and W. C. Fields (vaudeville juggler) as well as the general "nonliterary" backdrop of silent comedy forms and filmmakers from Mack Sennett to early Frank Capra. The Keystone Kops, after all, lived and romped *in the street,* receiving their sanctioned freedom not from the Catholic church feast day calendar but from Mack Sennett himself, who, like those practitioners of another carnivalesque form, commedia dell'arte, raised improvisation to an artistic peak. Clearly the Marx Brothers work, joke, and "destroy" in a carnivalesque freedom and frenzy as well. For them, every day is a holiday, uncontrolled by society's schedules and norms.

The pure fun of the carnivalesque seems apparent. Yet it is Bakhtin's insistence on the high seriousness of such release that is also worth studying. Even though Federico Fellini is usually labeled a surrealist or social satirist, a consideration of his work in light of carnival laughter and festive forms should prove even more illuminating. His concern for clowns, whores, grotesques, circuses, and nonlinear construction of narrative is in part a reflection of Italian festive culture. *Amarcord* (1974) begins with a village festival burning "old man winter," a framing scene that thereby casts the entire film as an outgrowth of a village celebration of death and renewal. The depth of feeling and nostalgia generated by Fellini, on the other hand, is a result of his awareness not only of the passing of time but also of the clash of such a traditional festive world with the nonfestive demands of contemporary European culture.

"Literary" comedy began with the Romans as the carnivalesque elements were separated out and the "well-structured" plays of Terrence and those who followed remained. Certainly when film turned from the silent image to the sound movie, much of American comedy (and, one suspects, that of other countries as well) derived directly from playwrights shipped to the West Coast to reproduce on film the kinds of success they had enjoyed on the stage. At its best, as in the screwball tradition, Hollywood comedy has managed a tricky balance between the carnivalesque and the literary. As Brian Henderson suggests in his chapter, "Cartoon and Narrative in the Films of Frank Tashlin and Preston Sturges," nobody wrote better comedy than Preston Sturges, and yet much of our pleasure in watching and rewatching *Lady Eve* (1941), *Miracle at Morgan Creek* (1944), and *Hail the Conquering Hero* (1944) derives from the loony bevy of "street" folk, complete with their dialects, malapropisms, and puppet show–like movements, who inhabit his films.

William Paul and I make use of Bakhtin's approach to suggest how the sexual (the "lower bodily stratum") is represented or repressed on the screen. Ruth Perlmutter examines Woody Allen's carnivalesque sense of parody. She traces how all of modern history becomes the plaything of his Jewish protagonist's frail or nonexistent sense of identity. Peter Brunette also finds that Bakhtin's remarks help explain how the Three Stooges work against any "logical" sense of narrative as Hollywood has traditionally constructed it.

Class Consciousness and Comedy

What are the political relations between comedy and society? Bakhtin clearly roots his theory of carnivalesque laughter in culture and history. "Every act of world history was accompanied by a laughing chorus," he remarks (474). Thus for him, folk humor is universal and has never been "merged with the official culture of the ruling class" (474). To a large degree, therefore, an analysis of the carnivalesque in its many manifestations and implications is a study of class conflict, of hierarchies of power, of the need for group celebration and individual expression. The kinds of broad-based dialectical studies of literature practiced by such observers as Terry Eagleton and Fredric Jameson surely can aid a closer comprehension of cinematic comedy as well.

If comedy has often been described as a dramatic and/or narrative form ending in triumph, then the proverbial "happy ending" of Hollywood narratives bears scrutiny as a conscious or unconscious ideological requirement in a highly commercialized culture and industry. Is it an accident that film comedy may be capitalistic America's finest cinematic hour? And on a broader scale, what implications can we draw from the split between popular tastes and critical acclaim (particularly in the form of the Academy Awards) when year after year comedies such as *Beverly Hills Cop* (1984), *Raiders of the Lost Ark* (1981) (comedy-adventure-romance), *Ruthless People* (1986), and *The Naked Gun* (1988) top the box office charts only to be snubbed at Academy Awards time.

"Arretez cette comédie!" (Stop this comedy!) orders the marquis at the height of the confusion in Jean Renoir's *La règle du jeu* (Rules of the Game, 1939). "Which one?" replies the butler, ironically named Corneille, as a multitude of sexual "gag sequences" are in full swing before him.

So much of comedy does depend on perspective. And the dialectical critique of the range of possible perspectives that a Marxist or politicized orientation offers is definitely of value. In Renoir's comic drama (which ends with the hero's death rather than marriage), romantic and sexual interests abound between the upper class of aging aristocrats and the pretentious nouveaux riches, among the servant class, and in the combinations in between. The latter is depicted by two figures outside the highly class structured French society on the verge of World War II: Octave (played by Renoir), who describes himself as a parasite on his wealthy friends, and Marceau, who enjoys poaching other men's wives as well as their game. As presented by Renoir, every character is part of one farce or another. Which farce to focus on does depend, as the majordomo wryly suggests, on one's point of view. A Marxist perspective need not dwell only on the obvious social dichotomies.

On the aesthetic level a Marxist "boundary" helps us to see that the breakdown of the comic formula based on classical romantic comedy is in part due to the increasingly fragmented sense of the old order in the interwar period of the 1930s. Following in the distinguished comic French tradition that includes Pierre Carlet de Marivaux, Georges Feydeau, and Victorien Sardou, however, Renoir shows a modern hero (trans-Atlantic pilot-adventurer), André, who ends up as a fool for love on the ground in matters of the heart and so becomes a victim of the rules of the game of aristocratic behavior. A politicized point of view could indicate that although classical Athens could tolerate Aristophanes' sharp but inventive comedies, those in power in France in 1939 were too fragile and sensitive to allow Renoir's razor-sharp critique to be screened (it was not seen in France until after World War II).

Charles Eidsvik's chapter on European leftist comedy ("Mock Realism") makes us aware that a political viewpoint is always ambiguous or double-edged. What seems a radical leftist comedy to one generation may seem conservative propaganda to another. And socialist regimes believing in the value of labor and the perfectability of the individual are, as Eidsvik demonstrates, every bit as much easy targets for comedy as are puritan cultures of the past.

Feminism and the Comic Perspective

We can also observe the implications of a politicized view of comedy through a feminist lens. Joe E. Brown's splendid response in Billy Wilder's *Some Like It Hot* (1959) when he learns that by marrying Jack Lemmon, he will be marrying a man—"Nobody's perfect"—suggests the complicated and intriguing (in all senses) topic of gender and comedy. As Lucy Fischer admirably discusses in her chapter, not only are women's mothers often missing in film comedies; an integrated sense of women or "woman" in general is also distorted, masked, and repressed in much of the comic (patriarchal) tradition. Because so many women writing about film (and literature) see their discourse as a "counter-history, or re-vision" (Doane, Mellencamp, & Williams), like much of comedy itself, their writing has necessarily existed in a "space" outside, around, and in opposition to the implied and stated norms of patriarchal society.

A feminist perspective necessarily involves a critique of the comic film canon. Beyond the facile observation that most comedies, like most films in general, have been made by men, and perhaps almost exclusively from a male perspective (the so-called male gaze), lies the more challenging work of examining how gender is used and abused in comedy and how other forms of comedy more sympathetic and less repressive of human potential (male or female) might be constructed. (I am here acknowledging the strongly felt conviction of many feminist critics that it is not enough to simply criticize but that at an ideological/aesthetic level new possibilities should be identified and encouraged.)

The playful consideration of gender is evident in our Western tradition beginning with Aristophanes; consider the productions of *Lysistrata, Assemblywomen,* and *Thesmophoriazousai* in particular. But Aristophanes was hardly a feminist, and his comic treatment of gender was a means to an end rather than the goal itself. We remember, for instance, that all actors at the time were male; thus, Aristophanes could count on the added irony in a comedy such as *Lysistrata* that while "women" were staging a protest against their men who are off at war, the women were being played by men all along. This assumption of female roles is familiar to us in Shakespeare's times as well. And we should note that such a "men in drag" tradition has been a standard one in film comedy also, from the silent comedies through such classics as *Some Like It Hot* and on to the 1980s, which witnessed the forefronting of the question of gender in films as diverse as *Tootsie* (1982), *The World According to Garp* (1982), *Working Girl* (1988), and *Big Business* (1988).

We need more carefully considered feminist studies to suggest how much of a change these more recent films indicate or how much they may still be solidly within the partriarchal comic tradition. Linda Martin and Kerry Segrave in *Women in Comedy*, for example, detail how American comediennes since the early days of vaudeville have had to fight against a strong sexist bias against women in comedy; "Comedy is aggressive and hard," they write, and "women are not supposed to be hard" (21). Thus, most comediennes have had to get laughs by being much more self-disparaging than their male counterparts.

Tootsie, for instance, does bring out such lines as Dustin Hoffman's comment near the end, "I was a better man as a woman than I was when I was a man." Yet the film is told from a male point of view, is made by men (director and writers, except for Elaine May who was one of eleven who worked on the project!), and presents a conventional "romantic" ending in which the female lead, Jessica Lange, is clearly involved with another man, Hoffman, before we see her having a chance to live fully on her own.

Some women filmmakers with comic talent have begun to appear in the American commercial cinema. Susan Seidelman, director of *Desperately Seeking Susan* (1985), is clearly one example behind the camera, and Bette Midler has emerged as a representative of strongly self-assured women in films such as *Outrageous Fortune* (1987), *Big Business* (1988), and *Beaches* (1989).

How far women have to go, however, in the world of Hollywood comedy can be seen in the case of Whoopi Goldberg. A film such as *Jumpin' Jack Flash* (1986) allows Whoopi room to do what she does best as a spirited black woman with a sharp tongue: talk tough and dirty to those men (mostly white) who attempt to put her down, take advantage, or make unwarranted advances. But there is a double danger here. One concerns narrative: for despite all her streetwise New York independence, the film's narrative requires that she finally soften, compromise, and walk off with a . . . white man in what is a traditional romantic (Oedipal) comic Hollywood ending. There is also the danger that in capitalizing on Whoopi's acid tongue, the film never allows her to be more than a negative concept of "woman." All we know is that she can outargue, outcurse, and outthink (she is a computer expert) the males who surround her. Is she a New Woman or a Tough Man? It can be said that the *elasticity* of the Hollywood system is evident here. The potentially threatening force presented (black/ strong/intelligent female) is allowed a certain amount of "free play" but is ultimately integrated into the traditional patriarchal social and aesthetic norms of a "happy" romantic ending.

Finally, a feminist perspective could aid us in viewing such a film as an update of the screwball comedy tradition. Even though the films in this tradition usually highlight the union of a couple from divergent social classes (aristocracy and the middle class in most cases), *Jumpin' Jack Flash* accomplishes the same task according to race, with, one might add, an ironic twist. The white male is not American, but British.

It is perhaps fitting to end an overview of feminism and comedy by returning to origins. Feminist commentators might well make more use of studies, such as those by Jane Ellen Harrison, into the origins of the celebrations and ceremonies dedicated to the god of comedy and tragedy, Dionysus. Dionysus was twice born: of Semele, his mother, and of Zeus (placed in Zeus' thigh for protection), his father. Tragedy grew from the tradition of dithyrambs, group lyric praises to Dionysus, and comedy from phallic songs sung by a *komos*—that is, a band of male revellers. In actual fact, both the dithyrambs and *komos* served a similar function: they were group (thus social) invocations (sacred and profane) to Dionysus for rebirth, fertility, and protected growth to maturity.

But who is Dionysus? It is significant that he is not a Greek god but an Asian one and that instead of being a patriarch, as is Zeus the "father," Dionysus is always represented as a *kouros,* a young man who is masculine as well as delicate and feminine (he has, for example, long, flowing, golden hair). Analysis of these rituals further shows that in addition to being a *kouros,* Dionysus is represented as a *son.* Thus, in their origins both comedy and tragedy are concerned with a form of initiation rite that aids Dionysus in moving from a sphere of influence associated with the mother (Semele and, by extension, the matriarchal cultures that preceded classical Greek culture) to that of the father, Zeus. This "second birth" is thus necessarily symbolic and mimetic: hence drama. Jane Harrison sums up by relating the Dionysus cult to an earlier *kouros* cult from Crete:

> Both are the reflection of a group religion and of social conditions which are matriarchal and emphasize the figure of Mother and Child. The cardinal doctrine of both religions is the doctrine of the New Birth, and this doctrine is the reflection of social initiation. (49)

Dionysus, the twice-born god, offers us a double vision. In origin, comedy and tragedy—that is, drama as an aesthetic form—are about "growing up": we view the movement from the biological and emotional connections with the mother to the socialized world of the father (the realm of the symbolic). Comedy and tragedy are also, it would appear, about the evolution of Greek culture from matriarchy to patriarchy.

Certainly none of this discussion of the ritual origins of comedy may seem directly related to Burt Reynolds's Good Ole Boys comedies, Jerry Lewis's "hysterical" farces, or Cantinflas's (Mario Moreno) long reign over Spanish-language comedies. Yet from a theoretical viewpoint, such ancient patterns of gender behavior do have contemporary implications that should not go unexamined.

That's Not All, Folks!: Comedy on Film

The boundaries I have discussed are not established by treaties. In practice, we would do well to draw from several perspectives at once. Indeed, these chapters reflect such challenging merges of theoretical influences. Much of the preceding exploration has necessarily treated comedy in general, with specific examples drawn from cinema. But it remains for us to ask what is there *specifically about cinema* that may contribute to comedy and the comic.

Film comedy is deeply rooted in the comic traditions of the cultures in which it is produced as well as in the tradition of film comedy itself (Luis Buñuel imitates Buster Keaton in several key sequences in *Un Chien Andalou* [1928], for example). But there is at least one aspect of film that has helped to shape film comedy. I am speaking of film's ability to destroy and manipulate time and space for its own purposes. If, as I have suggested, much of the comic involves fantasy, festivity, wishes, attempts at wish fulfillment, a turning upside down of the norms of everyday society, and thus a joyous, free-wheeling sense of pleasure and freedom, then the ability to "play" with time and space offers the comic filmmaker an almost limitless spectrum of possibilities. From the comic surrealism of Keaton's *Sherlock, Jr.* (1924), in which the movie projectionist protagonist is buffeted about by the changes in "locations" while he attempts to climb into a film from the movie theater (a concept that Woody Allen more recently played with in *The Purple Rose of Cairo* [1985]), to the carefully controlled soundtracks to Jacques Tati's French social farces, cinema as a medium has made possible what a Giovanni Boccaccio or a Ben Jonson could only dream about.

References and Additional Reading

Aristotle. 1947. *Aristotle on the Art of Poetry*, trans. and ed. Lane Cooper. Ithaca: Cornell University Press.

Bakhtin, Mikhail. 1968. *Rabelais and His World*, trans. Helene Iswolsky. Cambridge, Mass.: MIT Press.

Barber, C. L. 1959. *Shakespeare's Festive Comedy*. Princeton: Princeton University Press.

Bazin, André. 1982. *The Cinema of Cruelty*, trans. Saline D'Estrec. New York: Seaver Books.

Bermel, Albert. 1982. *Farce: From Aristophanes to Woody Allen*. New York: Simon and Schuster.

Brunette, Peter, and David Wills. 1989. *Screen/play: Derrida and Film Theory*. Princeton: Princeton University Press.

Cook, Albert. 1949. *The Dark Voyage and the Golden Mean: A Philosophy of Comedy*. Cambridge, Mass.: Harvard University Press.

Corrigan, Robert W., ed. 1971. *Comedy: A Critical Anthology*. Boston: Houghton Mifflin.

Culler, Jonathan. 1982. *On Deconstruction*. Ithaca, N.Y.: Cornell University Press.

Derrida, Jacques. 1981. *Positions*, trans. Alan Bass. Chicago: University of Chicago Press.

Doane, Mary Ann, Patricia Mellencamp, and Linda Williams, eds. 1984. *Re-vision: Essays in Feminist Film Criticism*. Los Angeles: American Film Institute.

Eagleton, Terry. 1983. *Literary Theory: An Introduction*. Minneapolis: University of Minnesota Press.

Freud, Sigmund. 1938. *Jokes and Their Relationship to the Unconscious*, trans. A. A. Brill. New York: Random House.

Frye, Northrop. 1968. *Anatomy of Criticism*. New York: Atheneum.

Gurewitch, Morton. 1975. *Comedy: The Irrational Vision*. Ithaca, N.Y.: Cornell University Press.

Harrison, Jane Ellen. 1963. *Themis: A Study of the Social Origins of Greek Religion*, 2nd ed. London: Merlin Press.

Hartman, Geoffrey H. 1981. *Saving the Text: Literature-Derrida-Philosophy*. Baltimore: Johns Hopkins University Press.

Harvey, James. 1987. *Romantic Comedy in Hollywood from Lubitsch to Sturges*. New York: Knopf.

Huizinga, Johan. 1955. *Homo Ludens: A Study of the Play Element in Culture*. Boston: Beacon Press.

Jameson, Fredric. 1972. *The Prison-House of Language: A Critical Account of Structuralism and Russian Formalism*. Princeton: Princeton University Press.

Janco, Richard. 1984. *Aristotle on Comedy*. Berkeley: University of California Press.

Kael, Pauline. 1974. "Raising Kane." *The Citizen Kane Book*. New York: Bantam.

Kerr, Walter. 1967. *Tragedy and Comedy*. New York: Simon and Schuster.

Koestler, Arthur. 1949. *Insight and Outlook*. Lincoln: University of Nebraska Press.

Lacan, Jacques. 1979. *The Four Fundamental Concepts of Psychoanalysis*, trans. Alan Sheridan. Harmondsworth: Le Seminaire Livre XI.

Ladurie, Emmanuel Le Roy. 1981. *Carnival in Romans: A People's Uprising at Romans, 1579–80*, trans. Mary Feeney. New York: Penguin.

Lang, Candace D. 1987. *Irony/Humor: Critical Paradigms*. Baltimore: Johns Hopkins University Press.

Levin, Harry. 1987. *Playboys + Killjoys: An Essay in the Theory of Comedy*. New York: Oxford University Press.

McFadden, George. 1982. *Discovering the Comic*. Princeton: Princeton University Press.

McLeish, Kenneth. 1980. *The Theatre of Aristophanes*. New York: Taplinger.

Marc, David. 1989. *Comic Visions: Television Comedy and American Culture*. Boston: Unwin Hyman.

Martin, Linda, and Kerry Segrave. 1986. *Women in Comedy*. Secaucus, N.J.: Citadel Press.

Mast, Gerald. 1979. *The Comic Mind: Comedy and the Movies*, 2nd ed. Chicago: University of Chicago Press.

Merchant, Moelwyn. 1972. *Comedy: The Critical Idiom*. London: Methuen.

Metz, Christian. 1974. *Film Language: A Semiotics of the Cinema*. New York: Oxford University Press.

Mulkay, Michael. 1988. *On Humor*. Oxford: Basil Blackwell.

Palmer, Jerry. 1988. *The Logic of the Absurd: On Film and Television Comedy*. London: British Film Institute.

Rosen, Philip, ed. 1986. *Narrative, Apparatus, Ideology*. New York: Columbia University Press.

Swabey, Marie Collins. 1961. *Comic Laughter: A Philosophical Essay*. New Haven: Yale University Press.

Sypher, Wylie, ed. 1956. *Comedy*. Garden City, N.Y.: Doubleday.

Todorov, Tzvetan. 1984. *Mikhail Bakhtin: The Dialogical Principle*, trans. Wlad Godzich. Minneapolis: University of Minnesota Press.

Turner, Victor. 1982. *From Ritual to Theatre*. New York: Performing Arts Journal Publications.

Truffaut, François. 1967. *Hitchcock*. New York: Simon and Schuster.

Van Gennep, Arnold. 1960. *The Rites of Passage*, trans. Monika Vizedom and Gabrielle Caffee. Chicago: University of Chicago Press.

Winnicott, D. W. 1969. *The Child, The Family, and the Outside World*. Harmondsworth: Penguin.

Wittgenstein, Ludwig. 1968. *Philosophical Investigations*. Oxford: Basil Blackwell.

Problematics of Film Comedy

Notes on the Sight Gag

Noël Carroll

Although claims about "firsts" always seem disputable when it comes to the history of film, a case can be made that the first film was a comedy— depending on whether one dates *Fred Ott's Sneeze* as having been made in 1889 or 1892. In any case, comedy appeared early in film history. Thomas Edison provided peep shows of clowns and a kinetoscope series entitled *Monkeyshines,* which, at least, suggests comic doings. In terms of films made for the screen, the first Lumière show in 1895 contained one comedy, *L'Arroseur Arrosé,* in which a hapless gardener gets a face full of water when a prankster toys with his hose.

Comedy of a sort, of course, also figures largely in the films of Georges Méliès—although not comedy of the variety one usually associates with gags or jokes. It is more a matter of joy borne of marvelous transformations and physically impossible events: bodies blown apart and then reassembled—with unwanted fat emulsified. This is comedy that derives from exploiting the magical properties of cinema, a comedy of metaphysical release that celebrates the possibility of substituting the laws of physics with the laws of the imagination. Méliès's experiments gave rise to the early genre of the trick film, which promotes levity by animating the inanimate and by visualizing a fantastic physics. Here, the undeniably high spirits evoked seem less concerned with what we typically call humor and more involved with indulging a newfound freedom, the power of molding the physical world in accordance with the fancy—in short, a kind of cosmic wish fulfillment.

Early comedy also gravitated toward roughhouse and slapstick. Here the major theme was mayhem. Buffoons, marked by only slightly disguised clown outfits, would be set into exaggerated fisticuffs, discharging pistol shots into each other's behinds, jabbing each other with pitchforks, and clunking each other on the head with bricks. Because these clowns were signaled to be not quite human, they could be pummeled, dragged, hurled, hosed, burned, and stomped with impunity. Their fantastic biologies allowed the free reign of sadism in terms of either comic debacles or sprawling accidents, after the fashion of the Keystone Kops. In these cases, comedy was generally less a function of structure than of the transgression of social inhibitions about the proper way in which to treat the human body.

Whereas the trick film transgressed the laws of physics, films by people such as Mack Sennett tended to transgress the laws of society, especially in terms of the norms of respect appropriate to the handling of persons. In both cases, the comedy in question proceeded simply by displaying transgressive material. Gradually, however, a more structural type of comedy became a major source of humor in silent film. This was the sight gag.[1] And it is about the sight gag that this chapter is concerned.

The sight gag is a form of visual humor in which amusement is generated by the play of alternative interpretations projected by the image or image series. Sight gags existed in theater prior to their cinematic refinement, and sight gags, although they are regarded as a hallmark of the silent comedy, can occur in films that are neither silent nor comic. To orient our discussion, consider a famous example of a sight gag in Alfred Hitchcock's *The 39 Steps* (1934). The character played by Robert Donat has been manacled to a woman who positively hates him. They come to an inn, where the landlady takes them to be intensely affectionate newlyweds. Their closeness is in fact mandated by the handcuffs, and when Donat pulls his prisoner toward him, this is in order to get more control over her. The landlady misinterprets these gestures as further signs of the "lovers'" infatuation, although we hear them exchanging hostilities. The scene is shot and blocked in such a way that we not only know how things actually stand between these "lovers," but we also simultaneously see how someone in the landlady's position could systematically misinterpret the situation. Our amusement is generated by the fact that the scene is staged to show not only what is actually going on but how that set of events could also visually support an alternative, and in this case conflicting, interpretation. And it is this play of alternative, often conflicting interpretations, rooted first and foremost in the visual organization of the scene, that primarily causes the amusement that attends sight gags.

The type of humor of which the sight gag is a subcategory is often analyzed in terms of incongruity. On this view, amusement is provoked by the juxtaposition of incongruous elements. Comic duos, for example, are often composed by pairing a very fat man (or woman) with a thin man (or woman), or a tall, thin actor with a short, fat one, and so on. In the preceding example from Hitchcock, what is juxtaposed are two incompatible interpretations: that of a loving couple versus that of a hateful couple.

Stated schematically, the incongruity theory of humor says that comic amusement is an emotional state. Like all, or at least most, emotional states, comic amusement is identified by its object. The object of comic amusement is humor, where among the central criteria for what can be humorous—its *formal object*, to revert to philosophical jargon—is incongruity. The perception of incongruity in an event or situation amuses us, which in turn causes the risible sensations—laughter, for example—that we feel in response to humor. With sight gags, the loci of the relevant incongruities are the alternative, generally opposed interpretations put in play visually by the image.

Sight gags differ from verbal jokes. Verbal jokes generally culminate in a punchline that at first glance is incongruous by virtue of its appearing to be nonsense. Once the punchline is delivered, however, the audience has to give it an unexpected, although latently predictable or retrospectively comprehensible, interpretation that makes sense out of the incongruity. Succeeding in this, the audience is amused and the result is standardly laughter. For example: what do you get when you cross a chicken with a hawk? Answer: a quail. At first, this answer is nonsensical until you realize that "quail" is a pun on "Quayle" and that "chicken" and "hawk" are being used metaphorically, not literally. In order to appreciate this joke, one must reinterpret the riddle in light of the punchline in a way that effectively amounts to retelling the joke material to oneself. One is initially stymied by the incongruity of the punchline, which leads to a *re*interpretation of the joke material that makes it comprehensible.

Sight gags also involve a play of interpretations. But with sight gags, the play of interpretation is often visually available to the audience simultaneously throughout the gag; the audience *need not* await something akin to the punchline in a verbal joke to put the interpretative play in motion.

To get a better handle on the nature of the sight gag, let us examine some major recurring types of this sort of cinematic humor. The following list does not pretend to be exhaustive; nor would I claim that some of these categories might not be so interwoven in specific cases that classifying a given gag neatly under one or another of my labels might not become daunting. In other words, I am aware of some conceptual slippage in this incomplete taxonomy, but I offer it nevertheless in the hope that future researchers will use its shortcomings to develop more precise formulations. So, without further ceremony, some leading types of sight gag include the following.

(1) *The mutual interference or interpenetration of two (or more) series of events (or scenarios).* This is far and away the most frequent form of the sight gag. It does not originate in cinema; in 1900 Henri Bergson identified it in his book *Laughter* with respect to theater. Nevertheless, this form is a staple of cinema, especially of the Golden Age of Silent Comedy. The previous example from *The 39 Steps* exemplifies this type of sight gag. One way to characterize it is to say that it is staged in such a way that an event, under one description, can be seen as two or more distinct, and perhaps in some sense mutually exclusive, series of events that interpenetrate each other. Thus, the event of the couple's seeking lodging at the inn in *The 39 Steps* can also be seen as two events—one from the perspective of the landlady and the other from the perspective of the couple—which events interpenetrate each other (i.e., have overlapping elements) in such a way that two interpretations of what is going on are comprehensible. This is not to say that even within the fiction both interpretations are equally sound, but only that we can *see* how both could be plausible, often plausible relative to different points of view.

Many of the most famous sight gags in silent comedy fall into this category. For another concrete example, let us look at the second gag depicting Harold's arrival at Tate College in Harold Lloyd's *The Freshman* (1925). Harold, yearning to be popular, has just mistaken a group of students at the train station to be welcoming him to Tate. Then a tight shot follows of a man at the train window lighting his pipe. He strikes a match along the edge of the window, and he drops the match out of the frame. Next there is an extreme close shot of the match landing on a white woolen background. The ensuing medium shot identifies the white woolen background as Harold's sweater. Lloyd cuts back to the shot of the match; the sweater is starting to burn. Back to the medium shot—the man with the pipe looks down and sees that his carelessly dropped match is burning Harold's sweater. The man with the pipe bends out of the train window and slaps Harold on the back in order to snuff out the flame. The blow is a hard one, and it momentarily knocks Harold off balance. By the time Harold turns around to see who hit him, the man with the pipe has recomposed himself and sits reading his paper. Standing behind Harold is a man previously identified as the Dean of Tate. His back is turned toward Harold; he is talking to a distinguished-looking group. To Harold's mind, we suppose, the Dean is the only possible person who could have slapped him on the back, a slap, by the way, that Harold seems to interpret as a robust greeting. Harold hits the Dean on the back, nearly knocking him over. Lloyd cuts to a close shot of the Dean's face; he is astounded and enraged. Lloyd cuts to a close shot of Harold attempting to introduce himself. The ensuing close shot of the angered Dean, identifying himself, bodes badly for Harold's future at Tate.

Within this single event—call it Harold slapping the Dean on the back—there are three interlocking events or scenarios, each correlating with the perspective of one of the scene's leading agents. There is the event of the smoker stanching the fire, the event of Harold reciprocating a welcoming slap on the back, and the event of the Dean being insulted. Each of these events or scenarios causally interpenetrates the others in significant ways; none of the characters appears to be aware of views of the event alternative to his own. Indeed, none of the characters has the overall interpretation of the event that the audience has, for the simple reason that none of the characters is positioned in the fiction to see everything we see. Moreover, some of these event descriptions, as relativized to characters' points of view, directly conflict. Harold thinks that he is making a friend just as he is making an enemy. And it is this incongruous conflict of interpretations rooted visually in the play of points of view that gives the scene its humorous edge.

Because this particular type of sight gag is so pervasive, discussion and analysis of a further example of it may be fruitful. Johnnie's entry into Northern territory in Buster Keaton's *The General* (1926) comes to mind here. The scene begins with the title, "The Southern army facing Chattanooga is ordered to retreat." There is a shot of Southern cavalry troops waving a retreat signal. Then a shot of the Union spies shows them crouching in the cab of The General (the hijacked locomotive). Finally we see Johnnie. In an overhead shot over the timber car, he can be seen cutting wood. Keaton then cuts to a shot of the retreating Southerners. Initially it is a long shot. Then all of a sudden the front of The Texas (the locomotive with which Johnnie is pursuing The General) pulls into the foreground from screen right. The Texas drives past the camera, revealing that Johnnie is still chopping wood with his back to the battle. This is quite an ingenious shot not only in its use of foreground and background to set out the significant facts of the situation but also in its channeling of the relevant facts to the audience sequentially, thereby effectively replicating the detailed, phased selectivity available in editing in the context of the realism of the single shot.

The battle ensues behind Johnnie's back. The Southerners retreat entirely, and the Union troops triumphantly spill onto the field behind Johnnie. Now he is in enemy territory. Yet he continues to chop. At one point, he breaks his ax handle. But even at this rupture in his work pattern, he remains unaware that he is completely surrounded by hostile Union troops. In all, it takes twelve shots before Johnnie realizes his predicament. He is so absolutely engrossed in his work that he never once glances outside his narrow work area.

Here again there is a striking incongruity between two interpretations of the shot, both of which are made visually comprehensible to the audience. On the one hand, Johnnie's fortunes have changed dramatically; he is in the grip of the enemy. On the other hand, from his perspective, which we can understand by noting the fixity of his attention, his position remains relatively benign. The disparity of viewpoints, made evident in the staging of the action, gives rise to a play of conflicting interpretations of the situation, and this gives rise to amusement.

Key to this Keaton gag, as to many other Keaton gags, is the character's inattention or unawareness of the surrounding environment—an inattention that is palpably portrayed in the shooting.[2] Often sight gags rest on this sort of monumentally unaware character. We laugh at the clown headed for a pratfall as he approaches a discarded banana peel because we see the banana peel and he doesn't *and* because we see that he doesn't see the banana peel. This gives birth to two divergent interpretations of the scene: one in terms of what we see is the case and another in terms of what we see the protagonist sees and takes to be the case. This incongruity, available visually to the spectator, is the source of humor in the situation. Our amusement is not purely sadistic pleasure at someone taking a fall. Rather, the pleasure comes of a visually motivated conflict of interpretations over the nature of the scene. Two different interpretations of an event collide, or, to put the matter differently, the actual situation or event interferes with the protagonist's imagined picture of the event, with the net effect that the protagonist's expectations have been reversed.

Yet another way to put this is that the event progresses under two scenarios—here, notably, that of the comic butt, on the one hand, and of "reality," so to speak, on the other. For our purposes, we will require of candidates for this sort of sight gag that there be at least two scenarios (visible in the image or image series), that these scenarios be at odds with each other, and that the disparity between them portends a mishap (i.e., one of the scenarios *interferes* with the other).

Generally, sight gags of the mutual interference of two series of events (or scenarios) variety often occur where the character's view of the situation diverges from the reality of the situation. Thus, the relevant conflict of interpretations emerges from the disjunction of the character's point of view—which is a function of the situation being laid out in such a way that the spectator can see why the character fails to see it properly—and the way the situation is. Again, this structure differs from the standard case of verbal jokes. For with verbal jokes, our second interpretation deals with the incongruous punchline, whereas with this sort of sight gag we have two or more alternative and often conflicting interpretations before us throughout most of the gag.

(2) *The mimed metaphor.* Silent film, of course, employed a great deal of pantomime. Sometimes pantomime was engaged to produce a very spe-

Charlie Chaplin in The Pawnshop *(1916)*

cial sort of sight gag, one in which the audience came to see an object metaphorically equated with something that it was not. Mime functioned figuratively to produce visual similes between disparate sets of objects. In *The Gold Rush* (1925), Charlie Chaplin treats a boot as a meal. The shoe laces become spaghetti; the nails, bones; the sole, a filet. In the same film, candle wicks become eggs. In *The Rink* (1916), Chaplin holds a chicken aloft in a way that suggests a bird in flight; when the stuffings fall out of the rear and hit a customer in the eye, it is hard to resist seeing them as bird droppings from on high. And in *The Pawnshop* (1916), Chaplin does a virtuoso number with an alarm clock. His surrounding gesticulations make the clock seeable as a heart and then as a sardine can. And when its inner cogs rush about on the counter like so many insects, Chaplin turns his oil can into an insecticide. Earlier in the same film, Chaplin transforms doughnuts into barbells and teacups into dish towels. In such cases, humor arises through seeing objects in their literal aspect at the very same time that the miming gesticulation enables us to see them otherwise: to see cogs as bugs or nails as turkey bones. The operation here is essentially metaphorical; disparate objects are identified for the purpose of foregrounding similes, in this case visual similes. This abets the play of incongruous interpretations. For the selfsame object can be seen either literally or figuratively.

The preceding examples all hail from Chaplin. And this is no accident. For Chaplin is particularly invested in the theme of imagination, and it is an essential feature of his character that he can see things differently from others, that is to say, imaginatively. But the device is evident throughout silent comedy. In *Cops* (1922), Keaton beautifully metamorphoses an accordion extension (of the sort associated with telephones) into an arm while also portraying a ladder as a seesaw and then as a catapult. This type of sight gag is probably more popular in silent film than in sound film—in contrast to the mutual interference gag, which is crucial to both—but it has exemplars in sound film as well. One recalls the house with eyes in Jacques Tati's *Mon oncle* (1958) and the tire as funeral wreath in his *Mr. Hulot's Vacation* (1953);[3] there is also the metaphor of glass as nothing in *Playtime* (1967), when the doorman, with only a handle to speak of, acquits his duty as if he had a door at his disposal. And, indeed, the very glass he has not got, shattered as it is, is recycled as ice cubes.

With the mimed metaphor, the audience is invited through the prompting gesticulations of the mime to consider objects under alternative interpretations. This is not akin to the famous duck-rabbit examples discussed by psychologists, however, for we can see the nail as a bone at the same time we see the nail as a nail. The humor in the situation rides on the possibility of its simultaneous play of interpretations, which interpretations are nevertheless delightfully opposed, allowing and even encouraging alternative—literal versus metaphorical—views.

In speaking of mimed metaphors, a distinction is meant to be marked here between what is mimed and mimes that provoke metaphors, that is, mimes that are implicit similes. When Keaton's Steamboat Bill, Jr., attempts to tell Steamboat Bill, Sr., that he has given him a saw, he mimes sawing off his thumb. This is not a mimed metaphor. For no object is being analogized to a disparate object. This is miming pure and simple. With mimed metaphors, it is important that the audience has before it, imaginatively speaking, radically disparate objects that are being equated for the purpose of analogizing them in a context where the point—the very wit in question—is that the audience appreciates the success of the analogy in the face of its unlikelihood. Ordinarily, this will require that we be able to identify the literal object and the metaphor independently and that we speak of two objects. Chaplin's "sailboat" turns constitute a real problem here. For when he pivots, throwing out his leg as if to shift a sail, it is not easy to describe that movement literally—that is, independently of saying it is a "sailboat" turn. Perhaps a different category—body metaphors?—will have to be introduced to accommodate examples such as this.

Mimed metaphors may also function by evoking linguistic idioms or verbal metaphors. In *College* (1927), Keaton plays a high school valedictorian who speaks on the evils of sport. As his diatribe revs up, he lurches exaggeratedly from left to right while standing in place. We note that the assembled local dignitaries in the background shift position with him. Keaton is, so to speak, "swaying the audience," and we view this scene both literally and under the aegis of the unexpected and amusing metaphor.[4]

Mimed metaphors differ from mutual interference gags in that the alternative points of view need not be relativized to any characters, that they need not result in mishaps, and that they are directed more at objects than at events, although as the last example from Keaton indicates, they may operate on situations.

(3) *The switch image.* A famous shot in Chaplin's *The Immigrant* (1917) shows the Tramp leaning over the railing of a boat and lurching to and fro. We think he is seasick and vomiting; but he turns around, and we see that he has been struggling to land a big fish. Or, again from Chaplin—more than once—we see his shoulders heaving. We infer sobbing and sorrow. But the figure seen frontally is mixing a drink. In Lloyd's *Safety Last* (1923), we initially think that we are to be witnesses to an execution, but we soon realize that we have been fooled into regarding a farewell scene as death row, just as in Keaton's *Cops* we initially think that the suitor is in prison when he is only on the other side of a gate. Or Tati shows us an airline terminal that we initially think is a hospital waiting room. Likewise, in Keaton's *The Boat* (1921), we first take him to be caught in a storm at sea, whereas a subsequent image shows him to be the victim of his children pulling on the ropes in his garage.

In these cases, the image is given to the audience under one interpretation, which is subverted with the addition of subsequent information. The initial image is subsequently shown to be radically underdetermined. At first, it seems to mean one thing unequivocally in terms of its visual information, but then it means something entirely, and unexpectedly, other. Switch images are lessons in visual ambiguity.

Unlike most mimed metaphors, switch images pertain to events rather than objects, and their dual aspects are generally perceived sequentially rather than simultaneously. Unlike mutual interference gags, switch images need not be relativized to any character, and they may involve no mishap. Switch images may be thought of as the interpenetration of visually distinct events without interference. That is, the two alternative interpretations of the scene—the literal and the metaphorical—are not embedded in the narrative in such a way that disaster befalls anyone. Or, to put it differently, the alternate interpretations are not narrativized in a way that they causally impinge upon each other.

Buster Keaton in The Boat *(1921)*

Switch images tend to be found at the *beginnings* of films and sequences. An obvious reason for this may be that at such points the filmmaker does not have a large number of narrative commitments and implications that need to be camouflaged in the imagery.[5] But, there is no reason in principle that a switch image cannot occur in the middle of a shot, perhaps by way of a playfully deceptive scale variation.

In some ways, the switch image resembles a verbal joke. For once the initial image is subverted, part of our pleasure involves noting the way in which our first identification of the image was misguided. That is, switch images abet a limited play of reinterpretation. Nevertheless, switch images are distinct from verbal jokes in that the first image, unlike the punchline of a joke, need not be absurd or incongruous.

(4) *The switch movement.* In Chaplin's *The Pawnshop,* the Tramp spends a great deal of time fighting with his office mate. On one occasion,

the boss walks in, and, midair, the Tramp's punch changes its trajectory and heads for the floor, where he falls to his knees and begins scrubbing. One movement—the punch—is transformed into another—washing the floor—in one seamless line of movement. Or, again, the Tramp has his adversary straitjacketed between the rungs of a ladder. He feigns high-class, dancerly boxing poses, torturing his helpless opponent with tweaks on the nose. A cop appears behind the Tramp, and, aware of the cop's presence, the Tramp's pugilistic dodges become swaying, waltzlike steps—as if the whole time he had been dancing rather than street-fighting. The Tramp, continuing this deception, glides back into the pawnshop, and seeing the disapproving visage of his boss, he transforms his prancing pivot into a businesslike strut.

In all these cases, the Tramp is out to deceive an authority figure by seamlessly metamorphosing a questionable movement activity into an innocent one—as if to say, for example: "You thought I was fighting, but I was only dancing," or "You thought I was dancing, but I am really off to work." Such switch movements often occur in narrative contexts of deception, although they need not.

Switch movements are to actions as puns are to sentences. They derail one line of thought and send it in another direction. The gesture or series of gestures upon which a switch movement pivots are like a pun in that they can take different meanings in different movement contexts. Switching from one meaning potential of a movement to another provokes an alternative interpretation of initial action. Just as our earlier pun—quail/Quayle—plays on the aural similarity of two different words in order to prompt interpretive amusement, the Tramp exploits the visual similarity of boxerly dancing with ballroom dancing to compel a reinterpretation of his activity.

That this reinterpretation is purportedly "forced" onto observers, like the policeman, shows, as indicated previously, that different types of sight gags can be segued in larger comic constellations. For insofar as we attribute the reinterpretation of the action not only to ourselves but also to the cop, this byplay can also be seen as a mutual interference gag.

Switch movements are like verbal jokes in that they involve a sequential play of reinterpretation. But they are unlike verbal jokes insofar as they are not prompted by anything like an incongruous punchline. Indeed, we start out initially unaware that we are interpreting an action, and we only become retrospectively aware of our initial interpretation when it is undercut. That is, unlike a verbal joke, our reinterpretation of the gag does not begin with the perception of nonsense. Nevertheless, our amusement at the gag still rests on the incongruous play of interpretation. For we are delighted by the way in which one line of movement may be made to yield two, often conflicting, glosses, for example, the Tramp wasting his boss's time fighting versus dutifully washing the floor. Switch movements often reverse the interpretive meaning of an action; but they need not. They may merely transform one action into another as when a silent comedian, beaned on the head, turns his doddering into a modern dance à la Isadora Duncan.

(5) *The object analog.* This category is very much like the mimed metaphor. Some readers may in fact see little point in drawing a distinction here. A famous example of the object analog is the moment in *The Pawnshop* when the Tramp drops his cane into the tuba as if it were an umbrella stand; or in the same film when he puts his derby in a bird cage as if it were a hatbox; or in *The Rink* when he removes his coat from an oven as if it were some kind of closet. In these cases, one object is equated with another. One object, that is, can be seen under two aspects: one literal and the other metaphorical.

Essentially, the comic dynamic here is the same as in mimed metaphors. I have not assimilated these examples to the mimed metaphor, however, because they do not seem to require mime to do their work. They do not need enabling gesticulations of the sort that must accompany the perception of a doughnut as a barbell. The objects analogized bear their similarities close enough to the surface, so to speak, that the metaphorical interpretation does not require much staging. Unlike verbal jokes but like mimed metaphors, the object analog affords a simultaneous play of interpretation—seeing the object literally and metaphorically at the same time. In the Chaplin example, the audience focuses on the visual similarities of tubas and umbrella stands while remaining peripherally aware of their differences.

The object analog gag should not be confused with another technique common to much action-oriented comedy (silent and otherwise). Call this technique the refunctionalization of objects. Very often at the height of an action sequence, when disaster seems inevitable, a comic will seize upon an object and use it triumphantly in a way that deviates from its ordinary employment. For example, when the back of the boat breaks away in *College,* Keaton realizes that he can use his behind for a rudder. Or, for a less action-packed example, in *The Navigator* (1924) Keaton redeploys crab traps to cradle boiling eggs in the galley's outsized cauldron. Here an object is used successfully for a purpose for which it was not designed; the object is, in a manner of speaking, refunctionalized.

Such refunctionalizations are undoubtedly amusing, but I am not sure that they should be considered *sight* gags. For the object is not being redeployed in order for the audience to see it as something else. With object analogs and mimed metaphors, the point of the humor appears to rest on visual metaphors; refunctionalization of objects does not. The humor in the latter case rests on the comic's unexpected—incongruous but sufficient—ingenuity rather than on any particular visual byplay. In *The Frozen North* (1922), when Keaton turns the guitars into snow shoes, or the snow shoe into a tennis racket, the point of the routines (which I count as mimed metaphors) is to remark on the physical resemblances of the items in question. Refunctionalizing objects would not necessarily have this dimension of paraverbal wit. That said, however, let me also admit that the refunctionalization of an object may also be yoked to the projection of an object analog or a mimed metaphor. At the end of *College,* Keaton uses a pole supporting a laundry line as a vaulting pole and a lamp as a javelin. These involve not only refunctionalization but mimed metaphors, for in the context of the film it is hard to miss the similarity, indeed the visual similarity, that is being drawn between these events and the earlier sporting episodes.

(6) *The solution gag.* The discussion of the refunctionalization of objects reminds me of another type of gag, albeit rare, that appears in comic films—the solution gag. I am of two minds as to whether it should be considered a *sight* gag, for like refunctionalization it concerns unexpected, indeed brilliant, reversals based on practical ingenuity rather than play with the presentation of visual ambiguities. But I may be too narrow-minded in this case. So I will discuss the structure of the gag and leave it to the reader to determine whether it belongs on this list.

The most famous example of what I am calling a solution gag occurs in Keaton's *The General.* Johnnie (aka Buster Keaton) sees a railroad tie strewn on the tracks in front of him. The Union spies have thrown it there, hoping to derail him. Johnnie slows his locomotive down and runs along the side of the engine. Carefully, he slides down the cowcatcher of his locomotive. He runs to the foreboding tie, and with much difficulty, he pulls it off the track. Unfortunately, he has not worked fast enough. His engine has inched up behind him while he struggled with the tie. By the time he lifts it, his locomotive scoops him off his feet, and he falls on the top of the cowcatcher. The beam he removed from the track, moreover, is so heavy that it pins him to the front of his own engine. Suddenly, he sees there is another railroad tie on the track less than ten feet ahead of him. The locomotive seems destined to derail with him on the front of it. Yet Johnnie, but not the audience, in a flash of brilliance sees an avenue of escape. He realizes that the tie on the track is straddling one of the rails. Thus, if he can hit the overhanging end of the tie on the track, he can catapult it out of the way of the oncoming train. He lifts the tie on his chest overhead and bangs it down on the beam on the track, thus casting two worries aside with a single blow.

This is an immensely amusing routine. And its effect rests on the lightning reversal of one interpretation of the situation by means of an unexpected, economical, and effective reconceptualization of the situation. It depends on Johnnie seeing that the beam on his chest is not a burden but a tool. Johnnie sees this, but the standard viewer does not until Johnnie demonstrates it. The reconceptualization of the situation surprises the audience, which also would appear to derive pleasure from the situation by reinterpreting the scene in light of the absolute fitness of Johnnie's action. If Johnnie's lifting the beam, rather than, say, trying to roll off the cowcatcher, strikes us as initially incongruous, once the beam is flung, the action strikes us as the most perfect and neatest solution available. In this respect, the solution gag is akin to a verbal joke insofar as it enables the viewer to pleasurably reconceive the situation, although the solution gag is not exactly like a verbal joke because in the process of appreciating the gag and the sequential reconceptualization of the scene, the audience does not exercise its own wit but rather admires the wit displayed by Keaton.

Whether this gag counts as a sight gag probably depends on the degree to which one thinks a sight gag depends on visual play. On this basis, one might reject it as a sight gag because the gag is more a matter of physics than of perception. Or if one takes the gag to derive from a kind of visual thinking—seeing the situation as a catapult—one might be prone to call it a sight gag. Moreover, if one wants to use the phrase "sight gag" to denominate all the recurring gag structures of the great silent comedians, then this sort of solution gag counts as a sight gag.

Nevertheless, however one decides this terminological point, it is important to note that the solution gag does differ interestingly from the standard cases of mutual interference gags. For with mutual interference gags, it is generally some comic character in the fiction whose interpretation of the event is limited, whereas with solution gags, it is the audience whose vision is limited. Moreover, with solution gags the play of alternative interpretations comes sequentially, whereas with mutual interference gags and switch images the audience can contemplate incongruous alternative interpretations simultaneously.

The preceding taxonomy of sight gags is admittedly rough. It does not claim to be exhaustive, nor are the categories as precise as I would like them to be. Furthermore, it is not systematic in the sense that these distinctions could be deduced from an underlying set of formulas. The lack of systematicity in part derives from my method, which has been primarily descriptive. Whether a system could be developed for the sight gag really depends upon getting a more comprehensive picture of the range of variations within this form. The purpose of advancing this confessedly informal cartography of the sight gag is to elicit the kind of criticism and refinement of terms that will foster a more comprehensive and rigorous classification of the phenomena, which may in turn allow systematization.

It is also important to note that this chapter does not pretend to say why the sight gag is amusing. Rather, I have attempted to assimilate the sight gag to the incongruity conception of humor. Thus, explaining why the sight gag is funny relies on an account of why humans find incongruity amusing. Though by attempting to assimilate the sight gag to the humor of incongruity we have not *explained* the sight gag, we have, however, I believe, enhanced our understanding of it by situating the sight gag in the appropriate conceptual framework.

I began by noting that the sight gag appears in art forms other than cinema, in films other than comedies, and in periods other than that of the silent cinema. At the same time, however, most of us probably have very strong associations between the sight gag and silent film. One reason that might be offered for this is that that is just where you happen to find sight gags. However, I distrust this answer. Sight gags are everywhere in the history of film (and television), and they recur frequently in our own day in films such as *Back to the Future* (1985), *Big* (1988), and the works of Pee-Wee Herman, not to mention their standard use in all sorts of television comedy shows. So in concluding, I would like to speculate on whether there might be a deep thematic connection between the sight gag and silent film that underlies our sense that these phenomena, so to speak, "go together."

In looking over the preceding taxonomy of the sight gag, I see that one motif running through all the examples is what might be called the "double (or multiple) aspect." Sight gags seem to presuppose the possibility of visually interpreting the image in two (or more) ways. I have argued that the incongruousness of these interpretations is the feature of these gags that gives rise to amusement. But at the same time, the theme of the multiple aspect is relevant to important debates about the artistic prospects for film in the silent era.

As is well known, early film suffered what might be called "the anxiety of photography."[6] That is, because film is a product of photography and photography cannot be art, then film is not art. The reason for supposing that photography could not be art was that it was believed that photography could only slavishly reproduce reality. The task of silent filmmakers and of theoreticians of the nascent art form was generally to refute these charges by showing that film need not slavishly reproduce reality; it could also creatively reconstitute it.

Within this context, I hypothesize that the sight gag, with its exploitation of the multiple aspects of the image, has an especial, symbolic pride of place. For the donneé of the sight gag is that the film image is open to various interpretations, can show more than one point of view, and can be creatively ambiguous (albeit in a highly structured way). In other words, the sight gag flies in the face of the prejudice that movies can only brutishly recapitulate from a single point of view what stands before the camera. In celebrating the ambiguity of appearances, sight gags in effect undermined the uninformed conviction that cinema was capable only of mechanically, unequivocally, and unimaginatively recycling something often infelicitously called "reality." The ethos of silent film culture—its commitment to cinema as a means of interpretation rather than of recording—was, in other words, the operating premise of the sight gag. This, I submit, is the reason silent film theorists generally have an affectionate, if sometimes unexplained, place in their hearts for the masters of the sight gag. At the same time, I think that the rest of us may intuit some of the urgency of this dialectic when we laugh at the great silent clowns. That is, we feel them trying to transcend what were often perceived as the period-specific limitations of their medium. We do not feel the same about sight gags in our own time, however, because we are as yet unaware of our limitations.

Notes

1. The historical claims here are meant to be quite tentative. Roughly, it seems to me that the earliest stages of film comedy were aimed at generating laughter through an exploitation of the fantastic capacities of cinema and/or through a kind of amoral, antisocial transgressiveness. But this is only to speak of major tendencies. Sight gags—for example, Feuillade's *Une dame vraiment bien* (1908)—were certainly in evidence in early film.

Similarly, when I speak of sight gags emerging as a key form of silent comedy, I do not mean to imply that trick films and roughhouse slapstick ceased to be made. I merely wish to note the prominence that the sight gag form gradually assumed as it was refined by people such as Chaplin, Lloyd, and Keaton. Of course, the sight gag form is not inhospitable to either the machinations of the trick film or roughhouse. The sight gag often incorporates these elements in the kinds of structures discussed in this chapter: Keaton's disappearance in *Sherlock, Jr.* (1924) is surely one of many survivals of the trick film in the period of the sight gag, and a great many sight gags are basically structured roughhouse. And, as well, films notable for their sight gags can also employ trick devices and sadistic slapstick independently of their sight gag structures.

Given all these qualifications, one might begin to wonder about the point I am trying to make. It is this: the sight gag, although evident in very early comedy, gradually comes to be refined in such a way that it, rather than trick comedy or slapstick pure and simple (the more dominant earlier tendencies), is seen as the most important form of silent comedy. This is a process that gains steam in the later half of the 1910s so that by the 1920s the sight gag is the leading type of film comedy.

Needless to say, the preceding historical hypothesis may require even further modification as we learn more about very early film comedy, such as the work of the Italians.

2. For further discussion of the role of inattention in Keaton's humor, see Noël Carroll (1976). (This is available through University Microfilms, Ann Arbor, Michigan.)

3. Mention of Tati's wreath gag gives me the opportunity to make a comment about comic conventions, especially with respect to sight gags, not discussed above. Clearly, this gag with the tire succeeds in large measure because we are dealing with a black and white film. In a color film, a tire with wet leaves stuck to it would not be visually confused with a funeral wreath; this sight gag is persuasive only because the film is black and white.

But this leads to an interesting point—that the characters in the world of the fiction insofar as they are confused by the tire appear to be seeing their world in black and white. This suggests that there may be an implicit convention with respect to sight gags—that the perceptual capacities of the characters in silent films are presented as roughly the same as the perceptual capacities of the silent film audience, unless otherwise signaled. That is, just as the silent film spectator cannot hear, smell, or feel cues in the fiction, so the silent film character, unless otherwise marked, is similarly deficient in these regards.

This would explain the comprehensibility of the spectacular inattention that characters in, for example, mutual interference gags often evince. In *Fatty's Magic Pants*, a comedy of the middle 1910s, for instance, someone sews a rope down the seam of Arbuckle's slacks from behind. And he does not notice this! Nevertheless, it seems to be accepted by the audience. Why? I hypothesize that it is because it is being implicitly supposed by the filmmakers and the audience that Arbuckle has available to him only the perceptual capacities that are available to the film viewer with respect to the fiction—here, specifically vision. In this gag, his touch receptors are bracketed just as in the Tati gag the characters' color receptors are bracketed. And unlike real-world humans, characters in silent film with astounding frequency seem to be unaware when other people and animals are standing behind them. We might call this convention perceptual leveling. Whether there actually, rather than hypothetically, is such an implicit convention, however, is a topic for further research.

4. For a discussion of this sort of interplay between word and image, see Noël Carroll (1980–1981).

5. In *Wild and Woolly* (1917), the film begins and ends with switch images, ones with reversed significations. In the opening we initially take Fairbanks to be on the range but then learn he is in the city; at the conclusion, we think he is in the city, but he is really out West. For analysis of this, see David Bordwell (166–169, 202–203).

6. This is discussed at greater length in Noël Carroll (1988, chap. 1).

References and Additional Reading

Bergson, Henri. 1956. "Laughter." In *Comedy,* ed. Wylie Sypher. Garden City: Doubleday.

Bordwell, David. 1985. *Narration in the Fiction Film.* Madison: University of Wisconsin Press.

Carroll, Noël. 1976. "An In-Depth Analysis of Buster Keaton's *The General.*" Ph.D. dissertation, New York University.

———. 1980–1981. "Language and Cinema: Preliminary Notes for a Theory of Verbal Images." *Millennium Film Journal,* nos. 7/8/9 (Fall/Winter).

———. 1988. *Philosophical Problems of Classical Film Theory.* Princeton: Princeton University Press.

Penis-size Jokes
and Their Relation
to Hollywood's Unconscious

Peter Lehman

"I hope his dick is bigger than his IQ," a woman remarks to her friends near the beginning of *The Witches of Eastwick* (1987), and the joke inaugurates a whole series of penis-size discussions. Later in the same sequence, the three central female characters talk about their ideal man. One of the women (Michelle Pfeiffer), referring to penis size, says he should be "huge." Another (Susan Sarandon) says "small" because she likes it better aesthetically and because she was physically uncomfortable with her former husband, who was large. Completing this democratic survey, the woman in the middle (Cher) says that she is in the middle on this issue. When the central male character (Jack Nicholson) invites Cher to his estate in the hopes of seducing her, he begins the discussion by telling her that his servant has a huge penis, adding however, that he has heard that women do not care about that. Later when Cher is with Susan Sarandon, she says that she was sore for days after making love with Nicholson and goes on to describe the unusual curvature of his penis.

Although *The Witches of Eastwick* is obsessively laced with this kind of talk, such chatter about the penis is a common characteristic of films of the 1970s and 1980s. Not surprisingly, no one has commented on this because little attention has been placed on the representation of the male body in the cinema. Furthermore, this talk frequently takes the form of penis-size jokes, and many people are willing to dismiss jokes as not worthy of serious attention. Finally, many of the films in which these jokes occur are not prestige films. Thus, some may dismiss the phenomenon as an uninteresting feature of films aimed at the teen market. From this point of view, such jokes may simply exploit adolescent anxiety about changing bodies and sexual discovery.

As *The Witches of Eastwick* should make clear, generalizations about the kind of films in which penis-size jokes occur are inaccurate; they have been laced throughout virtually every type of film in the last decade or two. In *The Decline of the American Empire* (1986), women in a sauna talk about their sexual experiences. The scene is structured around a woman who tells of the time she picked up a handsome man only to discover that he had a very small penis. Both she and the woman to whom she tells the story break out in laughter and concur that that is the worst possible thing. In *Flashdance* (1983), a man in a bar propositions the central female character, and she replies by quoting to him the size of the smallest penis on record. In *A Nightmare on Elm Street* (1984), a high school boy tells a girl that he woke up with an erection with her name written on it, to which she replies that this is impossible because his penis is not big enough for the number of letters in her name. In part four of the same series (1988), a high school girl calls a boy "needle dick" and tells him that he is the only boy in school who suffers from penis envy. *Porky's* (1981) contains numerous penis-size jokes that commence at the film's beginning when we see Pee Wee (guess where the character gets his name?) measuring his penis. In *The Godfather* (1972) and *The Cotton Club* (1984), we hear women speak in awe of the large size of someone's penis. In *Blood Brothers* (1978), when a character urinates on the street, another says, "Looks like a penis, only smaller." And so it goes.

In a survey of the usual terms in which our culture constructs sexual difference, Stephen Heath notes the emphasis placed on the visible. Psychoanalysis stresses the significance of the penis, the sight of it, and the concomitant concept of the female "lack." In Sigmund Freud's terms, "Little girls . . . notice the penis of a brother or playmate, *strikingly visible* and of *large* proportions, at once recognize it as the superior counterpart of their own *small* and inconspicuous organ" (quoted in Heath, 53; emphasis added). Such an account of sexual difference can only be called dramatic, and where we have drama, we all know, comedy cannot be far away—if only because one source of comedy is the failure of drama.

Freud's assumptions and language both clearly establish the basis for such comedy with his emphasis on visibility and size. The two, of course, are connected; if one is going to stress the visible, then the larger something is the more visible it is—especially if one presumes the spectacle is *strikingly* visible. As Dr. Freud might well have known, not all penises are strikingly visible and certainly not all the time. If we believe that the sight of the penis is the basis for the ultimate psychoanalytic drama, it is no wonder that we are anxious about the collapse of this dramatic spectacle, something that emerges in the "peniscope" cartoon.[1] During the early

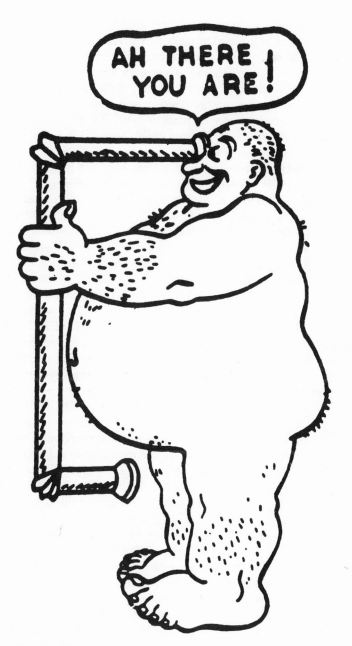

The Peniscope

1970s, Paul Harvey, a conservative radio news commentator, reported with relish a story about two women who streaked a public event. They were caught, taken to the police station, and booked, whereupon it was discovered that only one of them was a woman. In his unique style, Harvey told the story as a joke that spoke for itself, the assumption being that of course any long-haired man who would engage in such disgusting behavior would turn out to be inadequately marked as being a man. Similarly, when a man streaked the Academy Awards while David Niven was speaking on live television, Niven joked about the size of the man's penis. These jokes reveal a paradoxical nervousness. On the one hand, the penis should not be shown and seen. On the other hand, if it is, it had better be a "strikingly visible" drama (a lesson that, incidentally, all the arts have learned well). What better way to put down a man who breaks the taboo and threatens the awe and mystique surrounding the organ than to joke about his inadequacy.

Ironically, then, the awe we attribute to the striking visibility of the penis is best served by keeping it covered up—that is, invisible. The relationship of hard-core pornography to Hollywood cinema perfectly illustrates this. Hard-core porno is the one place in our culture where the penis is always on display, and the conventions of the genre work to guarantee the supposed drama of the event. Actors are chosen because they are well endowed, they are usually shown erect, and close-ups emphasize the thrusting of the penis or the feat of women who, performing oral sex, can take the huge organ into their mouths. Small, unerect penises are seldom shown. If we see the male get undressed, he is frequently partially erect, or if he is not, we glimpse him only briefly as a precursor to the ensuing drama, which may even be heightened by the comparison. The striking visibility of male sexuality—right down to the obligatory climax when the man withdraws and ejaculates on the body of the woman—is at the center of the genre. In Hollywood the situation is reversed. The penis is almost always covered up, but, as I have indicated, there is endless fascination in talking about it: now you see it; now you hear about it. Not surprisingly, jokes and comedy emerge within the sphere of what we hear rather than what we see. This also structures the "Tootzie Roll" penis-size joke that appeared on a greeting card. If hard-core porno tries desperately to assert the visual drama, Hollywood jokes incessantly about its failure. Between the two, the mystique is left intact.

Talk about the male body in general and penises in particular quickly leads to joking. In her book *The Nude Male*, Margaret Walters notes, "I found men sometimes reacted defensively and sarcastically when told I was writing about the male nude; comments ranged from the crude joke— 'What a lot of old cock!'—to sophisticated analyses of my penis envy" (17). In his treatment of jokes and humor, Freud spends a good deal of

The "Tootzie Roll" cartoon—the dialogue balloon echoing Mae West's famous line.

time analyzing dirty jokes, what he calls "smut." He argues, "Smut is originally directed towards women and may be equated with attempts at seduction" (97). According to Freud, men who tell such jokes to other men derive pleasure from imagining what they are socially inhibited from doing, and men who laugh at those jokes do so as if they were spectators of an aggressive sexual act.

Freud's analysis has to be positioned historically because if it was true in Vienna in 1905 that men always told dirty jokes and women were always the butt of those jokes, the same is certainly not true in the present-day United States. Three examples will suffice. The first two are jokes that were recently told to me by women in social situations. The first, in fact, the joke teller introduced as "my feminist joke." "Why are women such bad mathematicians?" she asked me. Placing her thumb and forefinger a few inches apart, she continued, "Because for years they've been told that's eight inches."[2] The second joke involves Freud himself. His daughter, who has never seen a penis, asks him what one looks like. He drops his pants and shows her. "Oh," she responds, "like a phallus, only smaller." A third example comes from the early 1960s and was told to me by a girl in high school. "What are the three most ego-deflating words a man can hear?" she asked. The not very reassuring answer to an adolescent boy was, "Is it in?"

It is beyond the scope of this discussion to detail what may be transpiring when these jokes are told in actual social situations, but a few useful points can be made before I return to films. Most obviously, Freud's generalizations about smut are no longer accurate, if they ever were; women do tell jokes with the male body as the object of those jokes. Nor is seduction the goal of these jokes. This is important because Freud atttributes a great deal of significance to men displaying hostility toward women through jokes after being turned down by them in actual social situations. In fact, he theorizes that a man initially desiring a woman at a party, for example, would tell a dirty joke in her presence to embarrass her or in her absence to share a bond with other men at her expense. The hostility, in other words, came from frustrated desire. There is obvious hostility in the aforementioned jokes, but it is hostility of a different kind.

Freud distinguishes two kinds of jokes that are not "innocent" jokes told as an end in themselves but served another purpose: "It is either a *hostile* joke (serving the purpose of aggressiveness, satire, or defence) or an *obscene* joke (serving the purpose of exposure.)" (97). Women's jokes about men, however, seem to be a combination of the two, rather than one or the other. Women's jokes are certainly based upon "obscene exposure," and they are motiviated by aggressiveness and satire. They revel in the fact that the male body is not what it is cracked up to be. They do so, however, not out of frustrated desire for that body but out of revenge. These jokes speak more of a desire to get back at men than a desire for them. As such, they take their place alongside *Playgirl* and male stripping. Some women may derive a pleasure from *Playgirl* that stems from feeling that if men look at women that way, turnabout is fair play. Such a pleasure, which is conceptual and involves getting back at men, is, however, far removed from the intensely erotic, masturbatory response that men may have when looking at pictures of nude women or at strippers. We cannot simply slot women's telling of penis-size jokes into the categories Freud has developed for men telling dirty jokes about women. More important for my purposes, however, we cannot presume that whatever function such jokes serve when told by women in social situations, they also serve when told in films. Films entirely recontextualize such jokes, because even if a woman is telling a penis-size joke in a film, in the overwhelming number of cases she is telling a joke written and directed by (and for) men.

As my introductory examples of penis-size jokes in recent films show, these are not all teen films. Even so, we must be careful when we presume that we can always learn more from "serious" films than from various "disreputable" genre films. This need to talk about penises is complicated in cinema by its central aspect of visual representation. When novels such as *The Godfather* and *Gardens of Stone* assert that a character has a large penis, that assertion is uncomplicated by further questions of representation. In the cinema, however, one has to either see the large penis or be denied its view. Hard-core pornography graphically displays the penis, whereas mainstream cinema almost always chooses to cover it.

In *Once Bitten* (1985), a film aimed at the teen market, we see high school boys taking showers. Every shot carefully covers the view of all the penises. One is particularly noticeable in that it is a long shot with a thin shelf in the foreground that just happens to be both in the right place and thick enough to cover the groins of the boys who stand behind it. *Opposing Force* (1986), an adult action film, has a scene of prisoners undressing and being deloused. The scene includes long shots of groups of men as well as various closer shots, but in all cases either the physical positioning of the camera, the set design, or the gesture of the men holding their hands over their groins covers the view of their genitals. Once again, this structure is strongly in place in *Escape from Alcatraz* (1979), when Clint Eastwood strips in a prison and walks to his cell; he is either shot from behind, or only his lower legs or upper torso is shown in frontal views. Similarly, in *O Lucky Man* (1973) a table top just happens to be in the right place and of the right thickness when Malcolm McDowell strips in a police station. In any of the many sex scenes in *Last Tango in Paris* (1973), Marlon Brando's body is spared the full exposure given to Maria Schneider's.

The Last Temptation of Christ (1988) is significant in this regard because the film places repeated emphasis on the naked male body being looked at by characters within the diegesis, while always denying the view of that body to the spectators of the film. Near the beginning of the film, a man is prepared for crucifixion. A startling close-up shows his loincloth being ripped off immediately before the cross is raised up. Although we see those who have gathered to watch the crucifixion stare at the man who has just been graphically stripped, we see the man only from behind. Later, a group of men gather around a bed on which lies a naked male corpse. Although they look directly down at the body, we see it only from a long shot, side view. Before Christ is crucified, we see him naked while he is being beaten. Although his body is in motion, the way he moves and the position of the camera totally obscure his genitals. Similarly, the position of his legs when he is nailed to the cross allows frontal shots of the crucifixion while simultaneously blocking our view of his genitals. What makes this film somewhat unusual is the startling emphasis on others looking at the naked bodies that we do not see. Indeed, the scene with the viewing of the corpse is particularly extreme because most viewers are surprised that the groin is not at least covered.

Robocop (1987) supplies another extreme example of this structure. A male police officer and his female partner close in on a group of armed and dangerous criminals. They split up, and she comes across one of the men as he urinates. She tells him to put his hands up, and he immediately turns arounds and follows her command, asking if he can complete dressing himself. She glances at his penis, and this allows him to disarm her. Because of her look, she cannot carry out her part in the mission, which leads to her partner being sadistically mutilated and left to die. As a result, his body is transformed into the robot of the title. Thus, it is no exaggeration to say that the woman's glance at the penis set the entire narrative in motion. Yet we, of course, never see what she does. Nothing that we might see, it seems, could justify the magnitude of impact this moment has in the narrative.

Furthermore, the moment contradicts an earlier scene in the police station dressing room. In a remarkable tracking shot, we see men putting on their uniforms when a woman unexpectedly appears. Her shirt is open, and her breasts are momentarily visible as the camera moves by. Moments later we see other women and conclude that in this futuristic film men and women share the same locker room with no sense of embarrassment or vulgarity. Dressing together is a simple fact of being on a police force composed of men and women. Even more astonishingly, the woman who is briefly glimpsed is not eroticized in any of the usual ways. The camera does not dwell on her, there is no shot from the point of view of a man looking at her, and the lighting and positioning of her body do not create an erotic spectacle. Visually, we as spectators are in the same position as the characters. The nudity has no erotic interest for us.

At the simplest level, we might wonder why a woman used to sharing a locker room with men would be unable to resist looking at a man's penis in a life-threatening situation. Furthermore, the locker room scene treats the representation of the woman's body maturely and without embarrassment. Yet when the sight of a man's penis becomes the object of a woman's look and sets the entire narrative in motion, we are denied the sight of it.

Although I want to make clear the pervasiveness of this structure in a wide variety of films, a final example comes from a comedy and returns us to our main concern. In *Bull Durham* (1988), we see a woman go to bed with a baseball player she has just selected as a partner. As he undresses in anticipation of having sex with her, she tells him to stop and begin again, undressing slowly while she watches. He does, but he stops with his underpants on. Although the scene is structured around her both controlling the situation and deriving pleasure from watching him, the logic of the scene is entirely broken when he simply leaves his underpants on and she does not even remark about it. Later in the film, we see a locker room scene that exactly fits the pattern discussed in *Once Bitten* and *Opposing Force*. Finally, a player has a classic anxiety dream about pitching without his clothes on—with the exception that he happens to be wearing a jockstrap and garter. The garter makes perfect narrative sense because we know that the player has been wearing one under his uniform, and the jockstrap allows the visual humor of the scene to take place without exposing the genitals. As with *The Last Temptation of Christ*, the pattern in *Bull Durham* is significantly paradoxical: the aforementioned scenes all overtly raise the spectacle of others looking at the naked male (especially the undressing scene and the anxiety dream) but then awkwardly circumvent the view for the film spectator. Like so many recent films, *Bull Durham* simultaneously foregrounds the display of the male body while protecting it from view.

These awkward visual structures that deny the view of the genitals are compounded when we hear characters talk about the penis but we are denied the view of it. This combination opens a potentially interesting ideological space that is likely to be foregrounded even in the conscious perceptions of the viewer: what is at stake in so carefully and systematically denying us the view of what we are hearing about?

We should also wonder, however, why so much of the talk about penises in mainstream cinema takes the form of penis-size jokes. In many of the cases, the joke structure in these films involves women who make men the butt of their jokes. But as in *Flashdance* and *The Witches of Eastwick*, the films are written and directed by men. Although the women in these films may appear to threaten men, is there another structure at work wherein the threat becomes pleasurable for the male spectator?

Robert Altman's films provide a good starting point for a close examination of penis-size jokes in films. His films have been laced with references to penis size at least since *That Cold Day in the Park* (1969), in which we overhear a conversation between women in which one is surprised to discover that penises are not all the same. This quintessential reference is to a particular male anxiety that lies beneath one structure of penis-size jokes. As Phyllis Chesler notes, if women become aware that penises vary, they may become discriminating and judgmental. The moment at which the woman becomes aware is therefore particularly charged. In *California Split* (1974), a male employee in a bar asks the woman behind the cash register if he can borrow some money because he is a "little short." She contemptuously replies that he was born short. In another similarly displaced reference in *Popeye* (1980), Olive Oyl dreamily sings a song with the repeated lyrics, "He's large." The film, which seems to many a curiosity within Altman's ouevre, is actually consistent with his other films if one perceives Altman's concerns with body types and sexuality. Its cartoon source allows Altman to represent a world peopled with a startling array of unusual body types.

McCabe and Mrs. Miller (1971), however, most significantly raises and addresses this Altman preoccupation. The penis-size joke is centered, comparatively graphic, and direct. An unnamed cowboy (Keith Carradine) who has come to town to visit a whorehouse asks with relish, "Who's next?" We see a prostitute laughingly whisper in another's ear. The cowboy looks on with interest, and as they continue to laugh, one of them holds two fingers together to indicate they are laughing at the small size of his penis. When he, like us, realizes what they are laughing about, a look of dismay crosses his face. On the surface, this seems to be just one more Altman penis-size reference and one that again betrays the fear that knowledgeable women will become judgmental. What makes the joke different, however, is that it is carefully woven into the entire structure and thematics of the film.

In a later rhyming scene, we see Mrs. Miller (Julie Christie), the madam of the whorehouse, dressing Ida, one of her new, young prostitutes (Shelley Duvall). The scene begins with Ida saying, "Well, it just hurts so much. Maybe I'm small." Her emphasis is on the last word. Moments later, while looking at her body, Mrs. Miller remarks, "Oh yeah, you really are small, aren't you? Just like me." Aside from linking sexual smallness to both sexes, the scene unexpectedly links the young prostitute to Mrs. Miller. In a much more indirect and complex way, it also links the small cowboy to McCabe (Warren Beatty).

McCabe makes his initial appearance in the film as a powerful, mysterious figure. His riveting charisma quickly establishes him as a "man among men." We soon learn, however, that all this is an elaborate con job; he is not the man he appears to be. When he becomes involved in political conflict over his business enterprise (the whorehouse), he fears for his life and watches for a gunfighter who might be sent to kill him. When the cowboy rides into town, he looks like that powerful gunfighter. McCabe readies his gun for a fast draw and cautiously approaches the stranger. It is only after the man looks at him with a puzzled expression that McCabe suspects his error. He asks what the man wants and learns that he has simply come to visit the whorehouse. Shortly after that, the aforementioned scene occurs in the whorehouse.

Julie Christie, as Mrs. Miller, dresses a young prostitute (Shelley Duvall) in Robert Altman's McCabe and Mrs. Miller *(1971)*

The cowboy's entrance into the town rhymes with McCabe's. Just as the men in the town presume McCabe to be a gunfighter and a powerful figure, McCabe presumes the cowboy to be one. In both cases, we quickly learn otherwise. Neither is what he appears to be, but in the case of the cowboy, the misperception is specifically linked to his penis—he is not a big man. But the comparison between McCabe and the cowboy extends from their initial appearances in the town to their deaths.

Although we do not see any further scenes with the cowboy in the whorehouse, Altman lingers on the scene when he leaves. Several of the prostitutes, including Ida, come to the door with him, wish him well, and see him off. Ida, who is cheerful and smiling, is particularly emotional. "Be careful," she says warmly. The other prostitutes go back into the house with a new customer ("Here's Shorty," one of them says) while Ida stays outside watching and wistfully saying, "Bye cowboy."

This brief scene is crucial. Now the cowboy and Ida—the small man and the small woman—are linked together. Clearly, in her intercourse with him she has enjoyed sex for the first time, and we have not seen her in the film since the scene in which she talks about her smallness and the pain of sexual intercourse. The scene also includes the throwaway joke, "Here's Shorty." There is a virtual epidemic of shortness of every kind in Altman's films. Most importantly, however, the scene sets up the cowboy's death.

Walking away from the whorehouse, the cowboy starts to cross a bridge when he is confronted by a gunfighter who bullies him in the hopes of getting him to draw his gun. The cowboy is scared and blurts out that he cannot shoot well. The gunfighter tricks him into showing his gun and uses this as a pretext to draw his own gun and shoot the cowboy. Altman cuts to a slow-motion shot of the cowboy as his body crashes through the ice into the water below. The scene moves from the literal to the symbolic; the cowboy has a small penis and does not know how to use his gun. His death has even further sexual connotations because cold water can cause penises to retract and become smaller. The cowboy's death reveals him as a total fraud; he is lacking literally in the sexual realm and symbolically in the realm of masculinity.

McCabe dies similarly. He pursues his gunfighter opponents through the heavy winter snows of the town. He begins with a rifle, but when he runs out of ammunition, he switches to a derringer. He is mortally wounded and left to die sitting in the snow holding the derringer. This is the last image we see of him. As the cowboy is literally small, so McCabe is symbolically small. And both of these men die amid the shrivelling connotations of coldness, visual images that recall the common male expression, "I'm freezing my balls off."

In *McCabe and Mrs. Miller*, Altman draws complex parallels between the literal and the symbolic, making clear that the representation of the male body involves the problematic relationship between the penis and the phallus. It has long been a commonplace of genre criticism that guns in westerns are phallic symbols. Furthermore, *McCabe and Mrs. Miller* belongs to a group of films made in the late 1960s and 1970s that attempt to reformulate genre films, often commenting on their conventions in the process. This is precisely what Altman has accomplished with the sexual smallness motif in the film.

Penis jokes are usually throwaways, with unattractive male characters as their butt. This is the case even if a woman speaks the line, as in *Flashdance*. This structure is very clear in *Where the Boys Are '84* (1984). A college girl tries throughout the film to get her dream hunk, whom she sees on the beach during spring break. Finally, she meets him and goes back to his apartment with him. She is shocked to discover that he wants her to pay him for making love to her. Taken aback, she asks him to undress for her so that she can see what she is buying. He does so: she looks him up and down and contemptuously jokes, "So where's the rest of it? . . . I'll see you in small claims court." She later tells her girlfriend about the experience, remarking that the man "turned out to be just another jerk in a leopard bikini." "Something's got to hold him together," her friend responds, upon which we hear the predictable reply, "There wasn't much to hold." In this film and *Flashdance*, the audience identifies with the women who utter the remarks and laughs at the men at whom the remarks are aimed. This structure reinforces dominant presumptions that to be a man is to have a big penis. In both films, the undesirable man is put down for not being a real man.

In *McCabe and Mrs. Miller* something entirely different happens. The audience identifies with both the cowboy and Ida. Because each is marked as small, the characteristic is not just attributed to men. More significantly, however, each of the "small" characters is linked to the central character of his or her own sex—the hero and heroine of the film, each of whom is cast within the established codes of the star system. Mrs. Miller tells Ida that she is built like Ida, and McCabe is revealed to be just like the cowboy. Thus, smallness is not a simple sign of inadequacy; on the contrary, it comments on our very presumptions about masculinity and femininity. This is something rarely achieved in any of the other countless penis-size jokes that characterize current cinema.

Finally, I want to conclude with some indication of how a consideration of penis-size jokes fits into current issues in film theory and comedy. The chapters in this book are primarily concerned with comedies, but theoretical work on comedy should not be limited to films in that genre. Comedy is an important part of nearly all films, if only via traditional comic subplots or isolated moments of humor. A recent *Variety* film review asks, "*Thinkin' Big* is a B movie that poses the pointless question: can a full-length feature be constructed from jokes about penis size?" (Lor, 24). Given the topic of this chapter, *Thinkin' Big* (1988) might seem better suited as the primary example than *McCabe and Mrs. Miller*. But notice what results from that assumption. The B comedy is dismissed as tasteless, and the presence of related jokes in such critically acclaimed films as *The Decline of the American Empire* and *The Witches of Eastwick* goes unnoticed. But the wording of the *Variety* review unwittingly raises another theoretical question: might some kinds of comedy be more suited to isolated moments than to feature-length treatment? In other words, rather than minimize the significance of the brevity of penis-size jokes in films such as *McCabe and Mrs. Miller*, I find them all the more significant in that such jokes need to be told but require a structure wherein they will not be emphasized or, perhaps, even noticed. Many people who have seen the films discussed in this chapter will not remember or have thought about the penis-size jokes because the films in which they occur are not about penises (as *Thinkin' Big* apparently is). Paradoxically, then, penis-size jokes must fill an important need because so many films contain them, but they are not important enough for a film to be about them. Jokes, comedy, and humor of this kind should be carefully scrutinized rather than dismissed.

Paying attention to such comedy also has theoretical significance for other areas of film studies. Penis-size jokes clearly relate to work on the representation of male sexuality and the male body in the cinema. When these jokes are told by women but the male body is not shown, they are part of a structure that denies both objectification of the male body *and* female subjectivity. This denial can be situated at many textual levels including that of eyeline glances and point-of-view shots. It is, of course, common in the Hollywood cinema that when a man looks desiringly at a woman, a point-of-view shot that shows what he desires follows. The woman's body is therefore not just shown but shown through a particular circuit of desire. I suggest that something even more extreme than denying female subjectivity is happening with the missing point-of-view shot in penis-size jokes in Hollywood films. In place of the logical objectification of the male body, we have the fetishistic objectification of the woman who looks. Her very desire or contempt for what we never see becomes fetishized. This in part explains the attraction of the structure to men and also links penis-size jokes to another nonjoking dominant structure in the Hollywood cinema—a woman looks with desire at (rather than speaks desire for) the naked male body (for example, Jacqueline Bisset in *Rich and Famous* [1981]).

Even when no nudity is involved, posing the male body as spectacle has always been a problem within the classical cinema. Richard Dyer notes that "*Rebecca,* for instance, a film whose first half hour is entirely constructed around the never named female protagonist's desire for Maxim/ Laurence Olivier, nonetheless, entirely denies this character any point of view shots of him" (184). In *Rich and Famous,* Jacqueline Bisset picks up a young man, and they make love. As she sits on a bed watching, he undresses standing up. We see only a shot of him naked from behind, and although logically she is the desiring subject in the scene, her face as she looks at the man is the erotic focus of the scene.

It is no coincidence that this scene is structured around the look of an actress such as Jacqueline Bisset. Beautiful women and/or women who are marked within the narrative as being sexually desirable are almost always the ones who utter penis-size jokes (as in *The Witches of Eastwick* and *Flashdance*) or who are the center of the desiring look at the man's body. Their beauty and desirability are crucial to the fetishization of the woman's desire for and/or talk about the man's body. Counter to surface logic, these women become eroticized for the male gaze exactly at the moment when they seem to be eroticizing the man for themselves or, in the case of penis-size jokes, putting down the man for failing to live up to their erotic expectations. In other words, watching Jacqueline Bisset's face as she looks at the penis that we do not see may be erotically charged. If within the codes of the star system and the narrative structure, the scene were shot and edited the same way with an actress/character marked as unattractive, the effect would be entirely different. Indeed, in all the examples I have gathered of penis-size jokes and the elision of the object of the woman's desiring look, none involves unattractive actresses/ characters. The structure only seems to "work" if the woman can be fetishized. This suggests another possible area of investigation—namely, masochism.

Much recent work has emphasized masochism as an important structure of male pleasure in the cinema. Gay Lynn Studlar, for example, argues that Josef Von Sternberg's Dietrich cycle turns on a structure whereby the man's pleasure is determined by his subordination to and loss of the woman he desires. When beautiful, desirable women erotically look at and make evaluative judgments about the penis, the structure may be masochistically pleasurable for men. If this is the case, joking about a man with a small penis would be an extremely erotic possibility, although the structure is very similar to that in which the woman quietly looks with serious desire. In the latter case, her look makes clear that she is in the powerful position of seeing, knowing, and evaluating, and the filmic structure makes clear that we would rather watch her see, know, and evaluate than observe what she sees. That most of these films are written and directed by men certainly makes sense from this perspective. What is seemingly women's desire is drafted into the service of masochistic male pleasure.

From this perspective, penis-size jokes may also be related to the simultaneous rise of rape/revenge films. This includes such exploitation films as *Ms. 45* (1981) and the notorious *I Spit on Your Grave* (1977). Mainstream genre films such as *Sudden Impact* (1983) and, even, *Extremities* (1986) (with its pretenses of serious drama) fit within this category. In all of these films, and countless others like them, a woman's having been raped seemingly justifies her hunting down the rapists one by one and sadistically torturing and killing them. Once again, the actresses/characters are always beautiful and desirable, and the films are nearly always made by men, frequently in exploitation genres that make it all too clear that a sincere interest in rape victims is of no concern to the filmmakers. The pleasure that men get from the destruction of the male body by the sexually desirable woman in these films is the dramatic equivalent of her joking about the body in the films surveyed earlier in this chapter.

This use of beautiful and desirable women may also serve to mask homosexuality.[3] The concern with penis size that gives rise to jokes is predominantly a male anxiety and one that specifically begins with boys and young men looking at and comparing themselves with each other. Such activity may give rise to conscious desire for or homophobic fear of such other bodies. From this perspective, the jokes, looks, and even sadistic actions of the beautiful women in these films may create a quite successful heterosexual veneer for what may much of the time be unconscious homoeroticism.

Women in our culture may have no jokes about their bodies equivalent to penis-size jokes, which may indicate just how phallocentric such jokes are.[4] Even when told by men to men in contexts that clearly articulate male anxiety, the jokes affirm the importance and centrality of the very thing they seem to question. In the movies, men frequently draft women into their service with these jokes. Contrary to appearances, women who look, evaluate, and joke about penises in most films pose no threat to male pleasure; these women simply tell men what they have always told themselves about the importance of the penis.

Although Freud's work does not apply directly to much of the foregoing analysis, it is fitting to close by returning to his work on jokes. As with dreams and slips of the tongue, Freud found a much greater significance in jokes than most of his contemporaries did. Even today, almost as if it were a contradiction in terms, we have trouble taking comedy seriously. We should expect, therefore, that our initial response to fleeting moments of isolated joking might be to dismiss them without too much consideration. Can we not learn more, for example, about comedy and theory from studying the films of Woody Allen and the Three Stooges than we can from analyzing jokes that take less than a minute in a two-hour film? On the contrary, one of the most important functions of comedy in cinema is to sneak a joke by almost unnoticed, make us laugh, and then allow us to forget that we ever thought something was funny.

Notes

I wish to thank Melanie Magisos for her insight and generosity in helping me revise this chapter.

1. I found the drawing in a tourist shop in Tombstone, Arizona.

2. Since completing this chapter, I have discovered a 1988 film, *Gotham,* that includes this joke. In this film the question becomes, "Why do women have such poor depth perception?"

3. I am indebted to Chris Straayer for this observation. Straayer analyzes structures of lesbian activity that are achieved via a male intermediary.

4. I am indebted to Natalie Boymel Kampen for this observation.

References and Additional Reading

Chesler, Phyllis. 1978. *About Men*. New York: Simon and Schuster.

Dyer, Richard. 1986. *Heavenly Bodies*. New York: St. Martin's Press.

Freud, Sigmund. 1960. *Jokes and Their Relation to the Unconscious*, trans. James Strachey. New York: Norton.

Heath, Stephen. 1978. "Difference." *Screen* 19, no. 3 (Autumn): 51–112.

Lor. 1988. Review of *Thinkin' Big*. *Variety*, April 27, p. 24.

Straayer, Chris. 1986. "The Hypothetical Lesbian Heroine in Feature Narrative Film." Paper presented at the Florida State University Literature and Film Conference, Tallahassee. Forthcoming in *Jump Cut*.

Studlar, Gay Lynn. 1988. *In the Realm of Pleasure: Von Sternberg, Dietrich, and the Masochistic Aesthetic*. Urbana: University of Illinois Press.

Walters, Margaret. 1978. *The Nude Male*. New York: Penguin.

Sometimes I Feel Like a Motherless Child

Comedy and Matricide

Lucy Fischer

*Impatience kicks and thrashes inside the clown, like a
violent baby in the womb that cannot bring itself to term.*
(Kerr, 339)

The Incredible Shrinking Woman

In the 1981 comedy, *The Incredible Shrinking Woman,* Lily Tomlin
plays Pat Kramer, a housewife and mother who inexplicably begins to di-
minish in size. In the beginning of the story she is of average height; by the
middle, Lilliputian (living in an Ibsenesque doll's house); near the end,
invisible. Her corporeal reduction is ascribed to industrial pollution—
contamination by the combined ingredients of myriad consumer products: cleaning aids, cosmetics, synthetic foods, and the like. Within the
film, a standard sociological explanation is advanced for Pat's tragedy: one
newscaster speculates that she is a "metaphor for the modern woman" and
notes that "the role of the . . . housewife has become increasingly less
significant." Another inquires, "Did she begin to shrink because her role
as homemaker was belittling?" Pat's surname, with its reference to
Kramer vs. Kramer (1979)—a film about the male absorption of woman's
domestic function—seems to validate this reading. I, however, would like
to offer another interpretation of Pat's plight: that it represents not only the
position of woman in bourgeois culture but the fate of woman in traditional
comedy.

The notion of female absence has been a commonplace of contemporary film criticism. Woman has been seen to suffer a narrative lack in the
patriarchal cinema equivalent to her alleged physiological omission.
Canonical modes (such as the western or action picture) either ban women
from centrality in the scenario or include them in pernicious incarnations

(the femme fatale of *film noir*). Where women do populate the screen (the musical or melodrama), they are frequently fashioned as a patriarchal construct—the mere "pseudocenter" of the filmic discourse (Johnston; Kaplan; Mulvey; Dozoretz).

Even though these perceptions have illuminated numerous cinematic genres, they have rarely spotlighted comedy—as though the topic of misogyny were too grave to consider within a jocular light (Doane 1982, 1983; Leibman; Mellencamp; Modleski, 1988a, 1988b). I wish to add some levity to the subject (or at least some gallows humor) by approaching comedy with the lessons of feminist film theory in mind.

To pursue this, we must temporarily avert our eyes from the comic image and attend instead to its theoretical, off-screen space—a discourse honed on literature, drama, and verbal anecdote. In the critical milieu that surrounds the genre, we will detect the masculine biases familiar to us from other branches of narratology.

Central to this discussion is the work of Northrop Frye, who in *The Anatomy of Criticism* constructs a paradigm for the classic comic form. In so doing, he configures a story told from the male perspective in which the female is present only as subsidiary object of the hero's quest:

> What normally happens is that a young man wants a young woman, that his desire is resisted by some opposition . . . and that near the end of the play some twist in the plot enables the hero to have his will. (163)

Equal to the male youth in comedy is the patriarch—who generally poses some hindrance to the protagonist's romantic pursuits. This generational dynamic invokes another scenario—the Freudian Oedipal conflict, which is a struggle enacted between men.

Whereas Frye's theory favors the youth of this archetypal narrative, others have foregrounded the elder. Ludwig Jekels (174) sees comedy as opposing tragedy by displacing guilt onto the father, thereby enacting a vindicative drama in which the son takes revenge on his precursor. Similarly, Martin Grotjahn views the comic form as choreographing a degradation of the patriarch. "The clown," he writes "is a one-man comedy; he represents a depreciated father" (91).

Clearly, in the formulations of Frye, Jekels, and Grotjahn, there lurks an obsession with the male personae of the comic diegesis. But even in considerations of nondramatic humor, woman is erased from the theoretical decor. When Sigmund Freud executes his brilliant analysis of jokes, he consistently configures woman as the object (not the subject) of their production. On numerous occasions in his typology of wit, Freud's examples cast woman as humor's butt. For the category of double meaning, he relates the following jest (one worthy of Henny Youngman):

A doctor, as he came away from a lady's bedside, said to her husband with a shake of his head: "I don't like her looks." "I've not liked her looks for a long time," the husband hastened to agree. (37)

But it is with Freud's delineation of dirty jokes that the elision of woman is truly accomplished. For here, he initially imagines the female as indispensable to the comic process—as the locus of the male joke teller's desires. "Smut," he writes:

is directed to a particular person, by whom one is sexually excited and who, on hearing it, is expected to become aware of the speaker's excitement and as a result to become sexually excited in turn. . . . Smut is originally directed [by men] towards women and may be equated with attempts at seduction. (97)

According to Freud, this scenario obtains quite literally for lower-class males, who make off-color remarks in the presence of the opposite sex. At higher societal levels, where women are imagined more "proper," this dynamic is significantly revised.

The men save up this kind of entertainment, which originally presupposed the presence of a woman . . . till they are "alone together." So that gradually, in place of the woman, the onlooker, now the listener becomes the person to whom the smut is addressed. (99; my italics)

Hence woman—once the core of the joke structure (as the target of sexual desire)—is eventually eliminated from the scene entirely and replaced by the male auditor. If her specter rematerializes, it embodies psychic opposition. As Freud remarks, the obstacle to seduction "is . . . nothing other than women's incapacity to tolerate undisguised sexuality." Hence, the female is an emblem of repression; an intransigency that fuels the artistic evolution of smut into joke (Doane, 1982).

The circumvention of woman can also be seen in the theory and practice of female impersonation—a form of theatrical, sexual burlesque. As critics have noted, this direction of cross-dressing prevails over the obverse—in which women are costumed as men. In favoring this mode, comedy once more privileges the male and claims his dominance even when woman is apparently there. Annette Kuhn perceives deep psychological motives for this practice:

It is possible that such a spectacle . . . fulfills the primal fantasy of the fetishistic look, a fantasy which "real" women must always frustrate; it banishes the castration threat by gratifying a masculine desire for a woman to be . . . more like a man. (73)

Finding women "like men" is precisely what typifies Grotjahn's view of the comedienne. For he extends the association of transvestitism and comedy by seeing the male specter inhabiting the bodies of *all* comic women. "The comedienne of modern times," he writes, "seems to play the strange role of a woman impersonating a man" (98–99). According to Grotjahn, man laughs at such a woman because of her pathetic penis envy. She "confirms his superiority" and demonstrates that "what she wants to be" is him. For Grotjahn, the unconscious male response is to think:

> She may try hard, she may be witty and aggressive and even exhibitionistic like a man, but she still is not a man. She tries to be what I am. It is really funny. (99)

The excision of woman in formulations of comedy is particularly bizarre given the origins of the mode in female fertility rites. Frye speaks of the comic narrative as enacting a "return to the womb" (186), and Walter Kerr sees it as "derived from that portion of Greek ritual which sang 'the *hymen*eal hymn' " (64; italics mine).

The theorist who most privileges this view, however, is Mikhail Bakhtin in his influential work on Rabelais and the carnivalesque. For in characterizing the medieval grotesque, Bakhtin stresses the centrality of female birth imagery—a system counterposed to an iconography of death. Both poles express comedy's downward thrust—toward the earth and the lower bodily region. As Bakhtin writes:

> Degradation . . . means . . . the contact with earth as an element that swallows up and gives birth at the same time. . . . To degrade also means to concern oneself with the lower stratum of the body, the life of the belly and the reproductive organs. (21)

As Mary Russo notes, Bakhtin finds this aesthetic emblemized in certain terra cotta figurines of women: "senile pregnant hags" who embody "a death that gives birth" (Bakhtin, 25; Russo, 219).

Given this perspective on comedy's roots, the elision of one female character seems most shocking—the mother. Grotjahn explains this phenomenon by noting her saturation in taboo. As he writes, "It is difficult to distort the relationship to the mother in a way which makes us laugh" (102).

Frye's discussion of the comic family—of male generational angst—reveals little sustained consideration of the maternal dimension. At one point he notes that female *alazons* (impostors of a parental cast) are "rare" (172). And he mentions only in passing that comedy involves an Oedipal replacement of the mother by the hero's young lover:

> The fact that the son and father are so often in conflict means that they are frequently rivals for the same girl, and the psychological alliance of the hero's bride and the mother is often expressed or implied. (180)

Thus, the maternal is reduced to a spirit in comedy that haunts the hero's paramour—her diegetic stand-in.

Whereas Frye notes the erasure of the *hero*'s mother, Stanley Cavell examines the obliteration of the *heroine*'s mother. In the comedy of remarriage, he finds that "the price of the woman's happiness is the absence of her mother" (1987, 16). He also notices a "strict absence of children for [the heroine] . . . the denial of her *as a mother*—as if the woman has been *abandoned . . . to the world of men*" (1987, 17; italics mine).

If these filmic heroines have been "abandoned to the world of men," the same might be said of the comic genre. Although female sexuality underlies comedy's ancient rites, in the Greek elaboration of the form it is obscured and appropriated by the masculine erotic. It is well known that the costumes of comic actors were replete with oversized male genitalia. As Plutarch remarks in delineating standard comic types, "One carried an amphora of wine and a bough; another dragged along a goat; a third followed carrying a basket of dried figs; and, *to crown all, the phallus*" (quoted in Kerr, 155). It is not only man's organ, however, that is enlarged in comedy but his ego, which has executed an elaborate "substitution trick" on the figure of the mother. As the male role has stretched, the female position has shrunk—as incredibly as the body of Pat Kramer.

Adam's Rib

When we turn from the abstract frame of comic theory to the films themselves, we find a world shaped by the critical off-screen space. The figure of the mother is largely absent, suppressed, violated, or replaced. Thus, the genre urges us to "Throw Momma from the Train."

Woman's disappearance strikes us most obviously in the cinema's fraternity of comic stars: Charles Chaplin, Buster Keaton, Harry Langdon, Harold Lloyd, Max Linder, John Bunny, the Marx Brothers, Stan Laurel and Oliver Hardy, W. C. Fields, Dean Martin and Jerry Lewis, Eddie Murphy, and Pee-Wee Herman. Although comediennes appear on screen, few are invested with the consistent comic persona identified with the male pantheon—a feature that allows comics to anchor a series of films. Mae West was the notable exception (in American cinema) during the period encompassing the 1910s through the 1930s. Even today, when comediennes star in films, they seem stripped of the personalities that define them as stage performers. In that respect, Lily Tomlin shrinks as much as her alter ego, Pat Kramer, does.

Where comedies are thematically "domestic," the maternal woman does appear, but she is often pernicious and peripheral to the male comic focus. In *It's a Gift* (1934) and *The Man on the Flying Trapeze* (1935), W. C. Fields plays a henpecked husband accompanied by a castrating wife. In *Their First Mistake* (1932), Oliver Hardy plays a married man nagged by his spouse.

But it is those comic works that are *not* specifically domestic that assist us most in uncovering the real fate of the maternal. What happens to the mother when the humorous text does *not* mandate her presence through the exigencies of plot? In some films, the nuclear family exists as a shadow thrown upon the dramatic mise-en-scène. In Chaplin's *The Pawnshop* (1916), the Tramp works for a small business run by a father and daughter; the mother is nowhere in sight. In flirting with Edna (Edna Purviance), his boss's child, the Tramp is seeking not only a lover but a parent. At one point, when he mischievously fights with a co-worker, Edna enters the scene. The Tramp suddenly and willfully drops to the floor, playing the role of passive victim—relishing Edna's nurturing, protective response. As he puts his finger to his lips, rolls his eyes upward, and leans on her breast, he is more infantile than amorous. Perhaps if the maternal figure were scripted into the narrative, this psychic doubling of lover and mother would be jammed: after all, moms cannot be in two places at the same time.

In this superimposition of lover and mother, one is reminded of Jacqueline Rose's insights concerning *Peter Pan*. She foregrounds a scene in which the seductive moves of Tiger Lily, Wendy, and Tinkerbell are frustrated by Peter's misprision of their nature (37). When the women state that each wishes to be Peter's wife, he responds, "Very well—that's really wishing to be my mother." This slippage (between lover and parent) continues in *Throw Momma from the Train* (1988), in which two men trade murder assignments. Larry (Billy Crystal) detests his ex-wife, and Owen (Danny DeVito) loathes his mother—thus placing the women in a symmetrical relation. As though recognizing this, Owen decides that they should "criss-cross" slaughters and eliminate each other's nemesis. Clearly, the men are alter egos, and their mothers and paramours are doubled as well.

A suppression of the maternal is also apparent in the films of Buster Keaton. In *Steamboat Bill, Jr.* (1928), the hero (who has been raised by his now-deceased mother) visits the father from whom he has been separated since birth. (Ironically, as he arrives in town, the local florist shop advertises bouquets for Mother's Day.) The narrative that follows is devoted to the father's attempts to divest the son of maternal influence—to change him from a mama's to a papa's boy. Even the family of the heroine is motherless; she resides only with her father.[1]

This elimination of the maternal occurs in screwball comedies as well—

even those that avoid a domestic setting. In *His Girl Friday* (1940), although none of the romantic couple's parents appear on screen, gratuitous comments malign motherhood. When Walter Burns (Cary Grant) wants to convince Hildy Johnson (Rosalind Russell) of his false sincerity, he swears on his mother's grave. But Hildy reminds him that his mother is still alive, thereby unmasking his tendentious wish. When Hildy refers to her own "mother" (meaning her prospective in-law), Walter cruelly comments that her mother "kicked the bucket." When a columnist writes a sentimental poem about a criminal, Walter singles out the line about his "white-haired mother" to mock. And when Hildy wishes to criticize the mayor's sense of justice, she claims he would "hang [his] own mother." Finally, when Hildy's future mother-in-law appears on the scene, Walter orders his cronies to cart the lady away, at which point she is bodily carried from the room. These images (of kidnapping, sudden death, and hanging) are resonant metaphors for the fate of the mother in comedy itself.

Maternal exclusion goes even deeper in Howard Hawks's film. Hildy's decision to divorce Walter and marry Bruce Baldwin (Ralph Bellamy) is a clear response to her desire to have children—a possibility foreclosed with Burns. Yet within the terms of the film, this aspiration is ridiculed. When Hildy says she wants to "have babies" and "give them cod liver oil," the audience is positioned to find her remark retrograde. Similarly, its point of view is aligned with that of the male reporters who travesty the vision of her "singin' lullabies and hanging out didees." The complete erasure of her project is summarized in Walter's burlesque of her plans for "a home with mother in Albany, too."

Although contemporary feminist criticism has applauded Hildy for her professionalism (Haskell, 135), this victory is garnered at a cost: the devaluation of the maternal so ubiquitous in comedy. But if Hildy is denied parenthood, Walter is not, for it is he who is credited with symbolically recreating his ex-wife, with reviving her sagging joie de vivre, with educating her. Cavell has surfaced this pattern in the genre and related it to the birth process but has ignored its implicit sexism:

> The demand for [the woman's] education in the comedies presents itself as a matter of becoming created [by man], as if the women's lives heretofore have been nonexistent . . . as if their materialization will constitute a creation of the new woman. . . . Theologically, it alludes to the creation of the woman from Adam in *Genesis*. (1987, 17)

So while Hildy's generative possibilities are contained, Walter's are liberated.

Ironically, in the film's crime subplot, much is made of Earl Williams's hearing the radical political phrase "Production for use," which he misreads as signifying that all things fabricated must be utilized. It is ostensibly this statement that has caused him to fire a gun he has had in hand. When it comes to the case of the female body, however, this motto is powerless. Hildy rejects female "reproduction for use" and turns the job over to a man.

Bachelor Father

To pursue this issue further, it is useful to turn our attention to those comic films that sustain female absence while positioning maternity at center stage. Among the most curious of these are the movies of Laurel and Hardy. While in many shorts, the teammates fluctuate between postures of parent and child, in others they constitute an adult couple, and this status is given a parental twist. In *Brats* (1930), the men play double roles—cast both as themselves and as their own offspring. The film concerns an evening of game playing at (what appears to be) Laurel and Hardy's collective home. The comedy unrolls as Baby Stan and Baby Ollie (who share an upstairs bedroom) continually fight and misbehave. In this strange domestic setup, wives are rarely mentioned; it is as though (as Freud would have it) the men are simply "alone together." Neither is it ever explained how the Laurel and Hardy "clones" have been produced. At one point, Ollie complains to the uncooperative kids that when *mother* is home, they always go to bed. Baby Ollie replies that she always sings *them* to sleep— implying that the kids share one female parent. Precisely what, we may wonder, is the nature of this domestic and genetic arrangement?

Their First Mistake presents an equally strange portrait of familial life. The film begins with Mrs. Hardy enraged at her husband for spending time with Stan. Ollie goes across the hall to his friend's apartment to discuss the matter. As the two loll around on the bed, Stan suggests that Hardy adopt a baby to keep his wife occupied, thus allowing the men time together. In the next shot, the men approach the rooming house, babe in arms—as though they had ordered the child from the Sears catalogue. When Ollie returns to his apartment, he finds that his wife has gone. That evening, the two men retire to a comfortable double bed and try to put the newborn to sleep. Various comic bits ensue: Stan provocatively produces a bottle of milk from inside the bib of his nightshirt and sucks on it as frequently as he offers it to the child. Ollie attempts to extract an inverted rubber nipple in a manner worthy of sadomasochistic pornography. In so doing, he articulates a discourse of the convex and the concave that evokes the contrast between male and female bodies.

Although Laurel and Hardy's films are the most eccentric of this type, other comedies (more tamely) substitute the clown for mother. In Chaplin's *The Kid* (1921) an unwed woman abandons her baby. The Tramp

Stan Laurel, Oliver Hardy, and child in Their First Mistake *(1932)*

finds him, with a note that reads, "Please love and care for this orphan child." The Tramp proceeds to do this for the next five years, naming the boy John. Meanwhile, the boy's mother has become a successful actress, who does volunteer work in impoverished neighborhoods to atone for her parental sins. She routinely passes her own child without knowing it. When John falls ill, the Tramp calls a physician, who learns that the urchin is not the vagrant's natural or adopted son. The doctor alerts the authorities, who take the child away. The actress realizes that the boy is her own, and the two are reunited. The film closes abruptly with a shot of the woman's home as a policeman ushers the Tramp to the door. John and the actress open it, smile, and invite the Tramp in. But what compromise they will strike we cannot imagine.

What Chaplin initiated in the 1920s others have continued. Recall that *The Kid* was both comic and tragic: "A picture with a smile and perhaps a tear," as Chaplin deemed it. Taking his lead, the specter of male mother-hood first appeared in contemporary melodrama before propagating in the comic realm: *Kramer vs. Kramer*, *Ordinary People* (1980), and *Table for Five* (1983) were notorious cases in point.

Subsequently, a slew of comedies spawned in which men supplanted the female parent—a virtual "baby boom." In American cinema, one thinks of *Mr. Mom* (1983) and *Three Men and a Baby* (1987)[2] and on television of "Full House," "My Two Dads," and "Who's the Boss?" Eventually, in a film such as *Baby Boom* (1987), woman herself comes to be configured as the incompetent mom—as though to reclaim her maternal/cinematic role, she must now mimic a genre determined by men.

Although the male comic hero repeatedly elects a Tiresian passage by placing himself in the woman's position, he denies that the feminine impulse issues from him. In *All of Me* (1984), Roger Cobb (Steve Martin) imagines himself haunted by a female phantom, Edwina Cutwater (Lily Tomlin), who appropriates his body; thus, he disavows that he may have invited the possession himself. But *All of Me* is also provocative for a particular image that recurs throughout the diegesis. Whenever Roger looks at himself in a mirror, his own reflection is replaced by that of Edwina. In this trope, we sense a relapse to the state of the imaginary in which the infant cannot distinguish between himself and others. Hence, the mother is perceived not only as a continuation of the self but as a "mirror" in which one's being is reflected back. Kaja Silverman in fact likens the Lacanian mirror phase to an experience "in which the subject identifies with the mother's breast, voice, gaze" (158). In envisioning a female doppelgänger in the mirror, the male comic hero reveals a wish to return to a time of maternal union when "all of him" was "all of her." Interestingly, French theorist Charles Mauron finds all "comic art . . . founded on a triumphal game—originally the restoration of the lost mother" (quoted in Holland, 58). Perhaps that is why the comic hero tries to *be* her in his madcap mimicry of the maternal mode. Significantly, at one moment during Roger's bewitchment, he asks the $64,000 question: "What if I got pregnant?"

In this equation of comic hero and mother, I am reminded of René Girard's characterization of passion as essentially imitative. "Metaphysical desire is mimetic" (192), he writes, by which he means that a person does not directly desire another but rather wishes *to be an individual who is prized by the coveted other*. Girard uses the example of comedy to illustrate his point, specifically *A Midsummer Night's Dream* in which "Helena would like to be translated . . . into Hermia, because Hermia enjoys the love of Demetrius" (191). If we apply this notion to the comedy of male parenting, we can chart desire's circuitous route. Although the comic hero may think he seeks the love of a baby, he truly wants to be transformed into the one whom the baby loves—the primary care-giver, mother. Girard sees this passion as involving "the copy of a model," a model configured as rival.

Bringing Up Baby

Having traced the broad configurations of this mimetic trend, I wish to sketch its trajectory within the confines of a single text. The French film *Three Men and a Cradle* (1985) seems a more than likely candidate. For in this work, written and directed by Coline Serreau, we see the feminine reduced or repressed in both its erotic and maternal manifestations. As woman shrinks (incredibly) in our estimation, so man expands to prove that he is truly the nurturant gender.

The movie concerns three friends and roommates: Jacques, an airplane steward; Michel, a cartoonist; and Pierre, an office manager. One night during a party, an acquaintance of Jacques asks him to receive a delivery and hold the package for several days. Jacques agrees but forgets to tell his roommates. He recalls only moments before he boards a flight for Japan and telephones Pierre at work.

On the specified day, the doorbell rings, and when Michel opens it, he finds a baby. A note accompanying the child is addressed to Jacques from Sylvia informing him that the baby, Marie, is the "fruit of their passion." Sylvia will be modeling in the United States for six months and intends to leave the child with him. Thinking that Jacques has agreed to Marie's arrival without informing them, the roommates are furious. They realize, however, that they must tend the girl until the "package" is retrieved. Myriad comic scenes ensue that delineate the men's incapacities for mothering: they do not know how to comfort a crying baby or what formula to buy; they do not know how to feed Marie or change her clothes.

The roommates are soon stressed and depressed—a result of sleep deprivation. When the real package arrives, Michel is so distracted that he does not realize that it is the delivery to which Jacques had referred. It turns out to be a packet of illegal drugs—a fact that eventually turns this feminized domestic comedy into a male caper film. When Jacques returns from Asia and learns of his daughter's existence, he faces his friends' ire. He tries to pawn the baby off on his mother and is enraged when she leaves on vacation. He returns to his flat, and the men resign themselves to a period of joint custody. Their social life is entirely eclipsed.

When Sylvia comes back from the United States and collects Marie, the men find themselves surprisingly despondent; they are suffering from a postpartum depression of a nonbiological sort. (Interestingly, in the American version, one of the roommates refers to a "postparty depression" in the opening scene.) One day, Michel finds Marie unattended, as

Jenifer Moret as Marie, the baby girl in Coline Serreau's Three Men and a Cradle *(1985)*

her mother works at a modeling job. Another time, Jacques visits Sylvia's apartment and discovers a callous baby-sitter minding Marie. Ultimately, Sylvia appears at the men's flat and confesses her incompetence as a mother: "I'm freaking out," she admits. "I'm cracking. . . . I can't handle it alone." She explains that she must model to make money but cannot do so looking a maternal wreck. "How can I pose like this?" she inquires. The men gleefully offer to watch Marie until Sylvia recuperates, and they wander off to feed the child. When they next encounter Sylvia, she is asleep in her daughter's cradle (in a fetal position, sucking her thumb). On that regressive note, the film comes to an end.

In some respects *Three Men* conspicuously replicates the structure of recent paternal melodrama. Like *Kramer vs. Kramer, Three Men* begins with a woman's abandonment of her child and domestic duties, leaving them to a reluctant man. As the film progresses, however, the men rise to the occasion and are deemed superior to the woman at the job she has vacated.

Northrop Frye has noted how comedies often duplicate the structure of legal confrontations. In the genre's valorization of a new society, a "case" is made against the failure of the old. "The action of comedy," he writes, "is not unlike the action of a lawsuit, in which plaintiff and defendant construct different versions of the same situation, one finally being judged as real and the other as illusory" (166). From this perspective, the male maternal comedy enacts a symbolic court case—a custody battle—in which responsibility for the child is eventually awarded to the man. Woman is judged the "illusory" parent—real men do change diapers.

Beyond finding in favor of the masculine, *Three Men* performs a series of eradications of the feminine—be it configured as maternal or sexual. When Pierre and Michel first find Marie, one of them suggests contacting Jacques' mother; the other rejects the idea, labeling the woman an "old harpy." When one of them thinks of telephoning his own mother, the other urges him to "leave the moms out." Later, in desperation, the men call the Second Mommy Agency and hire a nanny. By the time Nurse Rapons arrives, they have become so proprietary about child care that they vilify her until she resigns. At another point, when Jacques and a paramour are in bed, he interrupts their lovemaking to check on the child. The unsympathetic woman makes a hasty and irritated exit, stating, "I'm no wallflower." Later, a female dinner guest is equally intolerant when her meal is interrupted by Marie's cries. "It's just a whim," she claims. "Put her in bed." Clearly, in all these cases, the women are conceived as nonmaternal. Although Nurse Rapons is "certified," fathers know best.

But (we should inquire) might we not see the men as merely *fatherly* parents rather than as necessarily subsuming the female position? Might we not see the comedy as delineating a progressive expansion of the paternal rather than a problematic contraction of the maternal? Within the logic of the film, this option is disallowed. The men never consider calling their dads for advice on child-rearing, and Marie's father, Jacques, is the least devoted of the three. Furthermore, although Pierre and Michel are devastated when Marie leaves, they never pursue the option of becoming parents themselves. The women in their lives continue to function only as potential lovers, not as potential mothers of their children. Finally, when the need arises for Pierre to cut back his work hours, the men suggest he request a "maternity leave." Hence, man is not a father but a "second *mommy,*" and the nurturant role he fills is seen in feminine terms.

Beyond these instances of literal banishment, woman is extracted from the film in more subtle ways. For if she is denigrated in her maternal role, she is equally humiliated in her status as spectacle. In the opening party scene, the camera pans over a picture of a female nude on the apartment wall. Jacques then tells his friends of his sexual exploits with Clementine. In this dramatization of a smutty exchange, we recognize the Freudian scenario: the woman is no longer necessary within the dynamic, she is entirely bypassed in the system of male relays. We also perceive the connection between the defamation of the maternal and of the female erotic. As Erma Bombeck has noted, motherhood is the "second oldest profession."

Although the men are romantically obsessed with women, they also seem to detest them. They have in fact made a "deal" with each other that forbids cohabitation with the opposite sex. "If a woman stays here more than a night," Pierre declaims, "I move out." The men's submerged hostility erupts at several points, when women are given such appellations as "hags," "whores," and "plagues." When Jacques returns from Japan, he telephones Sylvia in New York and is enraged when she hangs up on him. "Bitch!" he yells. "Women . . . I'd slap them back into place."

It is significant that much of the comedy in the film is of the "low" variety—focused on the body. Thus, most of the gags center on Marie's eating, sleeping, urinating, defecating, or sucking and the problems each act causes for her adoptive parents. As Pierre says at one point, the men are spending their lives "wiping a baby's ass." "What a fine mess" they have gotten themselves into.

Interestingly, in Walter Kerr's delineation of physical humor, he makes an analogy to a child's first encounters with its mother.

> Low comedy is a birth experience, and for a time traumatic. *It consists in the discovery that we have a backside and that it is going to be slapped.* Total humiliation comes with our first breath of air, is a condition of our breathing. We are embarrassed to have a body that can be subjected to such treatment, and whenever it is subjected to such treatment again—*in a first slap from a mother . . .* we are freshly outraged. (149; italics mine)

Thus, in dealing with Marie the men seem to relive and relieve the "humiliation" of their own bodily constraints—limitations that men first associate with women. Perhaps that is why Jacques is impelled to "slap" Sylvia "back into place" or why Hildy Johnson claims that Walter Burns renders women "slaphappy."

Marie's femininity is decidedly an issue and is featured in one of the most tasteless bits in the film. On the day she arrives, Michel leaves to buy supplies, and Pierre stays alone with the child. Before Michel can return, Marie has to urinate, and the camera renders a medium shot of her nude genital area with liquid spouting out—a literalization of the smutty joke as "exposure." Rarely in mainstream cinema has the camera focused so unflinchingly on the site of male anxiety, and here the camera does so because the subject is a child and the director is a female.

But this revelation of Marie's physiology brings up a related issue—the question of childbirth, an act that is also focused on that physiological terrain. Clearly, the men appropriate the role of mother, and the fact that Marie arrives as a "package" seems parodic of biological delivery (comparable to the visitation of the stork). We are in fact reminded of certain traditional comic sketches in which clowns give birth to children. Psychoanalyst Sidney Tarachow discusses a set of etchings by the eighteenth-

century Dutch artist Peter Schenk of a commedia del l'arte scenario entitled "The Marvellous Malady of Harlequin." The play begins with Harlequin ill. He is visited by the doctor, who gives him an injection in his
backside. Harlequin then bears a son, whom he raises along with the help
of the white clown, Piro. At the end of the sequence, Harlequin is visited
by Columbine, who openly mocks his behavior. This act obviously
prefigures several films already considered: *The Kid, Their First Mistake,*
and *Three Men and a Cradle.* Significantly, in the latter, Pierre, Michel,
and Jacques sing a three-part version of "Au Clair de la Lune"—a classic
song about Pierrot/Piro.

Bakhtin's theories are also relevant to this conjunction of comedy and
childbirth. For in surveying the grotesque, he finds its archetypal image
"two bodies in one: the one giving birth and dying, the other, conceived,
generated and born." Thus, for Bakhtin, the carnivalesque stands on the
"threshold of the grave and the crib" (21). Given this view, it is not surprising that he favors a section of Rabelais's writing in which Gargantua's
wife delivers a son and dies in the process:

> Gargantua at the age of foure hundred, fourescore fourty and foure yeares
> begat his sonne Pantagruel, upon his wife named Badebec . . . who died in
> childe-birth, for he was so wonderfully great and lumpish, that he could not
> possibly come forth into the light of the world without thus suffocating his
> mother. (quoted in Bakhtin, 179)

Bakhtin finds the duality of this primal image (its components of life
and death) doubled in Gargantua's emotions, which are split between the
joy of fatherhood and the grief of marital loss:

> When Pantagruel was borne, there was none more astonished and perplexed
> than was his father Gargantua; for on the one side, seeing his wife Badebec
> dead, and on the other side his sonne Pantagruel borne, so faire and so
> great, he knew not what to say nor what to do. (quoted in Bakhtin, 182)

Again, we find parallels for this medieval moment in *Three Men.* For the
male protagonists are both distressed by Sylvia's disappearance and elated
at the arrival of Marie; like Gargantua, they do not know what to feel.

At one point in the film, a commentary erupts on the subject of childbirth and man's appropriation of motherhood. After Marie has been returned to Sylvia, Jacques' life is empty. One night he becomes inebriated
and parades around his apartment with a pillow stuffed under his shirt that
makes him look pregnant. (It is possible that one thing Jacques envies
about motherhood is the fixity of its assignation; his paternity, on the other
hand, is continually in question.) Eventually Jacques delivers a speech
about Genesis, claiming that if he were God and could remake the world,

he would craft Adam out of Eve's rib and not the other way around. Then things would be "clearer" because no one would imagine that a being could emerge from a man's bone. Perhaps, Jacques muses, no one made man believe it; perhaps he simply wanted to.

Although Jacques' speech seems a vindication of woman's maternal role, a realization that men (beginning with Adam) have attempted to replace her, the film ultimately contradicts this reading. First, the phrasing of Jacques' speech is peculiar; despite its revisionist impulse, it implies that the world is really as the Bible represents it. Only if he "were God" could he change the present perspective. Second, he suggests reformulating the creation myth so that Adam issues from Eve's rib—still a denial of the female birth process. Third, if anyone is configured to resemble Eve it is Sylvia, who is punished for her sexual knowledge with the social and physical pain of birthing an illegitimate child. Significantly, her daughter is named Marie—in honor (one assumes) of Christ's mother—the only woman to have known immaculate conception.

Furthermore, despite Jacques' paean to woman's procreative powers, the film evinces a discomfort with female sexuality. It seems intriguing that when Michel must hide the packets of illicit drugs, he stuffs them in Marie's diaper, perhaps compensating for her genital lack (as Jacques' pillow did for his). Moreover, although the men have forbidden cohabitation with women, they have chosen to live with Marie. Thus, it is only immature female sexuality that they can tolerate. In the closing scene when Sylvia collapses in the cradle, they finally have woman where they want her—in a neutralized and infantile position, as child versus parent.

This notion sends us back to the theories of Walter Kerr. In *Tragedy and Comedy*, he delineates the relation between the two genres, which he sees positioned in a particular historical order. For Kerr, tragedy always precedes comedy, and the latter is formed in its image: "Laughter is not man's first impulse; he cries first. Comedy always comes second" (19).

Kerr anthropomorphizes concepts to such an extent that he configures tragedy as the *maternal parent* of the comic form: "We insist," he remarks, "upon honoring tragedy as though it were the root, the mother, the matrix" (33). When he notes that modern comedy has veered toward the tragic, he sees the phenomenon, once more, in familial terms: "Comedy has come home to its source—for which it must inevitably yearn. A child is drawn to its mother even when its survival depends upon its being independent" (248). Kerr remarks that in "returning to its womb . . . comedy and tragedy become one again"—like parent and child in the generic imaginary (262).

For Kerr, it is the comic mode that eventually triumphs—slaying tragedy, which is conspicuously absent from the contemporary artistic scene. Thus, comedy can be seen as the symbiotic child that fails to separate, the perverse, matricidal offspring that returns to kill (like Owen in *Throw Momma from the Train*). Comedy can also be seen as Pantagruel— the monstrous generic baby that suffocates the female parent in the throws of childbirth. As Kerr notes, "The clown cannot help himself; he was born to bring ambition down. *He will do it to his own mother*" (334; italics mine).

In works such as *The Kid* or *Three Men*, the mothers are decidedly tragic figures. The unwed actress in Chaplin's melodrama is haunted by "her first mistake," and Sylvia in Serreau's film is a maudlin individual. Thus, there is a match between Kerr's theory of comedy subsuming tragedy and those films in which the comic hero (like comedy itself) preempts the role of pathetic mother. Furthermore, as though to replicate the history of the two genres, the recent batch of male maternal comedies supplants a set of tragic predecessors: *Kramer vs. Kramer*, *Ordinary People*, and *Table for Five*.

But what is the fate of the female spectator in this scenario of masquerade and annihilation—a query posed in the recent work of Tania Modleski (1988a) and Mary Anne Doane (1982). How might *she* react to this generic/genetic joke? She might respond to the male procreative urge with the cynicism of Roseanne Barr, who, we suspect, would willingly surrender her maternal role to them. For in facing her own family turmoil, she declares, "I'm gettin' my tubes tied." Or the female viewer might assume the bemused and sardonic stance of Columbine, coolly observing the domestic farce enacted by Harlequin and Piro. Or she might approach the male maternal comic with the superior air that Grotjahn reserves for the comedienne. In this case, she might paraphrase him, thinking that the comic hero "may try hard but [he] still is not a [woman]. [He] tries to be what I am. It is really funny" (Grotjahn, 99). If the female spectator is transcendent, she may engage the male comic with the composure of Osgood (Joe E. Brown) at the end of *Some Like It Hot* (1959). For when he learns that his fiancée is not a woman but a man in drag, he mumbles generously, "Well, nobody's perfect"—thus inverting clichés of feminine anatomical lack.

Ultimately, however, in the female viewer's reaction we may look for the spirit of Mary Daly, who prizes the comic sense. Rather than avoid humor (with a grim feminist propriety), she openly confronts it—valorizing an aggressive, empowered, female response to the masculine grotesque.

> There is nothing like the sound of women really laughing . . . roaring at the reversal that is patriarchy, the monstrous jock's joke. . . . This laughter is the one true hope, for as long as it is audible there is evidence that *someone* is seeing through the Dirty Joke. (17; italics mine)

Regrettably, that female "someone" is not filmmaker Coline Serreau— who is laughing only on the way to the bank. For she eventually clones her reproduction of mothering in a lucrative American context—this time (like Sylvia) handing the job over to a man.

Notes

1. A similar absence of the heroine's mother is found in Keaton's *The General* (1926), while her father is depicted.

2. After this chapter was written, Tania Modleski (1988a) published an excellent article on *Three Men and a Baby*. Although Modleski's focus is not on comic theory per se, many of her insights extend, complement, and/or coincide with my own thoughts on *Three Men and a Cradle*.

References and Additional Reading

Bakhtin, Mikhail. 1984. *Rabelais and His World*, trans. Helene Iswolsky. Bloomington: Indiana University Press.

Bombeck, Erma. 1983. *Motherhood: The Second Oldest Profession*. New York: Dell.

Cavell, Stanley. 1981. *Pursuits of Happiness: The Hollywood Comedy of Remarriage*. Cambridge, Mass.: Harvard University Press.

———. 1987. "Psychoanalysis and the Cinema: The Melodrama of the Unknown Woman." In Joseph H. Smith and William Kerrigan, eds., *Images in Our Souls: Cavell, Psychoanalysis, and Cinema*, pp. 11–43. Baltimore: Johns Hopkins University Press.

Chodorow, Nancy. 1978. *The Reproduction of Mothering: Psychoanalysis and the Sociology of Gender*. Berkeley: University of California Press.

Daly, Mary. 1978. *Gyn/Ecology: The Metaethics of Radical Feminism*. Boston: Beacon.

Doane, Mary Ann. 1982. "Film and the Masquerade—Theorising the Female Spectator." *Screen* 23, no. 3–4 (September–October): 74–87.

———. 1983. "The Film's Time and the Spectator's 'Space.'" In Stephen Heath and Patricia Mellencamp, eds., *Cinema and Language*, pp. 35–49. Frederick, Md.: University Publications of America.

Dozoretz, Wendy. 1984. "The Mother's Lost Voice in *Hard, Fast, and Beautiful*." *Wide Angle* 6, no. 3: 50–57.

Freud, Sigmund. 1960. *Jokes and Their Relation to the Unconscious*, trans. James Strachey. New York: Norton.

Frye, Northrop. 1973. *The Anatomy of Criticism: Four Essays*. Princeton: Princeton University Press.

Girard, René. 1979. "Myth and Ritual in Shakespeare: *A Midsummer Night's Dream*." In Josué Harari, ed., *Textual Strategies: Perspectives in Post-Structuralist Criticism*, pp. 189–212. Ithaca, N.Y.: Cornell University Press.

Grotjahn, Martin. 1966. *Beyond Laughter: Humor and the Subconscious*. New York: McGraw-Hill.

Haskell, Molly. 1974. *From Reverence to Rape: The Treatment of Women in the Movies*. Baltimore: Penguin.

Holland, Norman N. 1982. *Laughing: A Psychology of Humor*. Ithaca, N.Y.: Cornell University Press.

Jekels, Ludwig. 1981. "On the Psychology of Comedy." In Robert Corrigan, ed., *Comedy: Meaning and Form*, pp. 174–179. New York: Harper & Row.

Johnston, Claire. 1977. "Myths of Women in the Cinema." In Karyn Kay and Gerald Peary, eds., *Women and the Cinema: A Critical Anthology*, pp. 407–411. New York: Dutton.

Kaplan, E. Ann, ed. 1980. *Women in Film Noir*. London: BFI Publishing.

Kerr, Walter. 1985. *Tragedy and Comedy*. New York: Da Capo.

Kuhn, Annette. 1985. *The Power of the Image: Essays on Representation and Sexuality*. London: Routledge & Kegan Paul.

Leibman, Nina C. 1988. "Leave Mother Out: The Fifties Family in American Film and Television." *Wide Angle* 10, no. 4: 24–41.

Mauron, Charles. 1964. *Psychocritique du genre comique*. Paris: Librarie José Corti.

Mellencamp, Patricia. 1983. "Jokes and Their Relation to the Marx Brothers." In Stephen Heath and Patricia Mellencamp, eds., *Cinema and Language*, pp. 63–78. Frederick, Md.: University Publications of America.

Modleski, Tania. 1988a. "Three Men and Baby M." *Camera Obscura* 17 (May): 69–81.

———. 1988b. *The Women Who Knew Too Much: Hitchcock and Feminist Theory*. New York: Methuen.

Mulvey, Laura. 1977. "Visual Pleasure and Narrative Cinema." In Karyn Kay and Gerald Peary, eds., *Women and the Cinema: A Critical Anthology*, pp. 412–428. New York: Dutton.

Rabelais, Francis. 1931. *The World of Mr. Francis Rabelais*. London: Navarre Society.

Rose, Jacqueline. 1984. *The Case of Peter Pan, or, the Impossibility of Children's Fiction*. London: Macmillan.

Russo, Mary. 1986. "Female Grotesques: Carnival and Theory." In Teresa de Lauretis, ed., *Feminist Studies/Critical Studies*, pp. 213–229. Bloomington: Indiana University Press.

Silverman, Kaja. 1983. *The Subject of Semiotics*. New York: Oxford University Press.

Tarachow, Sidney. 1951. "Circuses and Clowns." *Psychoanalysis and the Social Sciences* 3: 171–185.

In Search of Radical Metacinema

Stephen Mamber

Introduction

A recent segment of British critical literature has been primarily concerned with defining aspects of what has come to be called "postmodernist metafiction" and doing so largely in relation to theories of parody. These works have sprung up partly in response to Julia Kristeva, Mikhail Bakhtin, and Gérard Genette and together constitute a body of ideas with great applicability to film studies. I will draw upon three of the major studies to explore a related group of films: *Parody/Meta-fiction* by Margaret Rose (1979), *Metafiction* by Patricia Waugh (1984), and *A Theory of Parody* by Linda Hutcheon (1985).

I will use issues suggested by these three to establish and explore common parody elements in the works of four filmmakers. In the process, I hope to outline some possibilities easily extendible to a range of other films, from these directors and an easily assembled list of others. For the most part, I will stick to Stanley Kubrick and *The Shining,* Brian De Palma and *Body Double,* Martin Scorsese and *King of Comedy,* Woody Allen and *The Purple Rose of Cairo* (referred to from now on just as *Purple Rose*). All four are nearly identical in their attention to the following parody-related activities.

Intertextual Overkill

The term *intertextual overkill* is Waugh's (one component of her definition of radical metafiction) and signifies the wholesale incorporation of source materials from outside the created fictional work (145). In terms of the films explored here, overkill could more properly be labeled massive annihilation by multiple warheads. (Radical metacinema could occupy us for a long time in simply charting original sources.) As "students" of movies (and television and music), these filmmakers are preoccupied with the pointed inclusive reference, so as audience we play continual catch-up. We can't help but feel sorely taxed by the demands of spotting that TV screen as the heroine walks past a department store window or straining to identify the song on the car radio as it's driven off a cliff. Watching and listening to movies today are partly acts of cataloging because the days of innocent homage are long over.

Even though the forms of multiple intertextuality as parody are more than sufficiently varied to be worthy of extensive study in their own right, as in each of my subsequent categories I'll just describe the territory in terms of its principal peaks. I mark them as four, present in abundance in the films in question:

1. Inclusions of television
2. Use of source music
3. Film historical quotes
4. Inversions of star types

The appearance of TV sets and programs is fairly obvious: characters come close to tripping over them. What is important is not their continual presence but their direct parody functions. These include ironic reformulation of narrative structures, as when in *The Shining* a Roadrunner cartoon anticipates the same failed pursuit rituals Jack Torrance and his son will play out.[1] Other televised cartoons, soap operas, and perfectly banal Kubrickian TV newscaster banter also serve to mirror and ridicule our supposedly more serious and central dramatic activities. *Body Double*'s use of porno video before that world is incorporated into the film itself and the clearly central role of video from the opening of *King of Comedy*, which begins as a television show presented to us in video transferred to film, are equally as pronounced.

Although *Purple Rose*'s being set in the 1930s obviously precludes use of video, Allen has been a heavy TV user in the past.[2] *Purple Rose* is interesting in this regard for its similar interplay of film-within-film (of the same name as the film), its black-and-white/color split, and its use of movie "materials," such as the poster that is the first shot of the film and the many shots of the movie marquee. The criticisms of film as exploitive low culture in *Purple Rose* (even by characters in the film-within-the-film) provide the "inferior art" backdrop corresponding to television in the other films.

Robert De Niro as Rupert Pipkin in Martin Scorsese's King of Comedy *(1983)*

As with television, so, too, with music, especially for the quality of continual commentative presence. *Body Double* goes so far as to insert its own music video, so elaborately produced and disruptive we're not sure for a time if we're still within conventional narrative. *King of Comedy* has the kind of eclectic and dominating rock-and-roll-history soundtrack that was also present in *Who's That Knocking at My Door* and *Mean Streets.* *The Shining* never reaches the repellent glories of the use of "Singin' in the Rain" in *Clockwork Orange,* but there's never been a more obtrusive and overstylized prototypical horror movie synthesizer score than the one that beats down on us in that movie with nearly every footstep and glance.[3] *Purple Rose* begins with Fred Astaire singing over the credits and comes full circle when Fred returns to sing in the "new" film that Cecilia, the main character played by Mia Farrow, is watching at the very end.

Oddly enough, *Singin' in the Rain* does make another parodied appearance as one example of the intertextual overkill surely present in the frequent film historical references of these works. Along with *Sunset Boulevard, Singin' in the Rain* is openly quoted at the start of the "Relax" video number in *Body Double,* two films about films mimicked in yet another film-within-film sequence. Give Martin Scorsese a blank screen, and he'll probably put *Pickup on South Street* on it, as he does for quite a substantial time in the scene in Jerry Langford/Lewis's apartment.[4] *Purple Rose* is as evidently astute in its film clips as was *Stardust Memories* and *Zelig,* where Allen clearly knows his old movies so well he not only quotes them; he makes them over so adeptly you can barely tell the fake-new from the real-old. The film-within-film fits comfortably with the "real" Fred Astaire film that follows it.

Mocking inversions of star types or the invoking of star-associated references adds a further dose of intertextual overkill. Star images are brought up and simultaneously chopped down. In *The Shining,* Jack Nicholson's gleefully threatening "Here's Johnny" is a reference no one can miss, and of course Johnny Carson looms even larger as a phantom-parodied presence in the Scorsese film. In a touch of self-mockery, Jerry Lewis running legs akimbo down the street after his kidnapping conveniently wears remnants of his white bandages in just the places where his white socks always are in his own movies, an unsettlingly humorous intrusion at an otherwise fairly tense moment. In *Body Double,* Melanie Griffith can't help but stand in ironic relation to the roles her mother, Tippi Hedren, played in Alfred Hitchcock films, especially when in varied hair colors and occasionally high-fashion masquerades she replicates the appearance changes in *Marnie.*

Purple Rose takes mocking inversions to a glorious level in that it presents the actor and his creation as independent entities. (Tom Baxter is the movie character and Gil Shepherd is the actor who plays him, although we even find out that Gil Shepherd is not his "real" name. All are played by Jeff Daniels.) The movie star is nicely ego driven and full of pomposity, in marked contrast to his "character." The character also tells the actor at one point that he might have been played by another star, such as Fredric March or Leslie Howard, to which one of the film-within-film characters comments that the part is not big enough to have attracted someone of that magnitude.

Failed Artists

The nonheroes of these films—a writer, an actor, a stand-up comic, and a divided film star/film character—are themselves parodies of artists. The metafictional tendency to place the author near the center of his or her own unfolding fiction is here thrown even further off kilter by the element of mediocrity of the protagonists. These main characters are all chronically unemployed, frustrated in their career ambitions, and unbalanced by lack of talent.

The book we see Jack Torrance working on in *The Shining* deserves special mention in this regard. When wife Wendy makes her horrific discovery that his time at the typewriter has produced pages and pages of "All work and no play make Jack a dull boy," there's something rather beautiful

Dennis Franz and Craig Weston in Brian De Palma's Body Double *(1984)*

about the glimpses of elaborate typing patterns we see as she flips through the manuscript, especially those pages displayed meticulously as if in film script format. Perhaps Jack is an underappreciated artist rather than the crazed failure this moment makes him out to be (or Wendy's possibly imagined point-of-view of the manuscript suggests), although I doubt similar claims could be made for Rupert Pupkin's stand-up routine in *King of Comedy* when he finally gets his shot at the crown; it seems genuinely low level, even by the often lax standards of TV talk show guest appearances.[5] As for Jake in *Body Double,* the audition scenes, acting classes, and part-time film work he performs within the film provide abundant evidence for his deserved spot on the unemployment line. Bad acting becomes an important question on multiple levels within the film, is continually discussed and incorporated within narrative concerns, and perhaps is raised by questionable (unintentionally bad) casting as well.

In *Purple Rose,* the actor and character have at least one quality in common: both are marginal. The role in the movie Tom Baxter has walked out of is of questionable importance, and the actor, Gil Shepherd, is also in fear for his career and deservedly so, given the pretentiousness with which he is ready to discuss his craft. (He's also too minor to get any billing on the movie marquee.) Cecilia, herself fired from her waitress job because of movie-obsession problems, has not exactly fixated on the higher levels of the firmament. It is as if Rupert in *King of Comedy* had chosen Joan Rivers or Garry Shandling as the star to shoot for.

In all four films, the characters stand in a parodied relation to their frequent proclamations of substantial self-worth. The illusion of talent is abandoned by the audience much sooner than it's stripped from the characters, although they surely have their own doubts right from the start.

Daring to Be Bad

In one of Linda Hutcheon's few references to films, she correctly picks on the opening of the De Palma film *Dressed to Kill* for "its deliberately bad parody of Hitchcock's *Psycho,* which acts as a signal, as does the title, for the audience to look for parodic backgrounded text" (106). With De Palma we can take our pick of deliberately bad Hitchcock parody, and although some might suggest badness in this regard is all De Palma's capable of, the parody activity of excessively exaggerating what was already florid in Hitchcock might be not without its own intrinsic pleasures. Audiences invariably groan at the kiss in *Body Double,* when Jake finally holds the object of his obsession in his arms, while De Palma circles around them twenty times faster and more frequently than did Hitchcock at the obviously parallel moment in *Vertigo.* To cite Hutcheon again, it is knowledge that separates plagiarism from parody, and De Palma's knowingness can scarcely be in doubt, nor can his overt desire to tear apart his cinematic past.

Kubrick, of course, is the know-it-all who rubs our noses in horror movie conventions until we wonder why we ever went to one in the first place. Stretched out suspense, intrusive comedy, unexplained escapes, multiple motives, even title cards that move from the merely ominous to the madly random and unspecific—all point not to a failed horror film, as so many reviews stupidly labeled it, but to a deliberately subverted one.

The Scorsese trick is to ape the flatness of television style, abandoning the tracking shot mannerisms and elaborate noirish visual effects more generally characteristic of his style. Filming often as if he is shooting a three-camera video sitcom, Scorsese is so successful in recreating a TV style that once more the parody can become indistinguishable from the backgrounded text. TV within the film and film as parodied TV style continually interchange. Scorsese also makes an appearance himself as a TV director, which functions as parody on any number of levels, particularly as a Hitchcockian type of authorial self-inscription,[6] and we might even consider a TV director (especially when presented in a film) as a parody of a "real" director.

One of the first amazements of *Purple Rose* is how perfectly recreated the film-within-film is. We see just enough of it (or perhaps too much) to feel we've seen it all before dozens of times. The "interior" *Purple Rose* is purposely mediocre yet lovable, teetering humorously on the edge of true lousiness, as the characters within that film are all too ready to remark when problems occur. Also enjoyable in this regard are the complaints of the "audience" in the film, such as, "They sit around and talk and no action. Nothing happens." This sounds like lines from the Mel Brooks–narrated cartoon *The Critic* or, as is so often said of films Allen has emulated without parody, from Ingmar Bergman. Allen probably much prefers the inner *Purple Rose* after Tom Baxter has exited to the real world. It becomes more like *Interiors* or *Another Woman*.

These films certainly flaunt the dangers of such parodic activities; we don't expect imitation to be an insincere form of nonflattery. Risking comparison to the originals, these films can easily be thought of as "bad" by the unparody-minded, a risk openly engaged.

Parodic Cultural Juxtaposition

Hutcheon takes appropriate pleasure from what she calls "high-low self-reflexive fiction," the juxtaposing of wildly eclectic sources (81). Tom Robbins's *Even Cowgirls Get the Blues* is her favorite example in its pushing against each other of Roy Rogers and William Blake. These filmmakers do the same kind of shocking matchmaking with equal abandon.

Perhaps the most obscure disparate linkage ever in a popular movie comes in Scorsese's *After Hours,* so weird it's worth explaining. The possible robbers played by Cheech and Chong have finally gotten their hands on the wrapped sculpture they've been after throughout the movie. As they load it onto their truck, one of them remarks that he saw the sculptor play banjo on the "Tonight Show." To get the joke and the parodic reference one has to recognize that (1) the sculpture in question is in the style of *artist* George Segal and (2) the *actor* George Segal had often appeared on talk shows playing a banjo (badly).

If you're up on your pop trash and your high art, you might manage to keep up with Scorsese's joke, a giant step ahead of his earlier penchant for sprinkling the names of his favorite directors and film characters throughout his films, as when Robert De Niro in *New York, New York* tries to register in a hotel under the name Michael Powell. As annoying as these little games might seem, on such foundations parodistic activities have always been constructed.

The high-low juxtaposition is so deeply imbedded within Kubrick's style as to be an identifying characteristic. The music clashes are most obvious: Gioacchino Rossini and gang fights in *2001*, Béla Bartók and Krzysztof Penderecki over the gore in *The Shining*. *Barry Lyndon* presents the spectacle of an almost never-ending gulf between base human activity and breathtaking classical art and music.

In De Palma the trash may be trashy enough that the high art doesn't have to be too high for a clash to be felt, so dropping *Sunset Boulevard* or *Vertigo* into the middle of faithfully recreated porno scenes is sufficient in itself to generate dissonance. The actor who sets up the *Body Double* plot (the partial counterpart to *Vertigo*'s Gavin Elster) is off to do *Private Lives* (even if it's in Seattle), and art museums, classical music, and religious artifacts have shown up discordantly in other De Palma films.

Allen's humor, especially in his *New Yorker* pieces, has often been built around high-low conflicts, with his film *Love and Death* probably his most overt so far in pushing cultural twists. The grafting of borscht belt humor to Dostoevskian musings on spiritual rebirth has been Allen's near stock-in-trade. In *Purple Rose,* we shouldn't express surprise when the playboy in the inner film is named Henry Adams, as these name games are one of the easiest ways to identify this kind of parodistic artistic split.

Conflicted Obsession,
or You Always Hate the One You Love

These films share a long-noted parody characteristic: the simultaneous qualities of faithful appropriation and vengeful revisionism. In speculating on the double-edged character of parody, Hutcheon recalls two important views on this issue. Marcel Proust, accounting for his own obsession with Gustave Flaubert, described his reworkings as "the purgative antidotes to the toxins of admiration." Robert Motherwell ties the two emotions together in describing the role of the modern artist as "everything he paints is both an homage and a critique" (Hutcheon, 50).

In the four films I have been discussing, obsessive love/hate is an extensive activity within the film and strongly characteristic of the film itself in relation to its genre. Love or frustration in the characters generally turns to murderous intent, and in the process these conflicted attitudes pass into parody complexity: ambivalent (but also extreme) feelings are everywhere.

It's not accidental that critiques of fandom are built into these films, most obviously in *King of Comedy* and *Purple Rose*. In the latter, it may be Cecilia's (near Pupkin-like) obsessiveness that pulls Tom Baxter off the screen (that's his story, anyway) and her rejection that dooms him to a Promethean return to what is now a perpetual straitjacket of mechanical performance. Rupert's obsession with Langford nearly kills him, as was to occur in an earlier version of the script.[7] In *Stardust Memories,* Allen eerily anticipates this kind of fan-murderer as well. Careening acceptance-rejection obsessions clearly have their consequences on both sides. Indirectly, the "worth" of the recreated worlds is questioned, be it a star, a genre, or, in the case of *Purple Rose,* old-time Hollywood itself. We probably can't ever decide whether Kubrick hates horror films, whether De Palma is strictly idolatrous of Hitchcock ("body double" may have a certain literal meaning), how much time Scorsese still spends watching TV talk shows, or the extent of Allen's engagement with Golden Age movies. It is enough to see evidence of the closest study and imitation and the kind of ultimate rejection through revision that mature art encompasses. Doomed to imitate an artistic past and sufficiently reflexive to bracket the old experiences by means of parodic devices, love/hate becomes comedy/tragedy. Heavy doses of humor and violence intermingle in uneasy, shifting disharmonies, reflecting strongly ambivalent relations to artistic predecessors.

Self-parody as Signature

Identifying parody strategies can go a long way toward determining distinctive authorial style. One of the most interesting and peculiar links between parody and authorship is the propensity, first, to self-reference and from there to self-parody. Rose establishes self-parody as a preeminent activity in metafiction, and in terms of film it's not hard to see the extension. The troubled artists at the center of these films surely have troubled artists behind them; and although the heroes here are never directors, like Chaucer's self-inscription in *Canterbury Tales* that Rose refers to, the authors of these works seem to have left their tracings in all sorts of sneaky ways (97).

Only Scorsese appears himself, but *Body Double* has director figures throughout, including an Eric Von Stroheim stand-in, a director working over an actor at a reading, and a porno film director—all possible versions of De Palma himself. Kubrick has tantalizingly left his own playful mark before, as in the prominently displayed *2001* soundtrack album cover that pops up in *Clockwork Orange.* In *The Shining,* stylistic exaggeration is often self-parodic and is most easily seen in the exhilarating steadicam tracking shots as Danny tricycles his way down the long hotel hallways, so reminiscent of the spaceship corridors of *2001,* the wartime trenches of *Paths of Glory,* and the other perfectly symmetrical narrow passageways so dear to Kubrick.

The Shining also presents us with a series of potentially controlling figures appearing in a variety of guises, including a hotel manager, the ghost of a dead murderer who may be Jack Torrance in an earlier incarnation, and a bartender, each giving us a vacant feeling that someone's dealing the deck, but we're not sure who. Absent ultimate power figures are a Kubrick staple, whether it's which general is in charge, who stuck that monolith there anyway, or where that narrator went in *The Killing* and *Barry Lyndon*. The most absent figure is, of course, Kubrick himself, whose mythic image as a reclusive castle-inhabiting control-freak is the only media creation able to rival his own power-mad figures. Behind all the hotel doors setting ghastly images in motion, dripping blood out of elevators, providing the unexplained means of escape to frequently trapped characters, lies the director himself, a parody puppeteer in the shadows.

Although Allen's nonappearance in *Purple Rose* is likely because his overt self-inscription has been so frequent,[8] there is still a director for the film-within-a-film (amusingly named Raoul Hirsh, no doubt a Jewish Raoul Walsh) and a cynical set of agents and studio-employed hacks, historical precursors to the bunch who pop up in *Stardust Memories*. Gil Shepherd's falsely modest remark to Cecilia about his career to date that he "tries to do one a year" is a clearly self-referring and self-mocking Allen remark. For Allen as personality, obviously the most known to the general public of these four directors, the tendency to blur persona and character, including this kind of mocking self-parody, has also been the most extreme.

Conclusion

Distinctive cinematic parody style, the strategies of radical metacinema we can extrapolate from Rose, Waugh, Hutcheon, et al., is so broadly pervasive we bump into it more easily than the TV sets all over these movies. What is especially distinctive in terms of cinema is how eclectic the forms of intertextuality have become and how properly the activities of parody have been directed toward an exploration of the processes of creation. Whether we go to other films by these four, or to Arthur Penn, Robert Altman, Jonathan Demme, Bob Fosse, Stanley Donen, or Francis Coppola, to name a fast six contemporary Americans,[9] the incorporation of mediocre art and artists, show biz references, and eclectic cross-cultural juxtapositions into ambitious, risky, and very funny movies is a parody lesson we're still in the process of discovering.

A number of filmmakers working within mainstream commercial cinema today have been systematically employing parody devices more commonly discussed and appreciated in literary circles. The clear applicability of the Rose-Waugh-Hutcheon school to this body of films suggests that the cinematic forms of these devices are widespread and distinctive. By using parody techniques not readily recognized and by making difficult, seemingly "bad" films, they push the limits of the acceptable, especially in redefining the ways the films are to be viewed. This critique-from-within and testing of audiences make up our unlikely but prevalent radical metacinema.

Notes

1. A Roadrunner cartoon is also heard without being seen in a second scene, and Danny wears a Roadrunner shirt among his parody attire, which includes a spaceship sweater and a Philadelphia Flyers (!) jacket.

2. Allen plays a TV writer in *Manhattan* very much concerned with having frittered away his talents in that medium, as he's now trying to write a novel. In *Bananas,* and in early Allen generally, overt TV parody is a continual staple, as in, for example, the appearance of Howard Cosell to provide play-by-play commentary on the honeymoon night.

3. See Stephen Mamber for a section on parody in that film.

4. TV screens also make prominent appearances in other Scorsese films, notably the newly installed and barely working set in *Raging Bull.* (Later we see one of the boxing matches on it.) In *Alice Doesn't Live Here Anymore,* there is extensive television watching, including a long (and prescient) close-up of Johnny Carson.

5. Beverle Houston, in an excellent article that explores the television questions raised by the film, has a useful discussion of the "Is Rupert's monologue funny?" question.

6. Scorsese has made regular appearances in his own films, in addition to his well-known cameo appearance in *Taxi Driver.* In *After Hours,* he again has a parodied directorial role as a guy "shining" a light in the punk nightclub.

7. Jerry Lewis reported this at a University of Southern California screening of *King of Comedy.* Also cited in Houston.

8. Allen's role in *Zelig* is an interesting precursor to Rupert Pupkin in *King of Comedy.* The director Allen plays in *Stardust Memories* struck so many as being a Woody Allen stand-in that his interviews related to that film generally begin with Allen laboring to point out differences. Also, in *Play It Again, Sam* (which he wrote and starred in but didn't direct), he does put himself into a *Purple Rose* –like situation, playing a character taking cues from the Humphrey Bogart of *Casablanca* come to life, a clear warm-up for the more complicated on-screen/off-screen interactions here.

9. The films of each I most have in mind (in a list that could be much longer) are *Mickey One, Nashville, Melvin and Howard, Star 80* (or, obviously, *All That Jazz* or *Lennie*), *Movie Movie,* and *One From the Heart.*

References and Additional Reading

Houston, Beverle. 1984. "*King of Comedy:* A Crisis of Substitution." *Framework,* no. 24 (Spring): 88.

Hutcheon, Linda. 1985. *A Theory of Parody: The Teaching of Twentieth-Century Art Forms.* New York: Methuen.

Mamber, Stephen. 1972–1973. "A Clockwork Orange." *Cinema* 7, no: 3 (Winter): 48–57.

Rose, Margaret A. 1979. *Parody // Meta-fiction: An Analysis of Parody as a Critical Mirror to the Writing and Reception of Fiction.* London: Croom Helm.

Waugh, Patricia. 1984. *Metafiction: The Theory and Practice of Self-Conscious Fiction.* London: Methuen.

Mock Realism

The Comedy of Futility
in Eastern Europe

Charles Eidsvik

—A competition for the best political joke was announced.
—Do you know what the first prize was?
—No.
—Fifteen years.

(Banc & Dundes, 9)

To a Western viewer, the first experience of viewing Eastern European film comedies in the company of Eastern Europeans is apt to be unsettling. Often, the films do not appear to be comedies in the usual American sense. Not only is there no identifiable comic protagonist to guide the humor— no Charlie Chaplin or Groucho Marx or Woody Allen or Steve Martin; there are few of the conventions that for Western viewers signal that it is all right to laugh.[1] Furthermore, Eastern European audiences laugh at things that mean little to Westerners. For those who "get" the "points" of the films' humor, the films are indeed very funny. This chapter is a tentative attempt to explain how a selected group of Eastern European film comedies "work."[2] My concern is to describe at least some of the comic conventions that have evolved among people who have managed by and large to keep their sense of humor under what has passed for socialism in Eastern Europe. The films I discuss are primarily those from Czechoslovakia in the 1960s, when the mock-realist comic style that dominates Eastern comedy coalesced, and current films from Czechoslovakia and Poland, but I believe they have many links with films from Yugoslavia and other Eastern European countries.

The first thing to be said is that film comedy in Eastern Europe is more overtly political than we are accustomed to in the West. As the "first prize" joke cited at the opening of this chapter suggests, humor in totalitarian states often functions as, and therefore often gets treated as, an act of rebellion against state-sanctioned values and taboos. In Eastern Europe during the last three decades, humor has often ridiculed the official Stalin-

91

ist rhetoric and approved forms of social organization. Official Stalinist rhetoric promises a great deal. Yet for everyday life, the bureaucracy, the centralized party control, the virtual colonial status vis-à-vis the USSR, and a barter-based international trade system have been a mess.[3] As one joke puts it, in the West, fairy tales are told about the past; in the East, they are told about the future.

Not surprisingly, given their shared official rhetoric and social dilemmas, Eastern Europeans share an unofficial and often underground sense of humor, with jokes that originate in one country adapted to and retold in the next.[4] A key quality in this humor is skepticism raised almost to the cosmic level—as the following joke reveals:

> Ford, Brezhnev, and Tito, in a time of crisis, are each permitted to ask God one question. Ford asks when will the United States come out of crisis? God replies, "In fifty years." Ford breaks into tears saying, "Oh, I will never see the day." Brezhnev asks when will the economic power of the USSR equal that of the United States. God replies, "In one hundred years." Brezhnev breaks into tears exclaiming, "Oh, I will never see the day." Tito asks when will the dinar be a strong currency. At these words, God breaks into tears saying, "Oh, I will never see the day." (Banc & Dundes, 170)

Eastern European film comedies often share the sensibility of such jokes from their region, but unlike privately told jokes, the films are made and get shown through state-run studios and distribution networks. Their comic malice must therefore be masked. The straight-faced and puritanical world of socialist good intentions, to say nothing of the party's sense of itself, has little tolerance of irreverence and levity. Eastern European comedies (excepting those by Dusan Makavejev and Peter Bacsó) tend to be deadpan and sly spinoffs from "ordinary" realism. Some, such as the stunning *Pictures from an Old World* (Czechoslovakia, 1972), even pose as documentaries. The standard pose of the comic filmmaker is that of a recorder of ordinary behavior; the result, for lack of a better phrase, could be called "mock realism."[5]

Mock realism takes some getting used to. Its roots go back in literature to Anton Chekhov and in fiction film to Jean Renoir, both of whom loved the humor of the everyday. The most direct impulse, however, came as cinema verité influenced Czechs such as Milos Forman, Ivan Passer, and Jaroslav Papoušek. Noticing that when filmed with deadpan "neutrality," real people could be both funny and revealing about social realities, Forman and his friends began developing a style of comedy that hardly looks like Western fictional comedy at all. This kind of comedy does not need repartee or funny walks or clowning around as an invocation of the comic mood, as the film equivalent of "Did you hear the one about?" Moreover at the story level there is nothing at all funny or malicious or mocking about

Pictures from an Old World

the films. What creates the comic effect is that allusions to the real world of the viewer allow the viewer to react in terms of an imagined world suggested by the film—one that *is* incongruous and funny.

The viewer must of course grasp the social realities to which the film alludes and be willing to view the film playfully. Some films, such as *Fireman's Ball* (1967) or *The Apple Game* (1976), invite this playful mood by introducing an overtly humorous scene or situation early in the film. Others use humor-establishing mechanisms common in jokes. As Michael Mulkay demonstrates, often the hearer of a joke willingly joins the playmood of humor by accepting either implausible story elements or a wholly idiosyncratic viewpoint while agreeing to participate wholly in the terms of the story (16). In an early scene in *The Apple Game*, implausibility is too much fun to reject: two legs in the air indicate that sex is happening in a parked car, and a crowd of workmen gathers, gives advice, and cheers the couple on. The idiosyncratic viewpoints of *Pictures from an Old World* and *A Short Film About Love* (1988) signal that the mood of humor is acceptable. In *Pictures from an Old World* the characters often look conspiratorially at the filmmaker's camera as if to boast about their own orneriness and eccentricity and their own cockeyed but practical approach to everyday life. Their feistiness resembles nothing so much as that of Charlie Chaplin's Tramp; it is as if they have chosen to be comic as a way of facing life honestly.

In *A Short Film About Love* an opening scene showing the protagonist breaking into a university storeroom to steal a telescope is immediately followed by one in which we see what he wants to use it for—to spy on a pretty neighbor. The melodrama of the first scene is mocked by the second: an incongruity between means and motive, between activity and purpose, is established as a pattern that typifies the protagonist's life and makes him both sympathetic and comic. Equally important is the filmmaker's rejection of the unitary or linear conceptual structure of serious modes of discourse, putting in their place multiple and incongruous realities, perspectives, or modes of interpretation (Mulkay, 214). In serious films a unitary mode translates to a situation in which one aspect of a character dominates and one plot problem "drives" the main story (although, of course, secondary, sometimes comic, subplots can abound). In mock-realist films the characters do not really know what they are doing, so no single plot problem fully dominates the film. (I will illustrate how this works in terms of *Fireman's Ball*.)

One other element of Eastern bloc comedies also must be mentioned, if only because of the unfamiliarity of Western viewers with socialist economic realities. Eastern European comedies often differ from Western comedies by their emphasis on ambition (or lack of ambition) as a source of comedy and the workplace as comedy's locale.[6] Except in television situation comedies such as "The Mary Tyler Moore Show" and "Roseanne," American filmmakers rarely treat the workplace as a locus for comedy. In Eastern Europe only love and family—comic subjects good anywhere in the world—get as much comic treatment as the workplace does, perhaps because of the fundamentally comic inefficiency of the system; as the cliché puts it, "We pretend to work; they pretend to pay us." Nothing personally is gained by work, and little is lost by not working hard. The incongruity between 100 percent employment levels and marginal productivity is a standing invitation to the humorist. Equally important, people have grown deeply disenchanted with the incessant trumpeting by despised party politicians of "work" and "productivity" as goals. The omnipresent official "production plans" of each factory or enterprise meet head-on the realities of the workplace. Socialist countries are called "workers' states," although, in fact, nobody is working, and even those who might want to work cannot accomplish much. Especially in films such as Forman's *Loves of a Blonde* (1965), the work site (in this case, a shoe factory) provides a locus for the comedy of futility in nearly pure form.

For Western viewers, perhaps the two best-known examples of the Eastern European comedy of futility are Milos Forman's *Fireman's Ball* and

Ivan Passer's *Intimate Lighting* (1965). In *Fireman's Ball* a provincial fire department attempts to put on its annual dance, raffle, and beauty contest. At the coming ball the department will also present a ceremonial fire ax to the old chief. But the raffle prizes begin to disappear even before the ball begins. While the retired chief watches, one fireman holds the ladder for a second, who trims a paper banner by burning its edges with a lighter. A third fireman comes into the room, distraught because an item to be raffled off is missing. The first and third firemen squabble, leaving the man trimming the banner hanging (from the now-burning banner) without a ladder. "Oompah" music begins and so does the ball.

Nothing goes right. The firemen quarrel about the missing raffle prizes and about who should be contestants in the beauty contest. One beauty contestant has brought a bathing suit; the firemen cannot help but ask her to pose in it. Finally the young contestants try to run away to the women's room. Someone hears a fire siren, and the firemen rush off to the fire. The crowd follows, and the fire becomes a continuation of the entertainment. While the firemen save salvageable items, the bartenders from the ball bring drinks to sell to the crowd and try to collect for drinks already consumed. The house burns down. Everyone returns to the ball. The firemen decide to donate the raffle proceeds to the old man whose house burned. But almost all the raffle prizes have been stolen. So the firemen announce an opportunity for the anonymous return of the stolen goods while the lights are turned out. In the dark the remaining goods disappear. The firemen try again. When the lights are turned on this time, a fireman's wife is still in the act of returning a stolen headcheese. Her husband faints from shame. The firemen are angry at the embarrassment to the company. With nothing to be done about the raffle, the firemen decide to honor their chief. They bring him the case with the ceremonial fire ax and make a speech. He makes an acceptance speech. He opens the ax case. The ax, too, has been stolen. The old man whose house has burned returns to the ruin and crawls into a bed that has been salvaged, alongside a fireman left there to watch the ruins.

What is special—and comic—about *Fireman's Ball* is its multifold distractions as conflicting roles and semantic systems trip up whatever at any given moment seems to be the plot.[7] The firemen cannot simply be firemen; they are also husbands, fathers, lechers, compulsive rationalizers. They squabble incessantly. They profess altruism, but steal. They pretend to dignity but sneak looks at the young woman in a bathing suit. When they actually try to do their "real" job, they are too late: perhaps their ball has distracted them from hearing the siren; perhaps not. They botch this job, too: the old man's house is gone. Each of the characters is a bundle of ineptitudes and contradictions. Together, they are a disaster. Accomplishing *anything*—even a fireman's ball—in this sort of society is impossible.

The film (like many Eastern European comedies) ends up feeling strangely like a Western situation comedy in that the society the film dissects, like those in our situation comedies, is essentially static rather than dynamic.[8] Forman's comedy depends on the sense that nothing *can* change in the kind of world he depicts.

Forman's comically dour sensibility was shared by Ivan Passer in *Intimate Lighting* and (to a lesser extent) by Jaroslav Papoušek's *The Best Age* (1968). *Intimate Lighting* tells of the reunion of two old friends, both in middle age. One, a city musician with a young mistress, visits the other, Bamba, head of a provincial music school. Both are disillusioned; except when completely drunk, neither has much hope left of accomplishing anything. But the city musician's mistress and the country musician's family and surroundings make the story of a simple visit into a polyphonal collision of realities that at times becomes almost surrealistic. The musicians want to talk about music, but the older kids announce that the youngest, Kaja, has urinated in the bath. Bamba's family tries to put on a good chicken supper, but the kids all want the drumstick and so does grandpa; the women (who are the real powers in the family) get into dutiful self-sacrifice and give up their plates for others. Cacophony rules. The two old friends get drunk and try to change their lives by leaving home, but they are so drunk they forget they are wearing pajamas. The film ends with their hangovers: at breakfast the family and its guests try to drink a "special" eggnog the grandmother has prepared. Unfortunately it has jelled and will not come out of the glasses. They try to drink a toast, pretending they are accomplishing something. But the jelled eggnog is as obstinate as the other realities they face.

The style of *Intimate Lighting* is that of the lyric documentary. Except that the film is in black and white, it reminds one of the peasant scenes in *National Geographic* spreads on Slavic villages. The sun is bright; everything is gently, diffusedly pretty. Against this style the humdrum midlife crises of the two protagonists and their families resound bizarrely, poignantly, and comically.

More artificial is Papoušek's approach in *The Best Age*. Here the images are documentarylike. But the characters, who lie to themselves perpetually, are obviously speaking dialogue. Passer, Forman, and Papoušek are masters at using, and directing, amateur actors (working alongside professionals) so that the work has a "real" look. But Papoušek's theme—lying—demands almost set-piece encounters. In perhaps the most revealing scene in *The Best Age* an injured coalman works as a model for an art professor who wants him to pose with his mouth open.

Professor: Open your mouth. "Hurrah" for Slavia.

Vosta: I support Sparta.

Professor:	Sparta has scored.
Vosta:	Sorry, but they seem unable to score.
Professor:	Pretend they scored and shout "hurrah." (quoted in Hames, 146)

Like authority figures in Forman's Czech films (for example, a buck-passing colonel in *Loves of a Blonde*), the professor in *The Best Age* is both ineffectual and ridiculous. The model is what the socialist "workers' state" pretends that working people are not: in a word, stupid.

Of course not all Eastern European filmmakers from the first Dubček era built their comic scenes from documentary bases. Jiri Menzel's *Closely Watched Trains* (1966) appeals to realism but within the freest genre in socialist countries: the anti-Nazi film. Although set during World War II, the satirical humor in *Closely Watched Trains* is not (according at least to friends of mine within the Czech émigré community) *only* about fascists. The railroad and political officials in the film seem little different from officials in Stalinist Czechoslovakia: bullheaded and ineffectual. Menzel contrasts these characters with Hubička, the station guard. Hubička cares little for promotion; what is important to him is his sex life. Constantly horny, Hubička cares little that a night with his "cousin" wrecks the stationmaster's beloved couch. Hubička also belongs to the resistance and is the man entrusted with the job of blowing up a Nazi munitions train. Hubička's independence from conformist and regimented thinking in personal matters carries over into an ability to act creatively in political situations. In the world of *Closely Watched Trains,* any expression of the comic or erotic is an act of subversion against oppression, and any rebellion is a step toward liberation.

In a film by Menzel's friend, Vera Chytilová, *The Apple Game* (1976), rebellion against authority takes a feminist direction: for women the work ethic has clearly meant an ethic of subordination. In *The Apple Game* images of strong physicality—of sex treated as physical farce, of a breast oozing milk—stand in direct opposition to the empty rhetoric of males, particularly those in charge of the hospital in which the protagonist works. The males all speak in the buzzwords of socialism, talking of "progress" and "objective problems" whether those are appropriate or not: for example, a doctor (played by Menzel) excuses his self-serving sexual behavior by talking of his "objective problems." Against this the protagonist, Anna, can only refuse the usual lures. She refuses marriage because that would make her a "washing machine" for her husband. She uses her physicality as a buffer against the world of rhetoric of the males who run institutions.

But for Chytilová, comedy stems only partly from documentary. Although she consistently worked with nonactors in films such as *Ceiling*

(1962) and *Something Different* (1963) and works with documented improvisation and an extraordinary eye for telling details in reality, Chytilová has never been satisfied with the conventions of ordinary narrative structure. She described *Something Different* as a "philosophical documentary in the form of a farce" (Hames, 211). But she departed from conventional forms altogether in her strangest and, I think, most interesting films, *Daisies* (1966) and *The Fruit of Paradise* (1969). In these two Chytilová borrowed from Louis Malle's anarchistic farce, *Zazie in the Metro* (1962); from Alain Resnais' *Last Year at Marienbad* (1961); and from comic strips and documentaries. Raunchy, funny, sad, disturbing, and dreamlike, these two comedies defy any theories of comedy, including mine. What is important here, however, is that within the Eastern European context, Chytilová, like Forman, Papoušek, and Passer, fought to find new ways of expressing the comic spirit. And her work, even at its strangest, looked to reality, not to theatrical, film, or literary convention, as the source of its comic motifs.

Even more physical than Chytilová's work is *Pictures from an Old World* (1967–1972) by Slovak director Dŭsan Hanák. Cast in the form of a grainy black-and-white documentary and including sections done with a still camera, with the "documented" people openly acknowledging the presence of the filmmaker, *Pictures from an Old World* is structured as a comic essay. The film vacillates between documents of the lives of people (playing versions of themselves) living in an isolated Slovakian region and a carefully structured set of variations on the theme of retaining inner freedom in the face of modern life. Self-sufficient, the characters in *Pictures* work hard. But one point of the film is that *this* work is of an entirely different kind from work in a city, modern work without personal meaning. The characters' physical relation to their lives stands as a stark contradiction to the normal socialist notion of work as an abstract good.

Hanák's images, some in still pictures, all in black and white, all with a strong sense both of the picturesque and of presence, are palpably physical. A man without functioning legs has rebuilt his farm so that he can manage alone. His family has left him, and as in "real" life, we do not know how that happened. He is ornery and solitary but rivets our attention as he goes about his life. For me, he is a phenomenon: there is nothing whatever I could tell him about his life that he does not know; I do not like the man, but I am staggered by a pragmatism raised to the heroic level. Another old man, who has no hot water, washes himself by holding well water in his mouth until it is warmed, then spitting it into his hands so he can wash with it. An old widow continues her husband's job taking care of a graveyard. She is unappreciated and alone but obstinate in her values and her commitment to the traditions she has loved. A lot of the characters in *Pictures* are almost grotesque in their age-bent individuality. But their

struggles are pitted not only against the cruelties of age and nature—
against such opponents these characters are formidable antagonists—but
against the specter of work (or retirement) in a modern world where one's
work is not one's own, where one's life is not one's own.

Although the structure of this documentarylike film is comic and there
are dozens of astonishing and funny moments, the film repudiates the
Marxist work ethic that removes work from contexts that are personal.
Defiantly Slovak (rather than Czechoslovak), Hanák's film celebrates a region of rebels getting along on their own terms. For Hanák the documentary mode did not remove him from censure; the film's message was obvious enough that the government suppressed the film until 1988.

Hanák's *I Love, You Love* (made in 1980, released in 1989) uses realist
conventions but invokes the spirit of Jean Renoir and Charles Chaplin as
much as it does that of documentary. Two friends work as mail sorters for
the railroad. Usually not just buzzed but authentically drunk, they putter
through their lives in a continual celebration. They both dream of women.
One is a successful seducer. The other, the film's protagonist, Pista, is not:
fat, ugly, and continually drunk, he cannot seduce anyone. He spends his
time getting along, playing with a pet pig, playing his tuba, and taking
care of his aging, senile mother, who, left unwatched, habitually tries to
run away. His railroad supervisors keep threatening to fire him but (as is
typical in socialism's world of 100 percent employment) never quite manage it.

His life goes on its blurry course until his friend dies. Shaken by news
that his girlfriend, Vera, is pregnant, the friend falls asleep with the gas
jets on. Was it suicide or an accident? Although we watch him do it, we do
not know. And neither do Pista and Vera. Both feel guilty. Consoling one
another, Pista and Vera become friends. Things blossom into a marriage
of affectionate convenience. But Pista cannot change a lot of his habits,
and Vera gets tired of Pista's connections to his old life. They separate.

Pista continues on his solitary way. He tries to reform but in his own
way. For example, at a kiosk he gets two beers—one for him, one in honor
of his old friend. Knowing that alcohol is a problem for him, he does not
drink his, only his friend's. Eventually at a carnival dance, Pista dresses up
in a costume. He is so ridiculous that Vera cannot help but embrace him.
And so they muddle on, dancing toward a life of compromise that is the
only hope for people for whom progress and officially sanctioned values
are forever chimerical and for whom the sense that there is nothing to be
done, that it is as well to play, provides a way of getting through life.

Even in *You Love, I Love,* the images Hanák presents are within a realist tradition. For the Czech government, however, works such as Hanák's
were, until recently, refused distribution, not because Hanák was not describing reality but because he *was*. The realities Hanák described were

I Love, You Love

unacceptable in terms of Czechoslovakia's public relations image as a "modern" state. Nevertheless, since Hanák's films were released, they have received broad festival and popular acclaim through Eastern Europe; the language of comic realism (or mock-realist comedy) has become a currency Eastern bloc audiences have learned to cherish.

Audiences in the East as well as the West have a harder time knowing how to take the humor of the Pole Krzysztof Kieślowski in his brilliant *A Short Film About Love* (1988). Part of Kieślowski's decalog on contemporary themes related to the Ten Commandments, *A Short Film About Love* has, like its companion *A Short Film About Killing* (1987), received wide theatrical release throughout Europe. Unlike *A Short Film About Killing,* winner of the first European Film Prize (the European answer to the Oscar), *A Short Film About Love* is structured as a comedy, but one that makes audiences squirm as well as laugh. Its viewpoint is never far removed from that of its protagonists, and its protagonists are (like the film's viewers) voyeurs. For me as well as others with whom I have seen and talked about the film, *A Short Film About Love* dredges up unwanted memories of how we made ludicrous asses of ourselves as teenagers when we first fell in love. But there is also something so recognizable in the desperate relationships between the characters that the laughter the film

A Short Film About Love

evokes has the rueful sound of people laughing at something in themselves.

The story is simple: Tomek, a nineteen-year-old postal clerk raised in an
orphanage, lives with his only friend's aging mother. His hobby is spying
on Magda, a pretty thirty-year-old weaver who lives across the way and
whose love life, although unhappy, is active. At the film's opening, we
watch Tomek break into a university storage room and steal a telescope so
he can see better. Smitten with love, Tomek concocts all sorts of excuses
to see Magda. He takes a second job as a milk deliverer for her building;
he sends her false mail pickup notices so she will have to come to the post
office. Jealous of her lovers, Tomek interrupts her lovemaking one night
with a prank: he reports a gas leak in her apartment and watches, ashamed
but delighted, as the gas inspectors come to see if Magda's stove is all
right.

Eventually Tomek confesses to Magda that he sent the false mail notices
and that he has been spying on her. Although irrationally fascinated that
anyone would be so interested in her, she is outraged and arranges to have
Tomek beaten up by her current boyfriend. Then, guilty, she agrees to go
out to coffee with him. In the cafe, Tomek gives her some letters he has
stolen from her. Astonished, and again angry, Magda brings him to her

apartment, gets him to touch her thighs, and when he immediately ejaculates, she ridicules him. He runs away. Suddenly ashamed, she puts a sign in her window for him to come back. Instead, he slashes his wrists. Saved by his landlady (who has used Tomek's telescope to spy on the encounter between Tomek and Magda), he is nursed back to some semblance of health. Now it is Magda's turn to become obsessive: using opera glasses, she watches Tomek's window for any sign that Tomek is again in the world. Initially rebuffed by the landlady (who has taken over Tomek's milk delivery job for him—a weird but oddly affecting demonstration of her love for him), Magda manages to get into Tomek's room to see him. As the film ends she looks at her own apartment window through Tomek's telescope and imagines the two of them together, comforting one another.

Peppered with outrageous humor but without in any way patronizing the protagonists, *A Short Film* bluntly refutes ordinary preconceptions. Tomek's behavior is, of course, outrageous, but as viewers we participate in it and share his fascinations. The landlady feels both motherly and erotic affection for Tomek, and this affection is treated with gentle, although humorous, respect. Tomek's confessions to Magda are as ridiculous as they are astonishing, but there is something painful about our laughter as he confesses. For Kieślowski's characters, all of modern life conspires against people reaching toward and touching one another; to get through the barriers a character *must* make a fool of himself.

Strikingly photographed in a compact, documentary-derived but carefully controlled style with jagged comic editing and rapid visual gags, *A Short Film About Love* is a comedy of desperation unlike anything I have seen from Eastern Europe. It is funny, especially in its treatment of the symbiotic relationship between Tomek and the landlady and in its insistence that voyeurism is both the natural state of contemporary (Polish) humankind *and* a first step for people who want to reach out toward each other. But unlike any other comedies I have seen from Eastern Europe, its characters' sense of their lived realities has no note of protest to it. The characters are beyond protest; there is nothing that can be changed, nothing to complain about. The world of Kieślowski's characters has been crushed by history. And so Tomek, Magda, and the landlady do not resent work even though they do not work for reasons of ambition. They work because work can help people to reach, however clumsily, toward each other. Work is an excuse for contact between ludicrous and funny but suffering human beings.

Yet there is something strange, something frightened in the laughter during *A Short Film About Love*. Long regarded as one of Poland's best documentarists, Kieślowski has emerged as perhaps Poland's best narrative filmaker. What I think frightens viewers is only partly that Kieślowski probes beneath the viewer's own lonely and voyeuristic surface. A deeper problem is that Kieślowski, unlike almost every other comic filmmaker in Eastern Europe, has stopped laughing at socialism. The mood of comic glee gained by juxtaposing official notions and rhetoric with documentary realities (or social realities viewed through a mock-realist sensibility) depends on at least the implicit existence of Marxist ideology as its antagonist. Life under socialism or even in general may be hopeless, and there may be little to be done except to play, except to laugh. But in the scheme of humor, it is best if someone in the establishment can be blamed for dumb values, a stupid semantic system, or mode of discourse that can become the butt of laughter. If there are idiots in charge of society, then idiocy can be blamed for why things go wrong the way they do, and the comedy of futility has, in its rebellious posture, a sense that things at least could be different.

But Kieślowski has gone beyond Marxism and beyond the demise of its advocates in Eastern Europe. He has inched toward a kind of comedy that has little or no glee in demonstrating the futility of socialist plans; rather his comedy simply admits that everything has failed and that we must start from zero. Tomek and Magda and the landlady have no one to blame for their helplessness and hopelessness. They can respond to their situation only by becoming ludicrous, by becoming comic.

For Eastern Europeans perhaps it is easier to laugh at films such as Kieślowski's and Hanák's than it is for Westerners. In Eastern Europe since 1947 Stalinist rhetoric has been the official and dominant form of serious discourse. Everything somehow could be related to or explained in terms of Karl Marx; everything would, with proper wisdom, get better. By the end of 1989 that rhetoric, those explanations, those promises, had died. Eastern Europe has begun to deal with the incongruous and conflicting realities and rhetorics of a post-Stalinist world. The result may be that the meaning of humor itself may change so that Western people will have an even harder time understanding Eastern European comedy than they have had until now. After Kieślowski, not to mention the events of 1989, there may be no way for Eastern Europeans to deny that they live in paradoxical, multiple, and incongruous realities. In such realities what is normally taken for humor is serious and seriousness itself is comic.

But such speculation also has its obverse. In Eastern Europe the mood of humor is ignited by an appreciation for the ridiculousness inherent in futile plans and hopes. Futile plans and hopes have a history far longer than that of socialism in Eastern Europe. So if Eastern Europe moves so far from Marxism that idealized notions of socialist goals disappear, they are bound to be replaced by capitalist notions that from an Eastern European perspective will seem equally ridiculous. Just as the contradictions of Marxism spawned comedy, so will realities in an area of the world that wants to espouse capitalism but has no capital of its own. Eastern Europeans like to laugh, even when it is virtually illegal, even when the first prize for political jokes is fifteen years. In Eastern Europe there has rarely been anything to be done. And now that new things are being done, their results may well prove a rich mother lode for new kinds of comedy.

Notes

1. See Maurice Charney for a typical account of Western comedy's dependence on comic character traits and a special kind of language. Although exceptions exist, the mainstream of American film comedy comes from the vaudeville and variety clown tradition and from theater comedy. Except in Eastern Europe, one can rarely talk of regional senses of humor; normally comedy traditions are national.

2. Unlike those of many film critics working in the area of comedy, my interests are primarily sociological. Although here I assume that humor is an act of rebellion or aggression, I make no claim that humor is limited to these uses: teenagers use sexual jokes as a way of sharing new sexual insights; men often use jokes about women to put them down. The variety of ways in which Eastern Europeans use humor of different kinds is beyond the scope of this chapter.

3. Banc and Dundes divide their book into joke sections for each of these categories. For example, an entire section titled "Big Brother" (pp. 107–131) is devoted to jokes about subordination to the USSR. The organization of this book reflects those of other collections of Eastern European humor published in the West.

4. The primary value of Banc and Dundes's anthology of Rumanian humor for this chapter is in its annotation of comparative jokes from Eastern bloc countries. The same jokes appear remarkably often in different countries. Variations from one country to the next differ relatively little, although jokes are often adapted to new events and local names. Russian humor in joke anthologies differs remarkably little from that common in Eastern Europe—although, of course, it lacks jokes with Russians as the butt. Yugoslavian humor, however, strikes me as often different from that in Warsaw Bloc countries.

5. Socialist realism, neorealism, and documentary are the strongest film traditions behind the Iron Curtain. For comedy to spring from realist styles therefore makes more sense than in the West, where fantasy genres in Hollywood have led to entirely different comic styles. The greatest difference between Western and Eastern film traditions, however, is in the importance of documentary in Eastern Europe. Large festivals (as at Leipzig) celebrate the form, and government and television support have given documentary a depth, variety, and visibility not common in the West. The documentarylike films I discuss in this chapter derive both from Eastern and Western forms because the cinema verité movement that so impressed Milos Forman and his friends was basically a French and an American movement. The American cliché that documentaries are inherently "serious" comes from watching those selected by American public television for broadcast. Because humor is often aggressive, and because people do not like being attacked,

public television has become a monument to humorlessness. There are, however, a few exceptions: much of Richard Leacock's work (such as *Chiefs* [1970]) as well as that of the Maysles brothers is hilarious at the same time as it is disturbing.

6. In the early cinema the workplace (and a distrust of work) was an important theme in comedy. For example, in Charlie Chaplin's *The Tramp* (1915), the Tramp rescues Edna from robbers, and at her home her father says, to the Tramp's dismay, "As a reward you can work." The Tramp of course does everything he can to avoid work. The theme of work is repeated in Chaplin films through *Modern Times* (1936) and occurs in a remarkable number of other silent or early sound comedies.

7. See Mulkay. In terms of older humor theory, Henri Bergson's view that we laugh when we see the mechanical "encrusted" on the living also explains humor in socialist countries. Stalinist theory applied mechanically to the running of societies produced a mechanical and inflexible social structure almost ideal for the humorist.

8. My guess is that our senses of humor are rooted in the realities of the traditional, isolated cultures that dominated history before the twentieth century and that our senses of humor are often archaic. Mulkay (221–222) suggests that the semantic inadequacy of serious "unitary" discourse for dealing with contemporary existence might well qualify what we now treat as serious as being better treated as funny, while what we now treat as funny—that is, discourses that accept or generate paradox and incongruity—should perhaps be considered serious.

References and Additional Reading

Banc, C., and A. Dundes. 1986. *First Prize: Fifteen Years!: An Annotated Collection of Romanian Political Jokes*. London: Associated University Presses.

Bergson, Henri. 1911. *Laughter: An Essay on the Meaning of the Comic*. London: Macmillan.

Bordwell, David. 1985. *Narration in the Fiction Film*. Madison: University of Wisconsin Press.

Charney, Maurice. 1978. *Comedy High and Low*. New York: Oxford University Press.

Goulding, Daniel J., ed. 1989. *Post–New Wave Cinema in the Soviet Union and Eastern Europe*. Bloomington: Indiana University Press.

Hames, Peter. 1985. *The Czechoslovak New Wave*. Berkeley: University of California Press.

Koestler, Arthur. 1964. *The Act of Creation*. New York: Dell.

Lewis, Paul. 1989. *Comic Effects: Interdisciplinary Approaches to Humor in Literature*. Albany: State University of New York Press.

Mulkay, Michael. 1988. *On Humor: Its Nature and Its Place in Modern Society*. Cambridge: Polity Press.

Young, Jeffrey T. 1978. *Classical Theories of Value from Smith to Sraffa*. Boulder, Colo.: Westview.

Comic Occasions

Charles Chaplin and the
Annals of Anality

William Paul

In Hollywood the collective enterprise engaged in making movies is known simply as "the industry." The appellation was perhaps inevitable. In creating a mass audience on a then unheard-of scale, the movies also made money in a way that could not have been previously imagined. From the romantic period on, the notion of the artist has been cultivated as someone in opposition to the dominant mores of society and certainly opposed to monetary motive by the nobility of his or her calling. In this context, the very profitability of mass art forms has in itself probably been sufficient to render them suspect to guardians of culture.

And yet throughout Western history there has been art offered to the people for consumption, art that very definitely has existed as economic production. It has included the traveling theater troupes of the Roman Empire, jongleurs, minstrels, troubadours, commedia dell'arte, and the fairs of medieval and Renaissance England with their theatrical spectacles and puppet shows in which were "inserted as many extravagancies, vulgarities and obscenities as the play would accommodate . . . even when the story was drawn from the Bible."[1] The one characteristic that all the items in my list have in common is that they represent arts of *performance,* and the most popular of the popular arts have all been performing arts.

Performing arts could be taken into the high culture only when forms conformed; theater could be made acceptable by being made drama to be read. The most apparent difference among the ways various manifestations of culture are held may be seen in contrasting the history of theater with the history of drama in the West as both are taught and written about: the history of Western theater—that which is *performed*—presents a continual flow from the Greeks onward, whereas the history of Western drama—that which is printed and *read*—moves along in bumps and starts, with some gaps lasting for centuries.[2] Performing arts are by nature transitory, disappearing in the very act of performance, and this at least offers a reason for the privileging of the printed over the performed in the records of Western culture.

Perhaps the most radical change opened up by the invention of film was its ability to record performance, to transform the transitory into permanence, and in the process to grant a performing art an unheard-of claim to importance by a durability that could match John Keats's Grecian urn and in the case of the new electronic media probably surpass it. Until this century we have been able only to read about the great clowns of the past, but now thanks to the invention of film we are blessed with a durable and extensive record of Charlie Chaplin's achievements as a performer. Of course, film enabled Chaplin to become something else as well, but it is the performer that we first get to know because it is the performer who most directly communicates with us.

For most of the performing arts, money is at least the spur if not the driving engine of the art. In Shakespeare's *Twelfth Night*, Feste the Clown, a one-man show who works outside any theatrical institution, generally earns money through witticism; in fact he's not beneath asking for payment in return for a witty remark.[3] Even though none of the arts and artists I have mentioned could approach the scale and economic ambition of film—and I don't wish to minimize the effect that scale could have on the works produced—most nonetheless existed within as precisely a defined economic context as movies have in this century. In the understandable desire to look for what was newest about the new forms of popular culture that the twentieth century has offered us, we have tended to overlook what was oldest about them, losing sight of powerful continuities between past performance and present practice.

These are, in short, art forms that speak, as Mikhail Bakhtin has aptly described them in *The Age of Rabelais*, in "the language of the marketplace."[4] As Bakhtin uses the term, the marketplace represents a culture that belongs to the people and is set against the Middle Ages official culture of high seriousness: "The marketplace was the center of all that is unofficial; it enjoyed a certain extraterritoriality. In a world of official order and official ideology, it always remained 'with the people'" (153–154). The art of the marketplace is the art the people choose by purchasing it, not the art that guardians of the state and culture impose on them. As such, for Bakhtin, marketplace art can become a tool for freedom.

In François Rabelais, Mikhail Bakhtin finds the culminating development in a tradition of "grotesque realism," a tradition that he believes more or less disappeared from most formal literature with the advent of the very different Romantic understanding of the grotesque. Nonetheless,

> the tradition of the grotesque is not entirely extinct: it continues to live and to struggle for its existence in the lower canonical genres (comedy, satire, fable) and especially in non-canonical genres (in the novel, in a special form of popular dialogue, in burlesque). Humor also goes on living on the popular stage. (101–102)

Chaplin's films derive directly from the popular stage, and my central concern in this chapter will be a consideration of the vulgar aspects of Chaplin's art. In particular, I am concerned with reinstating low comedy as Chaplin's greatest achievement, not a mere means by which he arrived at higher ends. In this regard, Bakhtin's exploration of Rabelais's low art offers a valuable lens through which to view Chaplin.

If "high" and "low" could be stripped of their evaluative connotations, they might well offer fine descriptive terms for differing kinds of art.[5] Yet official culture inevitably finds the high—the "noblest" aspects of experience, which are located in mind and spirit—as superior to the low—the body in its most grossly physical terms and located in the mouth, the genitals, the anus. An alternate view of experience may be found in grotesque art before the Romantic period, which Bakhtin believes aims to level this hierarchy by reversing it, by elevating the "material bodily lower stratum." In the process, "the essential topographical element of the bodily hierarchy turn[s] upside down: the lower stratum replaces the upper stratum" (309). In this reversal, the physical asserts itself over the spiritual and presses its demands to be placed at the top of the hierarchy.

The reversal Bakhtin finds in Rabelais suggests a radical challenge that may be seen most clearly by reworking Bakhtin's notion in Freudian terms.[6] I should say in advance of doing this that I realize the arguments of both Bakhtin and Sigmund Freud are too complex to force an exact fit, so I do not intend the Freudian terms to act as psychological analogues of Bakhtin. But Freud is close enough to Bakhtin in that he does regard the physical drives of the body as primary, the demands of the libido as the driving force of existence. The difference in Freud is that he sees the libido as always doomed to disappointment; the demands it makes must be tempered through repression: "Where id was, there must ego be," is one of Freud's most concise—and for that reason most often quoted—formulations.[7] And ego must be there because civilization itself is built on these repressions.

Because Bakhtin's concept of the grotesque reverses this formulation by asserting the ascendancy of the body, it in effect offers a challenge to the very foundations of civilization. In this regard it is at least understandable why works that aggressively elevate what is low, what in Freudian terms might be called the return of the repressed, should be regarded as dangerous. In a sense they are dangerous to the ways we think of ourselves as civilized peoples. But the elevation of the high is accomplished at the cost of repressing the low, although the very value we want to accord the high has generally necessitated denying the cost. Our claims to nobility as human beings, that which sets us apart from beasts, is built on a repression of what connects us to beasts.

It is perhaps this act of repression and the attendant psychological consequences that have caused the frequently paranoid quality in responses to popular culture, a dreaded fear that these new cultural manifestations will corrupt all that is good and valuable in high culture. In 1963 Fred M. Hechinger, the *New York Times* education editor, and his wife, Grace, gave fullest expression to this fear in an apocalyptically titled book, *Teenage Tyranny,* a tirade against this touted tyranny that blamed everything from permissive child-rearing to progressive education to the familiar villain of the culture industry. One of the worst aspects of teen culture for the Hechingers was the extent to which teens were managing to corrupt their unwitting elders. The repression on which high culture is built is so unsteady that it may succumb to animal assaults from out-of-control teenagers. This was made most dreadfully evident for the Hechingers by the fact that adults had begun to like rock 'n' roll and were even dancing the "Twist":

> The success of the Twist is a flagrant example of a teen-age fad dominating the adult world. . . . Probably the summit of success came for Joey Dee [a rock singer] when he was asked to play at the fashion industry's Party of the Year, a one-hundred-dollar-a-plate dinner held appropriately at the Metropolitan Museum of Art for the benefit of the museum's Costume Institute. Beside the serene pool and the classic columns, in the shrine of Rembrandt, New York's fashionable adults twisted to the tune of "You Can't Sit Down." (112–113)

Clearly for the Hechingers some kind of sacrilege was taking place through the juxtaposition of the Twist with Rembrandt and classic columns, even though the prototypes for those classic columns probably witnessed writhing Dionysian rituals that would have made these twisting socialites in evening clothes seem pretty sedate.[8] Nevertheless, I am quite taken with the Hechingers' juxtaposition because it unconsciously points to the inevitable confusion between the seemingly high and the seemingly low when art from the past, whether high, low, or in between, is preserved and venerated. There might be vulgar elements in Rembrandt's painting and classic columns that provided the backdrop for rituals we would now shun, but these elements are made secondary in modern valorizing of past art. Yet it is precisely what happens to the low as it is transformed to the high that is of interest to me here because Chaplin offers the most insistent example of a vulgar artist embraced by high culture. Shortly, when I explore the vulgar elements in Chaplin's *City Lights* (1931), I will discuss a metaphorical blindness that dominates the film's meanings. For now, I want to consider critical blindspots occasioned by looking at the low from too high a perch: when low culture is embraced by high critics, something inevitably gets repressed.

As Freud sees the lower bodily stratum repressed for the advance of civilization, Bakhtin charts something of a parallel repression in the post-Renaissance view of Rabelais. In particular, the function of laughter, Bakhtin believes, came to be understood in a different manner as laughter came to be opposed to seriousness. Bakhtin sees a "reduced" form of laughter taking hold of official culture from the Romantic period onward: "Laughter was cut down to cold humor, irony, sarcasm. It ceased to be a joyful and triumphant hilarity. Its positive regenerating power was reduced to a minimum" (38). Rabelais in particular and the grotesque in general came to be understood chiefly as satire, thereby making them more acceptable because satire irretrievably transforms the celebratory and challenging aspects of the grotesque into the tendentious, in the process yoking laughter to a sense of purpose that can ultimately be regarded as a social good. This is not to say that satire itself does not offer up challenges— clearly it does—but the challenge itself may be regarded as a benefit to society because it offers a corrective to behavior the satirist views negatively, whereas the grotesque humor that Bakhtin defines is both less purposeful but ultimately more radical.

Consequently, by the twentieth century laughter came to be seen chiefly as a kind of corrective, a view that necessarily elevates comic modes such as satire and irony over low comedy. This notion of laughter came to dominate most Western thinking, providing the foundation for the different but complementary theories of laughter by Henri Bergson and Sigmund Freud, who remain the two most influential writers on the subject. Yet there are ways of looking at laughter that enable us to reestablish ties to a repressed tradition of vulgar art.

For both Bergson and Freud laughter is to be considered chiefly in terms of its purpose: for Bergson the emphasis is on the social, with the stability of society as a whole the aim of laughter; for Freud the emphasis is on the biological individual, with the aim much like other biological mechanisms (screaming, for example) of maintaining a balance in "the economy of the soul." Although Freud discusses different kinds of humor, he privileges "tendentious wit," chiefly, I suspect, because it is easiest to talk about goals when the *targets* are always clear, as is the case with tendentious wit. Paralleling this, Bergson most of all privileges social satire. A wide range of laughter is necessarily left out of these discussions because it cannot be made to fit their teleologies. Looking at laughter in terms of teleology inevitably leads to a reduced understanding of it.

There is an honorable body of important art generally decried for its vulgarity if it is noticed at all. Occasionally works previously embraced by the masses are taken up by official culture, but when this happens the greatest appeal they held for the masses somehow vanishes. Although Charles Dickens achieved an early and extraordinary popularity, it took a good deal longer for his stature as a writer to be acknowledged. And even then, his work was transformed by critical reception so that he is viewed as great *in spite of* his sentimentality. "In Dickens," Dwight MacDonald cautions, "superb comedy alternates with bathetic sentimentality, great descriptive prose with the most vulgar kind of theatricality" (7). What for a nineteenth-century audience might have been key reasons for reading these novels becomes something for us to overlook. We of course possess discriminatory sensibilities the masses are incapable of, even though the masses probably did discriminate in favor of Dickens's "sentimentality." But by throwing out those qualities that made the novels most appealing to their audience we can congratulate ourselves on our ability to locate the "true" merit of these works. This kind of "discrimination" is as conformist in its aims as the mass audience it deplores is supposed to be.

Although sentimentality remains a value high critics frequently seek to expunge from low art, more often what is lost in the critical transformations worked on popular art is the lower bodily stratum. Consider, for example, the plays of Aristophanes. Three of his eleven extant plays use names of animals for their titles (*Wasps; Birds; Frogs*) and appropriately so because the plays are filled with a sense of animality. With their abundance of obscene sexual and scatological jokes, they present a joyous insistence on the lower bodily stratum. This obscenity should be seen as essential to any experience of these plays, yet criticism has tended to treat it otherwise. Writing in 1975 in a book aptly titled *The Maculate Muse,* Greek scholar Jeffrey Henderson notes:

> Obscene humor has always been something of an embarrassment to writers on ancient comedy. . . . To this day there has been no study that attempts comprehensively to elucidate, evaluate, or even to discuss the nature and function of sexual and scatological language in Attic Comedy. (ix)

The bawdiness of Aristophanes has always been recognized—after all, how could it be ignored?—but recognized in a way that effectively minimizes its significance and tones down the riotous fun of these plays. Earlier critics generally lamented the obscenity, whereas more recent commentators, keeping pace with the changing public discourse of the postwar period, have been more appreciative, but both have ended up making obscenity a secondary attribute of the plays.[9]

To point out the obscenity as insistently as I want to do here is not a matter of being a kind of smut sleuth like teenage boys looking up "dirty" words in a dictionary. I am not focusing on prurient details at the expense of an aesthetic whole. Rather, more often the distortions of these works takes place in the other direction, when obscenity is displaced from its central position. Henderson notes:

> The obscenity of Aristophanes is almost always integrally connected with the main themes of the plays; it is an important part of the stage action, the development of the plots, and the characterizations of personae, and can no more readily be excised from the plays than can any other major dramatic or poetic ingredients. (x)

The vulgar mass audience seems to understand this point better than the critics do. That, at least, seems implicit in the delight scholars take in pointing out how thrill-seeking audiences will be disappointed by Aristophanes, even though *Lysistrata* keeps on being performed for precisely those thrills.[10]

The general critical reception of Charlie Chaplin has always recognized the vulgar sources of his material, although usually to point out how much he transcends them. As with Aristophanes, the vulgarity is often acknowledged in order to be dismissed. Chaplin is most often praised for his abilities as a mime, his pathos, his subtlety of expression, his humanism, and, whenever the comedy is addressed specifically, most especially in his later films, his satire. As far as I know, no one has ever thought to praise him for the anality of his humor. A point that touches on this might be mentioned in passing but always in a way that ends up containing it; this aspect of Chaplin's humor is simply not regarded as fit for praise, certainly not to be made central to his art. In effect, there's a kind of censoring here of the lower bodily stratum. This censoring represents an astonishing distortion of his films.

Consider the following scene from *City Lights:* the Tramp is visiting for the first time the home of a poor blind girl, whom he has met on the city streets where she was selling flowers, her meager means of earning a living. Because she has mistaken him for a handsome millionaire, the Tramp tries to live up to the image she's formed of him by demonstrating his largesse with the gift of groceries, including, among other things, a naked, fleshy goose that he tries to describe to her. One oddity I should mention in passing: because this is a silent film, the Tramp inevitably describes things for the blind girl by means of mime, so there is paradoxically a suggestion that the girl has some power of sight. Here it comes up around the plucked goose, which anticipates the denuding of the Tramp that is soon to follow. I'm not sure how much I would want to ascribe this to conscious intent on Chaplin's part, but the use of mime here is not a minor flaw.

Charlie exposed

Rather, it nicely serves to underscore much of the tension in the scene between the Tramp and the blind girl, the danger that she will be able to see
him for the tramp he actually is rather than the millionaire she pictures him
to be.

Appropriately, then, the central action in the scene revolves around an
uncovering. As they sit down to talk, the blind girl asks the Tramp if he
will help her roll up a skein of yarn. As the Tramp obligingly holds the
wool, she mistakenly takes hold of a thread from his underclothes and
winds that up instead. The Tramp is indirectly responsible for what takes
place because he had pulled this thread loose from inside his vest and was
nervously toying with it while talking to the blind girl. Happy to be with
her, the Tramp nonetheless experiences some anxiety in her presence, an
anxiety centered on exposure, an act he both desires—he inadvertently
initiates it—yet dreads. Too embarrassed to point out that the blind girl has
taken hold of the wrong thread, the Tramp allows the accidental unraveling to take place. Wiggling his hips back and forth to allow free movement
of the thread and glancing down in dismay at his crotch, the Tramp makes
clear as can be, short of actual nudity, exactly what is being exposed.[11]
Nonetheless, one critic who has written quite extensively and with great
admiration on Chaplin has the blind girl unraveling the Tramp's *undershirt*, thereby neatly censoring out the lower bodily stratum and most of

the comic force of this scene.[12] Much as there is a fear of exposure in all of the Tramp's scenes with the girl, finally culminating in the actual exposure in the last scene when the girl with restored sight finally sees the Tramp for what he is, this is the one scene that specifies the nature of the exposure by casting it in terms of the lower body.

This is not an incidental detail any more than the obscenity in Aristophanes is incidental detail. The sexual innuendo in the comedy that I'm foregrounding deserves as much to be foregrounded as it has generally been ignored in the past. Without the foregrounding in this particular instance, the film would be incoherent because Charlie in this film, in fact all his films, rarely doubts himself in *social* terms: indeed, the chief point of his ragged but upper class costume complete with the dandy affectation of cane is that he sees himself as superior to all other society and for the most part also makes the audience accept that superiority. For the fear of exposure to make sense here, it must be presented in sexual terms, for it is only in sexual terms that Charlie can be made to feel inferior. The sexual imagery in the scene's emphatic pointing to the lower body is something far more important to the film than a simple bit of titillation thrown to the *vulgus* to ensure Chaplin's popularity. In fact, this "vulgar" humor both informs and forms the entire film through a richly articulated complex of sexual imagery.

The misunderstanding of this particular scene might appropriately be a blind spot, a lack of local insight that overlooks the connection between sight and sexuality the film is making here. Nevertheless, there are other ways in which the comedy of *City Lights* is distorted, turned to "reduced forms of laughter," to make it more acceptable to dominant critical standards and take it out of the realm of vulgar comedy. I want to look briefly at the opening scene—the public dedication of a grotesquely monumental statue on which the Tramp is discovered to be asleep—because it is one of the funniest set pieces in all Chaplin and, as such, one of the most frequently commented on. The commentary generally honors the scene for its satire, but if one comes to the film from reading texts on it, the most striking aspect of the scene is in fact the slightness of the satire.[13] Not that the scene isn't satirical, but next to, say, Jonathan Swift, George Bernard Shaw, or Bertolt Brecht, it's all pretty weak stuff, hardly the basis for any claims for Chaplin's art. And in any case, I'm not sure that even the sharpest satire can ever produce the kind of belly laughs we have here, rumbling forth from the lower body into convulsions that go far beyond the more intellectual appeal of satire. *Belly* laughs are the appropriate response here because what *is* very powerful about the scene, hilariously so, is the raucously insistent lower body imagery.

In a large public square, a statue to "peace and prosperity" is about to be unveiled. After a couple of pompous speeches by public figures, the film's

A shafted Charlie is held in place by patriotic fervor

first image of uncovering occurs: the great gray cloth is raised to display a grouping of figures in the early 1930s monumentalist style—a seated woman in the center (is she peace or prosperity?) surrounded by reclining male figures.[14] But more is revealed than the statue, for the Tramp has apparently taken refuge here for the night: he is discovered asleep in fetal position in the lap of the seated female. Whether peace or prosperity, she is clearly beneficent, although once revealed, she can no longer protect the Tramp. Awakened by the uproar of the respected gathering, he must emerge from this womb, and the climb down sets his troubles in motion because another figure in the grouping, a reclining male with an upended sword, interferes with the Tramp's progress. There is unfortunately—or is it functionally?—a hole in the Tramp's trousers directly over his anus, and through this hole he is impaled on the erect sword. At one point during his struggles to free himself the national anthem is played, which compels him to stand rigidly at attention until he can resume his struggle.

When he finally gets down from his impalement, he briefly sits on the head of the reclining male so that his anus fits directly onto the man's nose, a nice echo of the sword but also appropriate, albeit unconscious, revenge for it. Leaving this figure, he accidentally, although perhaps again with some unconscious intent, steps in the marble man's crotch. He tips

Unconscious anal revenge

his hat as if to excuse himself, but then as he leaves, he looks at his foot with a grimace, like someone who has just stepped in dog shit, seemingly concerned that something might have rubbed off on his shoe. There is in fact a confusion around this action that is typical of the Tramp: he had actually stepped in the crotch with his left foot, but then looked at his right as if that were the offending foot. Because the revenge against the phallic penetration of the statue must seem accidental, the Tramp distances himself from the agent of his own aggression, suspecting that the passive foot is the one that was contaminated by what the active foot stepped in. One last accidental aggression occurs while he talks to a public official about how to get down: he places his face against an outstretched marble hand that brings about an unexpected "Kiss my ass" gesture. If all this anal and genital imagery represents satire, it's hard to see exactly what's being satirized. It's clear something else is going on.

It might be enough for my purposes to limit my discussion to this scene alone because it is so insistent about something that has just as insistently been ignored in writings on Chaplin. And this limitation would be easy enough to bring off because Chaplin's dramatic structures often seem to break down into a series of set pieces. Nonetheless, the raucous lower body imagery that informs all the comedy of this scene takes on a retro-

The contaminated foot

spective resonance from the rest of the film. What I want to stress is some
concern for why the scene with its emphasis on womb, anus, and genitals
should open the film. This seems to me an especially problematic matter
for criticism that sees the scene primarily as satire: usually some attempt is
made to relate it to the scenes with the millionaire because some social
satire can be read into those sections of the film, but this effectively weak-
ens the force of the opening. If, instead, the sexual imagery is fully recognized, if the vulgar humor is embraced as central to Chaplin's vision, the
scene has great importance for the rest of the film.

I can get at this most fully by looking at something else that has been
generally ignored in *City Lights:* the homosexual theme that runs so pro-
nouncedly throughout the film. Even the couple of critics who have mentioned this at all end up dismissing it.[15] Yet at the least, any homosexual
theme in the body of the film should relate to the head of the narrative
where there is an explicit invocation of homosexual intercourse in the
Tramp's troubles with an erect sword. If it were to recognize the homosexuality at all, the satiric view of the film might see an anticipation of the
Tramp's getting shafted by the millionaire, who throughout the film wa-
vers between extremes of a lavishly bestowed affection and a cold denial
of recognition. This might in fact be an appropriate way of looking at some
of the byplay between the Tramp and his inconstant patron. At one point,

for example, a gun accidentally goes off as the Tramp is trying to prevent the millionaire from committing suicide. At the sound of the shot, the Tramp dives head first into a couch and immediately begins a protective probing of his backside as if this were the one area most vulnerable to the millionaire's aggression. There *is* satire here, and it has something to do with harm coming from the Tramp's attempt to do good, but why the satirical thrust should be cast in sexual terms still requires explaining.

Beyond that, satire could not account for the one other scene in which the homosexual theme is explicit: finding himself about to fight a boxer who towers over him, the Tramp, to curry favor, simpers, minces, and even makes flirting gestures toward his powerful opponent. The guy is so unnerved by this outrageous behavior that he hides behind a curtain to change into his boxing shorts, even though he has them on under his street pants. His sudden shyness is odd to the extent that he is clearly the Tramp's superior physically, yet he feels genuinely threatened by this display of feminized behavior. The scene, then, suggests that eroticizing a same-sex context endows the Tramp with a surprisingly aggressive power. The homosexual theme generally invokes an issue of power in the film, and as the confrontation with the boxer makes clear, this issue is something more than the opposition of social classes that the satiric view would suggest. In fact, this is an issue that could extend beyond *City Lights* because Chaplin's films are always filled with men who are bigger and stronger than he, men against whom he always measures himself and generally finds some inadequacy that expresses itself in something like coquettish behavior.

To get at what is going on with all these lower body issues in *City Lights* involves me in some speculation that I suspect will be resisted by those who admire the "beauty" and pathos of the ending. Let me state the proposition directly: the Tramp loves the blind girl precisely because she's blind. If you look at the scene where they first meet, you can see him being flirtatious with her as the Tramp would be with any pretty girl, but the point at which she becomes special for him is when he recognizes her defect. Suddenly his whole manner and bearing change; his face takes on an expression of deep concern and solicitousness that signal how much he feels her defect. But I question how much *we* in fact feel that defect; it seems to me one of the most important strategies of the film, both dramatically and thematically, that we never take the blindness seriously as an actual physical condition. The use of mime in conversation with her that I mentioned earlier suggests the metaphorical status of the blindness. The ease with which the condition is cured drives the point home.

If this is metaphor, then, and the metaphor can be interpreted psychoanalytically, which the insistent sexual imagery in the rest of the film should incline us to, it is not too much of a leap to see that the Tramp loves her for what she lacks, which is to say that the Tramp loves her because he sees her as castrated. This is one way of making sense of the homosexual theme that has puzzled other writers, but also of the very structure of the film, which alternates between nighttime scenes with the millionaire whom the Tramp is dependent on and daytime scenes with the blind girl, who is dependent on the Tramp. The two plot lines parallel each other, with each plot presenting one character who acts as the benefactor for the other, but in the nighttime plot the Tramp takes over the role occupied by the woman in the daytime plot. In the nighttime world of men, then, the Tramp becomes a woman, but in the daytime world of women, he at least has the possibility of asserting himself as a man.

In the film's rich sexual imagery, this problematic opposition of masculine-feminine relates to central issues of sight and voyeurism, which might be seen as a kind of phallic privileging.[16] Again, once the sexual imagery is understood, what might seem like an unintegrated set piece becomes central to the film's concerns. What I have in mind is the scene that immediately follows the opening, well before the main narrative lines of the film become clear. The Tramp is passing by an art gallery that has two objects in its window; a rather small figure of a horse on the left and a large statue of a naked woman at the right. The Tramp is immediately arrested by the sight of the naked woman but doesn't want this to be apparent to the passing crowds, so he looks instead at the horse, every now and then stealing a glance at the larger statue. Finally, to indulge his gaze more fully, he adopts the pose of art connoisseur, hand under chin, stepping back to take the measure of the aesthetic experience. Unbeknown to him, a sidewalk elevator has opened up, leaving a gaping hole behind him, but every time he steps back, the elevator returns to street level. The power of the Tramp's gaze is of course dependent on a blindness—the fact that the statue cannot look back—but it is also placed in the context of a danger to which he himself is blind.[17]

Much as the joke here revolves around the privileging of masculine vision, the power of that vision is itself placed in a potentially disempowering context: the capper to the scene foreshadows the homosexual theme that always places Chaplin in subservient position to larger and stronger men. Stepping back one last time, the Tramp finds himself on the elevator as it descends. Scampering back on the sidewalk for safety, he begins to yell and shake his fist at a workman who is riding back up on the elevator. When the elevator fully reaches sidewalk level, it turns out the workman is another one of Chaplin's imposing giants. Facing this greater physical power, the Tramp immediately loses his belligerent stance: he turns tail and runs. Facing the naked woman who cannot look back, the Tramp possesses power but must express it surreptitiously because he is constrained by propriety. Facing another man, he sees himself as powerless and openly displays his lack of courage.

The danger of voyeurism

The ending of *City Lights* presents the culmination of these interlocking themes of sight and power. And however consciously we might be aware of it, the insistent sexual imagery throughout the rest of the film is responsible for the devastating emotional force of the film's ending. The blind girl, having regained her sight, has clearly become empowered by the physical transformation: she moves up the social scale right into the bourgeois classes by becoming a shopkeeper. When the two of them finally see each other the mise-en-scène specifically invokes the scene of the Tramp looking at the statue. As in the earlier scene, the camera is inside a store looking through a display window toward sidewalk and street; once again the Tramp has his attention arrested by the female object in the window. This time, however, the woman can look back, and when the Tramp recognizes this he defensively starts to move away from her gaze. The power of sight granted to the woman is a power the Tramp feels he must protect himself from.

To set up this final meeting, Chaplin has deliberately introduced the two characters separately to define a new life for each. In contrast to the blind girl's rise in fortune, the Tramp is seen just after his release from prison, where he had been sent because of the money he had gotten for the blind girl's operation. The sequencing of events is important to our understand-

Glances away: unseeing and seeing

ing of the Tramp in the final scene because we see him in such an uncharacteristic fashion: for the first time in his screen life, the Tramp really looks like a bum—his clothes now ragged, his entire body bent over in a posture of defeat. Most important of all, he is now missing his cane, the most phallic-aggressive part of his costume.[18] Precisely because we have just seen the blind girl transformed into an independent woman, we must interpret the Tramp's unusual appearance as a loss of power. Clearly, the power has gone elsewhere.

Just before the Tramp meets this newly empowered woman, there is a gag, no longer funny, that deliberately echoes two earlier gags. Two newsboys who had teased the Tramp previously in the film, but to whom he displayed all his self-respect and dignity, again tease him, but now the Tramp can no longer defend himself. This loss of dignity is the greatest defeat for Chaplin because it represents a loss of the self-image that had always sustained him in all other films against the expectations of conventional social structures. The defeat is specifically tied in to the lower body imagery: as the Tramp bends over, one of the newsboys pulls a rag of torn underwear through the anus hole in the Tramp's pants.[19] The Tramp grabs the rag back from the boy, wipes his nose with it, neatly folds it, and places it in his jacket pocket. The Tramp's response is congruent with other attempts to assert his dignified view of himself, but for once it doesn't work; in effect he defiles himself as he rubs his nose with wipings from his anus. The whole routine recalls both the sword impalement from the opening sequence with its similar anal-nasal progression and the blind girl's inadvertent baring of the Tramp's privates. It is in this context, then, that their final meeting and her recognition of him must be understood as the film moves through an odd play of anal aggression, which the opening makes something passive by always assigning to accident, set against phallic aggression, which is understood as sight.

At its simplest, the cross-cut close-ups that end the film—alternating shots of the once-blind woman looking at the Tramp, slowly recognizing him, and the Tramp tremulously accepting the consequences of her recognition—serve to focus the central questions of the film: can the Tramp allow the woman to see him as he really is, and commensurately can Chaplin allow us in the audience such a privileged view without becoming emasculated? There is a fascinating stylistic figure in this final sequence in a jump cut that effectively isolates the two shots that bring the film to a close.[20] The shot that's angled toward the seeing woman is an over-the-shoulder two-shot, with the Tramp's profile on the left side of the screen; the shot angled toward the Tramp is effectively a single, although there is a slight indication of the woman's presence at the extreme right edge of the image. The sense of opposition gained by the two-shot/single contrast is extended by a mismatched action across the cut. In the single of the Tramp, he holds the flower he had picked up from the sweepings of the shop directly in front of his mouth, defensively covering the bottom of his face; in the two-shot, his hand has dropped to expose his face fully to her view. This opposition, this play between wanting to expose and wanting to cover up, can never be resolved as the jump cut fully separates the two conflicting desires.

Furthermore, there is an issue explored in this scene that ties into some of the central questions in Chaplin's art as I've outlined them here: the scene boldly articulates an opposition between the vulgarity of the grossly material world and the elevated quality of the more spiritual, at times sentimental, impulses implicit in Chaplin's treatment of character. As the now-seeing woman confronts the flesh-and-blood reality of the man she could previously see only in her imagination, as she must confront the apparent disparity between the material and the spiritual, the following questions emerge: How can upper and lower body be made whole? How can the spiritual grace we accord the eyes be made commensurate with the other organs that bring us into contact with the outside world and with other

The closing cut

people? There is no full embrace, no assurance of a future together. The film must end on a kind of suspension, a rift the jump cut will not allow to mend, because this is a question that for Chaplin cannot be answered: the demands of upper and lower body remain apart, and yet they also remain within the same body.

The Tramp is most at home in the world of material values; he is a character most fully defined by appetites, which accounts for the great emphasis on hunger in most of his films and the countless gags about eating.[21] Yet the Tramp's appetite also extends to a hunger for the spiritual, which has enabled critical appreciation of Chaplin to emphasize the spiritual over the material, a clear distortion of much of the impact of Chaplin's comedy. The vulgar humor is not merely decoration necessary for an artist who sought widespread appeal; in fact vulgar humor is close to the essence of his work. The kind of material-spiritual opposition that can be found in Chaplin has made it possible for critics to excuse his vulgarity. In focusing on the vulgar roots of Chaplin's art, the delight it takes in exploring the lower body, I have tried to establish that there are values inherent in the vulgarity itself.

Notes

1. Samuel McKechnie discusses the other forms of popular entertainment I've listed. For a more detailed description of fairground theater and the economic demands involved in it, see Sybil Rosenfeld.

2. Theater historian Phyllis Hartnoll notes makes clear that in the period when the theater was not producing drama the high culture could embrace, it remained a vital art for the masses: in the dark days of "the later Roman theater . . . the humbler entertainers of the classical world wandered across Europe, alone or in small troupes. Among them were acrobats, dancers, mimics, animal-trainers with bears or monkeys, jugglers, wrestlers, ballad-singers, story-tellers" (32).

3. Twice in the play—III, i and V, i; first with Viola, then with Orsino—he successfully begs money by making witty remarks.

4. This is the title of the second chapter of *The Age of Rabelais*.

5. Eric Bentley seems to be approaching something like this when he valorizes farce and melodrama, consciously elevating forms that had fallen into critical disrepute at the time of his writing and often doing so in ways that were clearly intended to challenge dominant critical opinion of the time. For example, he offers praise for self-pity as an emotion a worthwhile work of art might want to provoke. Nonetheless, for all that he sets himself apart from current critical opinion, he nevertheless retains a hierarchical view of the arts that sees the "higher" forms—comedy and tragedy—as inherently superior.

6. The chief source for what follows is *Civilization and Its Discontents*, the most appropriate work for my discussion because it is the most centrally concerned with social organization. In light of the comparison I make to Bakhtin, it's worth keeping in mind the point of departure for Freud in this work. Freud begins by citing an exchange he had with Romain Rolland over *The Future of an Illusion:*

> He entirely agreed with my judgement upon religion, but . . . he was sorry I had not
> properly appreciated the true source of religious sentiments. This, he says, consists in
> a peculiar feeling, which he himself is never without, which he finds confirmed by
> many others, and which he may suppose is present in millions of people. It is a feel-
> ing which he would like to call a sensation of "eternity," a feeling as of something
> limitless, unbounded—as it were, "oceanic." (64)

Freud admits he can't find this feeling in himself, so he sets out to find its sources
through a psychoanalytic investigation. In the process, the ideal is made real, the
high made low, and the spiritual turned into something more firmly entrenched in
the material world.

7. This sentence has received particular attention in the last decade or so because it is central to Jacques Lacan's reformulation of Freud. See Lacan (1977,
128–129; 1981, 44–45). My use of Freud's statement here is probably closer to
the ego psychology that Lacan sets himself in opposition to.

8. I wish to note that the "serene pool" the Hechingers mention is no longer
there, having been replaced by a high-priced restaurant that presumably earns the
Met more money than the cafeteria that surrounded the pool did. In this case, the
more adult drive for money has prompted a far more lasting desecration than could
the teenage libidinal drives the Hechingers deplored.

9. Rather than detail past opinions, I will let two examples from more recent,
more enlightened times suffice. Moses Hadas specifically denies the lower body in
Aristophanes, reversing the hierarchical reversal that I am claiming is common in
vulgar art: "Aristophanes is not prurient because his comedy is a comedy of pure
wit, which attacks the head and not the entrails. None of the characters engages
the audience's sympathy as human beings; with none can the audience identify itself" (100).

Cedric H. Whitman, one of the most astute writers on Aristophanes, wants to
separate this very vulgar artist from the appeal of contemporary vulgar art: "Old
Comedy dealt so freely with what we call obscenity, that one wonders why such
antics do not strike us as simply jejune and immature. Part of the answer may be in
the fact that there is never any question of 'daring,' that lurid word which today
sells so many mildly suggestive novels and movies" (209).

10. K. J. Dover, for example, notes, "Anyone who goes to the play in the ex-
pectation that continuous bawdy jokes will keep him laughing from the first line to
the last is likely to find that the choral lyric, after the first vigorous encounter between the old men and the old women, fall rather flat" (153).

11. In reviewing Chaplin's notes for the film in its early stage of composition,
David Robinson locates what seems to be the source for this scene: "There might
be a complex variation on the shame gag-nightmares: Charlie could lose his
trousers, but then realize that there is no cause for shame since the girl cannot see"
(394).

12. The scene is so described by Gerald Mast: "Charlie holds up hands to help
her. She, however, mistakenly grabs a strand from Charlie's undershirt, not from
the package of yarn she has just bought" (108). It would be most appropriate to
identify the garment as a union suit.

13. In a book-length analysis of the film, Gerard Molyneaux, drawing strongly

on Bergson's theory of laughter, provides extended analyses of the opening scene that concentrate on the satire and "social comment" (124–138, 212–218).

14. David Robinson identifies the male figure on the right as peace, although there is nothing in the statue that specifically indicates this. It is perhaps the presumption of satiric intent here that leads Robinson to assume Chaplin wants the figure with the sword to represent peace (400).

15. In "some notes on a recent viewing," Stanley Kauffmann observes "a surprising amount of homosexual joking" in the film but more or less throws up his hands in the face of it: "I can't remember this element in another Chaplin picture. I can't explain it here, but the hints are inescapable" (18). Kauffmann at least raises the possibility of an interpretation, but Gerald Weales mentions the homosexuality chiefly to deny it: "[Charlie's] flirtatious attempts to show how harmless he is, which his opponent (Hank Mann) takes as a homosexual advance, suggests nothing so much as the placating behavior with which animals assure the pack leader that they are not challenging his position" (26).

16. Although I think the ending of the film raises real questions about phallic privileging, the connection of sight with phallic aggression is congruent with Laura Mulvey's argument about the masculine gaze (305–315).

17. Julian Smith notes two "blind" statues, lumping the nude together with "Peace and Prosperity" and seeing both solely as foreshadowing (92). Weales also notes the statue's "blindness" and regards its purpose similarly (17).

18. Weales raises this point as well, again to dismiss the sexual meaning: "We do not need to play sexual symbology with the poor man's walking stick to recognize in his pathetic figure a loss of manhood" (27). The capacity for denial when dealing with the more vulgar aspects of Chaplin's art seems limitless.

19. Smith refers to this action as an "unveiling" to relate it to other scenes of exposure in the film, but he is curiously unconcerned with what is being unveiled. Once again, the sexual aspects of the action are ignored.

20. Walter Kerr terms the mismatch a fault, which expresses a narrow notion of film style (351). Given the amount of time Chaplin spent on production and the endless retakes he indulged in, it's unlikely the jump cuts were unintentional. Robinson provides some information on the shooting of this scene, which included seventeen retakes (409–410).

21. This is an issue I have explored more fully in an article on *The Gold Rush*.

References and Additional Reading

Bakhtin, Mikhail. [1965] 1984. *The Age of Rabelais*. Bloomington: Indiana University Press.

Bentley, Eric. 1964. *The Life of the Drama*. New York: Atheneum.

Bergson, Henri. [1956] 1980. "Laughter." In *Comedy*, ed. Wylie Sypher, pp. 61–190. Baltimore: Johns Hopkins University Press.

Dover, K. J. 1972. *Aristophanic Comedy*. Berkeley: University of California Press.

Freud, Sigmund. 1961. *Civilization and Its Discontents*. Standard Edition, vol. 21. London: Hogarth Press.

————. 1960. *Wit and Its Relation to the Unconscious*. Standard Edition, vol. 8. London: Hogarth Press.

Hadas, Moses. 1950. *A History of Greek Literature*. New York: Columbia University Press.

Hartnoll, Phyllis. 1969. *The Concise History of the Theatre*. New York: Harry N. Abrams.

Hechinger, Grace, and Fred M. Hechinger. 1963. *Teenage Tyranny*. New York: Morrow.

Henderson, Jeffrey. 1975. *The Maculate Muse: Obscene Language in Attic Comedy*. New Haven: Yale University Press.

Kauffmann, Stanley. 1972. "City Lights." *Film Comment* 8, no. 3 (September–October): 18–19

Kerr, Walter. 1979. *The Silent Clowns*. New York: Knopf.

Lacan, Jacques. 1977. *Écrits*, trans. Alan Sheridan. New York: Norton.

————. [1978] 1981. *The Four Fundamental Concepts of Psycho-Analysis*, trans. Alan Sheridan, ed. Jacques-Alain Miller. New York: Norton.

MacDonald, Dwight. 1962. *Against the American Grain*. New York: Random House.

McKechnie, Samuel. [1932]. *Popular Entertainments Through the Ages*. London: Sampson Low, Marston & Co.

Mast, Gerald. 1973. *The Comic Mind*. Indianapolis: Bobbs-Merrill.

Molyneaux, Gerard. 1983. *Charles Chaplin's "City Lights": Its Production and Dialectical Structure*. New York: Garland.

Mulvey, Laura. [1975] 1985. "Visual Pleasure and the Narrative Cinema." In *Movies and Methods*, ed. Bill Nichols, vol. 2, pp. 305–315. Berkeley: University of California Press.

Paul, William. 1972. "The Gold Rush." *Film Comment* 8, no. 3 (September–October): 16–18.

Robinson, David. 1985. *Chaplin: His Life and Art*. New York: McGraw-Hill.

Rosenfeld, Sybil. 1960. *The Theater of the London Fairs in the Eighteenth Century*. Cambridge: Cambridge University Press.

Smith, Julian. 1984. *Chaplin*. Boston: Twayne.

Weales, Gerald. 1985. *Canned Goods as Caviar*. Chicago: University of Chicago Press.

Whitman, Cedric H. 1964. *Aristophanes and the Comic Hero*. Cambridge, Mass.: Harvard University Press.

The Light Side of Genius

Hitchcock's *Mr. and Mrs. Smith* in the Screwball Tradition

Dana Polan

You can sign Minnie Q. Mouse on a marriage license [if you so wish]; you're still married.

Mark Rutland explaining the fictions of marriage to Marnie in Hitchcock's *Marnie* (1964)

Accident, excluded from tragedy, reappears, in comic constructions, as the negative principle par excellence: it is accident that sentences man and declares him impossible. It is not by accident that everything happens by accident. A human being affirms himself as a sovereign being with the conviction that he is capable of acting on the world and governing his own life. Accident steps onto the scene to denounce this illusion: the world is allergic to man, the comic gives witness of a process of rejection. . . . Man is lost in advance unless an accident saves him. In the service elevator of Modern Times, *these two opposed characteristics manifest their profound unity: whether the Macrocosm understood as pure* exteriority *crushes the microcosm or a lucky set of exterior circumstances comes together in time to save man without him knowing this, man is killed: he comes out the adventure dehumanized since his ends have been both stolen and restored him at the last minute by things. He can survive for a time as an object of the world but it has been demonstrated that the ideas of praxis and interiority are the dream of a dream and that the human object, an accidental assemblage that one accident conserves but another undoes, is exterior to itself.*

Jean-Paul Sartre (2: 1439)

What would it mean to treat the screwball comedy *Mr. and Mrs. Smith* (1941) as an Alfred Hitchcock film? How we might answer this question depends of course on what we mean by "mean"? Is our intent one of saving this film for Hitchockian auteurism, going against a tradition that sees the film as an aberration (for screwball, for Hitchcock's career)? In that case, the point would be to resist the kind of easy dismissal that Ted Sennett offers in his *Lunatics and Lovers:* "Early in 1941, RKO released a comedy that had one (and only one) surprise: it was directed by Alfred Hitchcock, whose views of marriage until then had been more menacing than mirth-

Robert Montgomery and Carole Lombard in Alfred Hitchcock's Mr. and Mrs.
Smith *(1941)*

ful" (73). Sennett, of course, approaches the comic tradition from an auteurism of his own (Frank Capra, Leo McCarey, and so on). Indeed, it is
precisely a brand of auteurism that leads him to find it surprising that
Hitchcock directs a screwball: auteurism here is the study of personal
affinities between certain directors and certain genres, each director (and
each genre) thereby compartmentalized off from all others as a pure space
wherein creative psychology and generic traditions come together in glorious artistry.

But in this respect, "saving" *Mr. and Mrs. Smith* for Hitchcockian auteurism would not be so much an overthrowing of Sennett's theory of
genre as a reaffirming of it: one could agree with his estimation that the
film doesn't fit the screwball tradition but only because the film belongs to
another tradition, a non- or anticomic *Hitchcockian* one that sees marriage
precisely as menacing rather than mirthful. The failure of laughter for this
film would then become a mark of Hitchcock's success,[1] a sign of his ability to take the most seemingly resistant material ("Hitchock's making a
screwball comedy?!?") and turn it to his own ends, the ends of the suspense genre that he is called the "master" of. This, for example, is the
gambit of Eric Rohmer and Claude Chabrol in their book on Hitchcock,

when they analyze the first shot of the film (a movement through the room in which Mr. and Mrs. Smith have been ensconsed for three days):

> The slowness of this first shot is a radical departure from the reigning laws of American comedy. It conveys a sort of anxiety, and might just as well be used to begin a "suspense" film. The rest of the movie follows the same principle: all the scenes are shot from a subjective point of view. On several occasions we even witness attempts at a "subjective" camera. This forced identification with the character undercuts the laughter. Generally speaking, American comedy gets its effects from the assumption of objective observation: it is a report on madness. Here, we are accomplices of the characters. The laughter, when it does arise, abruptly shrivels up: the "gag" is not funny to the person at whose expense it is carried out. (64)

It would be easy indeed to argue that specific sequences, if not the overall tone of the film, are eminently Hitchcockian *if* we mean by that a cinema that undercuts human pretense (especially the romantic-comic pretense to reach out across adversity to other humans) by emphasizing the isolation of each human, the cruelty of an existence in which finally one is always alone (like Marion Crane in her shower, missing her meeting with Sam Loomis by only a few miles). Rohmer and Chabrol's emphasis on the film's play with point of view suggests how the film's exploitation of filmic style works as deflation of existential mastery: where a "report" on madness comments on characters from without, the Hitchcockian style puts us within characters' subjectivity, sharing their desires, sharing the ways these desires are articulated through masterful acts of seeing, but then experiencing the closing off of the object of desire, the resistance of objects in the world to desire. A sequence in which David Smith sets out to triumph over his (estranged) wife by going out on a better date than hers well shows the deflating power of subjective point of view. From a shot of Smith arriving in the nightclub for his blind date, we move into a subjective shot that tracks in as he moves forward to a table where a (typically Hitchcockian) elegant blonde awaits. Suddenly, however, the voice of David's friend announces, "No, over here, David, over here," and the camera pans sideways to show us another table, another blonde: David's date, a coarse blonde busily and obnoxiously chomping away on a piece of food (and we well know the disgust with which food and vulgar femininity are often associated in Hitchcock).[2]

Here we are within a world where the self's mastery and the self's self-subversion are fully and inextricably intertwined. The scene has that existential quality that we can find so often in Hitchcock: the man's freedom, his for-itself, expressed but finding essential limits in its contact with, in the resistance of, a world of objects, of woman as a base materiality that counters all masculine projects and brings them down to the level of the in-itself. Not surprisingly, David's solution to his entrapment—a "solution" that turns into its own deflation—is to reduce his own being down to the in-itself materiality of the body. His own gaze deflated by its sighting of the nonobject of desire (the crass food-ingesting woman), David will suddenly be vulnerable himself to the gaze of the Other as his wife arrives with her date at the club and risks spotting David with his ridiculous partner. This leaves David no alternative but to regard his own self as nothing more than a corporeal matter that he tries to wound and bash with the salt-and-pepper shaker in the hopes that he will start bleeding and be allowed to leave the public space of the restaurant. All this seems Hitchcockian: sexuality as a battle of gazes; public space as an agonic site overrun by a crowd turned mob, mocking one's every project; the self as finally nothing but vulnerable materiality. (In so much Hitchcock, one is not spirit, the transcendent, but body, the all-too-earthy: hence, a whole concern with the need to turn people into bodies [for example, the protracted killing of a man dragged across the floor in *Torn Curtain* (1966)], the need to dispose of cumbersome bodies [for example, the very premise of *The Trouble with Harry* (1955), the disposing of Marion Crane in the viscous muck of the swamp, the struggle that Ann Smith has in carrying her seemingly frozen husband in from the cold in *Mr. and Mrs. Smith*].)

And yet what would we accomplish by following Rohmer and Chabrol in arguing a contrast between such techniques and a supposedly objective reportage on madness in the mainstream tradition of American comedy? As I've suggested, we would continue imagining genre and authorship *within boundaries,* inviolable realms shut off from each other. We would thereby cut off genre study from any possible connection to other forms of study such as a sociology of genres. (If each genre is a pure form, then it becomes difficult for us to explain how one social moment can produce a variety of genres; this has often been the problem with a sociology of *film noir* where by reference to the problems of returned vets, the accounting for paranoid narratives of men thrown into a world of dangerous sexuality fails to account for nonparanoid forms of the same moment—films of optimistic fantasy, for example.) We might note how Rohmer and Chabrol's very definition of mainstream American comedy as objective reportage operates a peremptory separation that misses the intricate play of point of view in many of the films from that mainstream. Take, for example, the opening of *His Girl Friday* (1940), by that director of supposed exteriority (as opposed to subjectivity), Howard Hawks (Hawks to *Cahiers du cinéma:* "I try to tell a story as simply as possible at eye level" [195]). Hawks's world is seemingly a fully material one in which men and women act physically in a world that acts and reacts physically to them. In such a world, psychology or subjectivity becomes pure lies, artificialities, processes of pretentious bad faith, factors of personality that block one's direct interaction with the world. The most that a Hawksian film will grant to psychology is its power as an unconscious force—a desire for objects that one consciously does not know one desires—that needs to be brought to transparent consciousness so that a character may physically strive after his or her truly appropriate object (hence, Lorelei in *Gentlemen Prefer Blondes* [1953] imagining that she desires a sugar daddy but discovering that she really wants love).

Thus, the Hawksian screwball film can entertain subjectivity—indeed, it can fully encourage subjectivity's representation—but only as a resistant force that has to be reduced down to the materiality of acting bodies. The opening, then, of *His Girl Friday* will not be about the objective point of view, about characters viewed simply from without, but about a dialectic of objective and subjective, Hildy's initial sense of her transcendence by new love over a coarse world of newspaper work undone by that world's very appeal to her, its triumph over her. The opening alternates between two sets of point-of-view shots (of Hildy walking confidently through the office, of the newspaper workers who greet her as she walks past) but also moves out of sync with subjective point of view (the angle of the camera and the angle of gazes not coinciding fully). As a result, the opening sets up a complicated play in which a number of attitudes exist together: Hildy's sense of newfound superiority over a world she quickly moves through and yet her appropriateness in that world. All this culminates in a moment when Hildy's look is simultaneously in control (she sees Walter Burns from behind, her gaze catching him in a pose that makes him look somewhat ridiculous) and lost to the control of the man she will finally come to admit she desires (Walter turns around, looking at her, looking at the camera, and Hildy loses her transcendence and enters into a game of dueling looks, dueling *praxes*). As Gerald Mast puts it in *Howard Hawks, Storyteller:*

> The simultaneous motion of character and camera establishes how she [Hildy] feels about that space (it is her domain, her milieu—she "owns" it), how the others in that space feel about her (they agree that the space belongs to her), and how the storyteller feels about her in that space (he also agrees—which casts severe doubt on her stated intention to leave that world in which she so perfectly belongs). . . . There is an alliance of storyteller and character (camera motion conveys her emotion) and another alliance of storyteller and viewer (we know more about the camera, her motion, and her emotion than she does). The gap between these two will allow the story (in which that gap closes) to be followed. (41–42)

Rohmer and Chabrol's valorization of Hitchcockian subjectivity (and a consequent contrast of that subjectivity with comedy's supposed objectivity) may well miss screwball comedy's own careful plays with subjectivities in space, with the battles of different egos.

In extreme contrast to Rohmer and Chabrol's analysis, Henri Bergson's

theory of comedy finds the effect of the comic to lie not in objective observation of a crazy world but in a subtle translation from subjective perception of the world to objective, or rather objectival, betrayal of subjectivity
by that world. Comedy for Bergson comes in acts of materialization
wherein the seemingly free human subject or spirit finds itself falling back
into mere body, its upward pretentions brought low by the sheer weight of
a body, mocked by a body gone mechanical. In this respect, screwball
comedy would seem eminently a dialectical genre, its effects coming from
its intersecting of two very different notions of the comic. On the one
hand, as Stanley Cavell's situating of screwball within Shakespearean and
nineteenth-century American traditions of transcendentalism (the call for
the green place of nature where desire can realize itself) argues, there is
comic as aspiration, as spiritual and spirited flight above the crassness of
the world. On the other hand, as in Wes Gehring's situating of screwball
within a pragmatic crackerbarrel tradition of folk comedy geared to the
ironic deflation of pretention, there is the comic as the materialization, the
rendering material of the spiritual. Or there is possibly the screwball as
the mediation of the two positions, a kind of mythic solution that allows
the spiritual and the material to exist together. Against the false spirituality of the pompous love choices that the main characters have made (for
example, the gentlemanly but unadventurous Jeff [Gene Raymond], whom
Mrs. Smith dates after splitting off from Mr. Smith), the plots of the
screwballs instruct the main characters by debasing them, by mocking
their pretentions, by showing how real spirituality resides in the earthy,
pragmatic love choice. This, indeed, is the lesson of American transcendentalism that Cavell sees the screwball emerging from: spirit suffuses the
ordinary objects of *this* world (for example, a Walden lake), and one has to
learn how to see in this material world, in its material and physical representatives (for example, Peter in *It Happened One Night* [1934]). One has
to be low enough to see what is really and truly high. And this mythology
is often easily the explicit ideology of the screwballs, especially in those
films termed *Cinderella comedies* by Ted Sennett, where rich people pose
as ordinary people and therefore allow the characters who love them to
have the best of both worlds (as the lower-class heroine of *Fifth Avenue
Girl* [1939] says as she falls in love with a family of millionaires, "I guess
rich people are only poor people with money").

If we return to our opening question, it might be most meaningful "to
treat *Mr. and Mrs. Smith* as a Hitchcock film" but not to separate this film
from the screwball tradition and to reinsert it into some other pristine tradition of which Hitchcock is an auteur. Quite the contrary, we might suggest that our real goal is to ask what it might mean *for comedy theory and
theory of screwball in particular,* not for auteurism, to associate Hitchcock
with this film. That a director such as Hitchcock can work in screwball

might be less a matter of surprise than a clue about structural affinities between genres. In such a view, each and every genre (and each and every film in a genre and each and every scene within the films) is easily rewritable, the tone of each work easily transformable into its opposite. We could note, for example, the sheer arbitrariness, grounded only by mythology and ideology, of the "happy ending" in comic film. In the screwball, for instance, the happy ending is a sort of fiat declaration that transforms strife into love, that imagines that strife was in fact love (like the Harlequin romance in Tania Modleski's analysis in *Loving with a Vengeance,* the screwball works out of an ideology in which one discovers that seeming hatred is really a mark of desire). The green place to which the quarrelers voyage to transform anger into admiration may seem to promise a rendering eternal of the couple's love, but it is always easy to be reminded that nothing is eternal. The very insistence on *re*marriage that Stanley Cavell finds so central to the screwball comedy can serve as a mark of the arbitrariness of any marriage: there can always be a fall from perfection that requires the whole process to start all over again (a film such as *His Girl Friday* seems particularly attuned to a repetitive or cyclical aspect of romance, Hildy's freedom in the present being little more than an interlude transitorily situated between endless ploys by Walter). And the ending in love is always exceeded by other endings or other narratives that go beyond the seeming eternity of the film's end titles. Most immediately, the end of the film usually coincides with the beginning of the remarriage, inviting one to imagine later moments, later transformations (this imaging is given ironic representation in at least two films, Buster Keaton's *College* [1927] and John Boorman's *Zardoz* [1974], in which the films continue on beyond the happy moment of the couple's embrace to show us the couples growing old and then dying, rotting away into nothingness).

There are several cases in which critics suggest the structural parallels between American film comedy and other forms of meaning-making, thereby suggesting that comedy is not a special realm but simply a specific option within a shared concern of all signifying forms to represent human endeavors. Much of the thrust of Cavell's *Pursuits of Happiness,* for instance, comes from his desire to see screwball comedy as invested in the same models of cognition as is post-Kantian philosophy, in which the subject tries to negotiate its way through a world of phenomenal forms in which it seeks higher meaning (see, for example, Cavell's excursus on Immanuel Kant in the beginning of the *It Happened One Night* chapter). In a sense, Cavell's approach takes structuralism one step further, restoring to the structural emphasis on an underlying pattern (for example, the one sentence that all plots might be reducible to) an existential underpinning in which each and every story becomes its own specific way of enacting a basic quest for sense.

In another respect, however, Cavell's step is also a step backward. Where poststructuralism takes a step beyond structuralism to argue that each and every plot is only an arbitrary (if socially motivated) form that can be deferred endlessly, deferred by other forms, other representations, Cavell's model can finally seem even prestructuralist in its apparent buying into the very American myths that it seems to take as grounding truths. Even if Cavell does acknowledge how often the screwball pinpoints the gaps between means and ends in the world of romance, he still believes in the existence somewhere of such ends and tends to see them as tied to American accomplishments: for Cavell in New England, as for the Henry David Thoreau who so inspires him, America comes closest to being that green place wherein romance can provide a meaning for human projects and wherein the screwball's instruction of the woman in the ways of earthy pragmatism comes closest to offering a model of emulable sense-making.

What is needed, is an approach that would respect Cavell's philosophical insistence on human activity as a quest for meaning-making while disavowing the American optimism that leads him to imagine the space of America as one in which meaning can most successfully be made. Within the analysis of American comedy, for example, Robin Wood's structural comparison of *Meet Me in St. Louis* (1944) and *The Texas Chainsaw Massacre* (1974) bears on a very general level certain similarities with Cavell in a shared emphasis on films as parables of bonding and a reaching out of subjects to their others. But Wood begins a relativization of categories that Cavell generalizes. For example, where Cavell sees the formation of the heterosexual couple as a solution to the material problems of the world, Wood insists on the very material oppressions that such formation can lead to: "The institution on which the Family in bourgeois capitalist society depends—legal marriage—appears flagrantly neurotic, its sole function being to make it more difficult for couples to separate if they are miserable" (6). Wood's analysis encourages us to understand the ideological cost at which American film can achieve its moments of optimism: the underside, the other scene, of such optimism is an "American nightmare."

In such an optic, we might note the similarity of *Mr. and Mrs. Smith* as screwball to some of the other American Hitchcock films that surround it: for example, *Rebecca* in 1940 and *Suspicion* in 1941. Female Gothics, these films depict the entrance into a woman's ordered existence of a seemingly menacing man, a lover rendered strange, and the transformation of the woman's world into an ambivalent space of ambiguous objects, words, gestures, that she must endlessly try to read so as to see if her environment (and the man in it) has really turned against her. We know of the arbitrariness within the form of the Gothic itself—for example, in the debates between Hitchcock and the studio over the ending of *Suspicion* (is Johnny a murderer or not? Is he exonerated by his last explanations to

Lina? And, even more complicated a question, does the exoneration of him as a murderer mean the same as his exoneration as lover, as husband? Does/should a woman's suspicion of a man extend no further than a suspicion directed at evidently murderous aims?). The exonerative nature of the screwball comedy—a man violently knocks a woman off her pedestal, out of her principled pretentiousness, but does so because he really loves her, and his seeming cruelty is really an educating of her into the appropriate mode of love—can seem less pure if one reads the screwball as an alternate version of the Gothic. (In a sense, *Psycho* is a nightmare version of *It Happened One Night:* the spoiled rich kid goes off on an adventure along the American highways, discovers the world of American mass culture [donuts and buses in the 1934 film, used car lots and motels in the 1960 film], and encounters a lower-class man who makes a mockery of her pretentions.)

Like the Gothic, *Mr. and Mrs. Smith* shows a woman's world turning strange when a man in her life turns strange (first, Mr. Smith suggests he would not have married Ann if he had it to do all over again; then he mysteriously invites her out for an evening that she endlessly misinterprets). As in the Gothic, the woman's dismay at her new world of estrangement is registered in the detail of isolated body parts reacting to the world around them: the nervous napkin twisting of the second Mrs. de Winter is similar to the close-up of Mrs. Smith's feet pulling back suddenly when her husband declares he would not marry her again. Just as melodrama, as Geoffrey Nowell-Smith suggests, works by means of a sort of conversion hysteria in which narrative excess is displaced "into the body of the text" (117), in the woman's film and in the screwball comedy, the body of the woman, and the textualized emphasis on parts of that body in close-up, becomes the site onto which tensions are projected. Wringing hands, nervous tics, darting eyes, withdrawn feet—in such attentions to the trivia of the body, the films lock into feminine structures of feeling in which the punctual momentousness of male narrativity is eschewed for another form of representation wherein the seemingly minor and the seemingly ordinary or everyday come to be charged with intense significations. And if the woman's body becomes the place in which the detailed alienations of her world become registered, there is no less a detailed attention to the seemingly small ways in which that world itself demonstrates its strangeness, in which the body of the world comes to threaten the body of the woman. In the Gothic, the man does not have to threaten death directly: for the woman, man's threat comes in the little details of his words and gestures, in the very ordinariness of the objects that surround the woman (for example, *Rebecca*'s most unbearable moment may be when the second Mrs. de Winter wears the wrong dress to the ball; the woman's world is one in which she, and every detail of her look, endlessly comes under the cruel and relentless gaze of others). Likewise, Mrs. Smith's suspicions of her husband come from a reading of objects around her, objects that because of her husband's strange behavior come to take on a strangeness of their own, a sexual implication especially (note, for example, how Mrs. Smith begins to twist between her hands the bottle of champagne that Mr. Smith has offered her until with horror she realizes that the drinking of this champagne will confirm her conversion into Mr. Smith's mistress; she recoils from the phallically upright bottle as if it condenses all the sexual charge of the new, nonmarital relationship between them).

At the same time, however, Wood's analysis comes to rest on essentializing gestures potentially no less dehistoricizing than those in Cavell. Although Wood substitutes for Cavell's sense of comedy's accomplishment of an American dream a much more critical sense of comedy's unveiling of the nightmarish qualities of that dream, he tends to work from a binary position that understands films to be either fully complicit with, or fully subversive of, dominant American ideology. Inspired by the English moralist literary critic, F. R. Leavis, for whom moral values can be unambiguously assigned to various works of authentic or inauthentic art, Wood offers a leftist criticism that is itself moral in tone and tends toward the same generalizing quality as moral criticism of other political persuasions. (If Wood's earlier apolitical criticism involved looking for an aesthetic moral richness in works of art, he now searches for a sexual moral richness, but the emphasis on rightness, on authenticity, on essential truthfulness to an unambiguous underlying meaning of the work, remains.) Indeed, for all his attention to the kind of art that a Leavis (or a T. S. Eliot) would see precisely as the degradation of morality, Wood's position is no less Leavisite or Eliotic in its assumption of art as possessing an essential core of value that is transmitted by objective correlative into the hearts and minds of spectators. As he argues in his "Introduction to the American Horror Film," "*The Texas Chainsaw Massacre,* unlike *The Omen,* achieves the force of authentic art, profoundly disturbing, intensely personal, yet at the same time far more than personal as the general response it has evoked demonstrates" (22).

In the case of comedy, the tendency is great to imagine the comic as outside of history, an essential force. On the one hand, the notion of comedy as transcendent celebration (as in Northrop Frye on William Shakespeare) imagines that history is but a contingent pressure or resistance that the comic impulse can always overcome. On the other hand, the secular tradition (as in Wes Gehring on screwball as merely the latest in an American tradition of comic satire) imagines that history always undoes pretention, that the pragmatic always triumphs over the idealistic. In both cases, comic tradition is imagined as self-contained, never losing its essential identity to the contingencies of a merely arbitrary history. Rarely have there been attempts to offer material, historically specific explanations of particular manifestations of the comic. Even Mikhail Bakhtin's notion of the carnival—so attractive in recent years as a way of situating comic in relation to social structures as a momentary and theatricalized reversal of the dominant values of those structures—tends to imagine the carnivalesque as an *essential* force. To be sure, Bakhtin does note a falling off of the carnivalesque in the twentieth century (and specifically under the pressure of the sort of totalitarian regime he feels himself to be living through), but this recognition of carnival's vulnerability goes along with a faith that the carnival always remains, even if certain moments render it less evident, less immediate.

One attempt at offering a contextually specific analysis of comedy comes in Jean-Paul Sartre's *L'idiot de la famille,* and this work, a three-volume study of Gustave Flaubert and the ways he turns to the imaginary realm of art to solve real problems in his material existence, is particularly pertinent to our concerns here.[3] Inspired by Sartre's turn to Marxism in the 1950s, *L'idiot de la famille* is driven in general by an attempt to find historical explanations for the very existential categories that govern Sartre's earlier work in such studies as *Being and Nothingness*. The very categories of subject-object, self-other, spirituality-materiality, in-itself–for-itself, that we suggested might underlie the human endeavor for meaning come to be inflected in such a way that we realize that there is no such thing as pure form of human endeavor, just a multiplicity of specific endeavors, each a response to the very specific historical situations in which they find themselves. For example, the fear of femininity that Sartre analyzes in *Being and Nothingness* (while participating in that very fear himself) and that I have tried to find a parallel for in Hitchcock and in the screwball comedy (Mr. Smith's disgust in the restaurant sequence) comes in *L'idiot de la famille* to be read in its historically manifested forms, rather than in some supposedly eternal state. Although Sartre doesn't want to deny cross-historical human phenomena (he terms much of the work of his Marxist period an "anthropology") and although he would certainly want to suggest that the male subject's domination over an other usually rendered as feminine is a domination not limited to life under capitalism, *L'idiot de la famille* provides an analysis of highly specific forms of fear of femininity in nineteenth-century France. For example, for the upwardly mobile bourgeois man concerned with career and accomplishment, the feminine can come to represent all that challenges his aspirations, all that he himself threatens to become if he slides back from success. In Flaubert in particular, Sartre finds a feminization that is both a mark of Flaubert's failure—he cannot be the striving businessman or professional man that his family wants him to be—and of his transformation of that failure into a weird sort of success—he becomes a successful writer in an age when the bourgeoisie can see such an activity only as a sort of leisurely, feminized waste.

Sartre's attempts to find historically specific explanations for seemingly existential phenomena has a special pertinence for our study here because part of his analysis is particularly focused on the social production of the comic impulse. Of course, to take Sartre's points about nineteenth-century comedy and simply apply them to the situation of 1940s screwball would be to rebetray the historicizing impulse that drives *L'idiot de la famille*. And yet, as Sartre himself insists, the intense specificity of *L'idiot de la famille* (2,801 pages of close reading of Flaubert's life) is intended to offer an example of a method that can be applied in other contexts. As Fredric Jameson puts it in a short journalistic review of the English translation of the first volume of *L'idiot:*

> It should not be thought that the nihilism of the imaginary, as it is elaborately anatomized in *The Family Idiot,* is a mere 19th-century curiosity or a local feature of some specifically French middle-class culture; nor is it a private obsession of Jean-Paul Sartre himself. Turning things into images, abolishing the real world, grasping the world as little more than a text or sign-system—this is notoriously the very logic of our own consumer society, the society of the image or the media event (the Vietnam War as a television series). Flaubert's private solution, his invention of a new "derealizing" esthetic strategy, may seem strange and distant, not because it is archaic, but because it has gradually become the logic of our media society, thereby becoming invisible to us. This is the sense in which *The Family Idiot*—at first glance so cumbersome and forbidding a project—may well speak with terrifying immediacy to Americans in the 1980s. (18)

Similarly, Hazel Barnes suggests how what may seem digressions from Flaubert in Sartre's analysis may actually work to imply the generalizability of the specifics of Flaubert's case. This seems especially true of Sartre's extended digressions, which are virtually full-length essays on, for example, other French writers, such as Leconte de Lisle. In Barnes's words:

> It is helpful to have Sartre's careful analysis of the qualities of *l'art névrose* as exhibited in the poems of a second Knight of Nothingness [like Leconte de Lisle]. Without this documentation, one might be tempted to wonder whether in fact Sartre's description applied fully only to Flaubert. As it is, we have a neat demonstration of at least two responses to the objective mind which show a harmony of basic qualities in spite of the radical difference between the authors, their backgrounds, and the formal qualities of the written texts. (297)[4]

In this light, what the analyst of screwball comedy might look for in Sartre's work are elements of a sociology of comedy that pinpoint what is common in capitalism across two continents and across two centuries, while keeping in mind all the specific differences from case to case. And in this respect, what is most striking about Sartre's theory of nineteenth-century comedy is his emphasis on the primary function of that comedy: to serve the interests of an ascendant bourgeoisie. Against approaches that see comedy as a subversive force that goes against dominant power, Sartre sees comedy as amply fitting the needs of dominant power. He is able to do this by recognizing that the bourgeoisie can have its own subversive function—to overthrow older aristocratic models so as to enact a social system in which hierarchies will still be maintained (there will be the rich; there will be the poor) but in which movement in this hierarchy will be possible for those industrious enough to seize opportunity. In a sense, Sartre pictures the bourgeoisie as a culture that imagines itself to be a new aristocracy or, to be more precise, the first real aristocracy; whereas the prerevolutionary aristocracy gains its positioning by artificial means (inheritance, the buying of power), the bourgeoisie comes to merit its position through dignified work. In Raymond Williams's terms, the bourgeoisie operates with a newly *emergent* ideology, but one that bears traces of the *residual* ideology that will be its most immediate critical target. Comedy here becomes a means by which the bourgeoisie can criticize its past and show up that past's nonpragmatic idealism. In particular, Sartre argues that the new middle class has as its raison d'être a pragmatist puncturing of all pretention, all high humanist valuations of Man, and, at the same time, all democratic strivings for community, for the human as open interaction. Under capitalism, human relations come to take on the form of market calculations; society is serialized into a nonorganic mass of egocentric actors, each governed by a profit motive, each regarding the other as either potential contributor to success or potential rival.

Anticipating Bergson's emphasis on comedy's rendering of the human as mechanical, Sartre then imagines the bourgeois function of comedy as one in which actors and objects all become reified as mechanical bits in a system of cold, calculating exchange. Indeed, Sartre borrows very closely from Bergson while suggesting that Bergson makes the mistake of treating the mechanical impulse of comedy as if it were a fully asocial, cross-historical phenomenon: "Bergson believes, correctly, that if one laughs [at someone who falls], this is because this unfortunate fall shows 'the mechanical grafted onto the living.' But he does not give us the social sense and intention of this hilarity" (1: 817). Significantly, Sartre gets at this by way of a twentieth-century example from film comedy—Charlie Chaplin (or "Charlot" in his French reputation) in *Modern Times* (1936). Chaplin's comedy serves as an emblematic figuration of the materialization of all relations of subject to others in a world where all such relations are rendered mechanical. At the same time, revealingly and in line with most readings of Chaplin as humanist (in opposition to, say, Buster Keaton), Sartre em-

phasizes the extent to which a residual humanism colors Chaplin's me-
chanicity. As Sartre explains in a footnote, "The comic in Charlie Chaplin
is never a pure form of the comic: there is a 'humanism' in his films that
shows us the vagabond humbly battling against all accidents in order to
affirm in spite of everything the possibility to be human" (2: 1439).

Comedy steps in each time Man has the bad faith, the pretention, to
imagine that he is anything more than a materiality. Whether a worker or
ruler, Man's goal is to function within the system of production, to become a machine (whether one that works or works at ruling those who
work), and comedy has as its purpose to deflate Man's aspiration to be
anything more. According to Sartre, "The comic appears then out of a
goal to make analytic reason triumph over the syncretic idealism of the
aristocracy, by the reduction of the interior to the exterior, of the subjective to the objective, of doxa to science, of historical temporalisation to
physical temporalisation" (2: 1439). (By this last distinction, Sartre seems
to mean that Man no longer works according to a temporality that is the expression of a human project—time organized according to personal or social needs—but according to a mechanical temporality controlled by nothing but physical laws—for example, the inexorable time of the assembly
line.) Working again to add a sociological dimension to Bergson's categories, Sartre suggests that the laugh that comedy elicits is a laugh that ex-
teriorizes and does so doubly: the laughter laughs with other members of
the society but never shares more than this because each member knows
that the laugh could next be applied to himself or herself; the laughter
laughs at the member of society whose inattention or whose slipping up
(literally and metaphorically in relation to dominant proprieties) has announced his or her separation from everyone else. In this respect, Sartre
argues that the comic accident (the fall, the spill) is read as an attack on society and that the laugh is society's revenge, a kind of scapegoating:

> When a member of the community . . . voluntarily or not caricatures the
> sort of *human nature* that is dominant in this community, the other mem-
> bers of the community find themselves suddenly endangered in their very
> person: if the "French character" is really only a tissue of lies, if all that it
> takes for it to explode open is that its principal traits be radicalized, then it is
> in *my* character as a Frenchman, the socialized structure of my Ego, that I
> am contested, and it is at the same time the entire national order that is
> gravely menaced since, all things considered, the French personality is
> nothing but the syncretic condensation of the history and structures of
> France. (1: 811)

To be sure, as the setting up of a social context within which to understand the specific practices of Gustave Flaubert, Sartre's analysis of

nineteenth-century comedy may appear paradoxical. After all, it seems to imply that Flaubert was nothing but a good boy of the bourgeoisie, a hard worker turning his sardonic, demystifying comic gaze on the pretentions of an older generation but never on his own. Yet Sartre gives his analysis one more twist: he sees in Flaubert evidence of even more newly emergent tendencies that are already beginning to take a distance from pure adhesion to bourgeois ideology. It is an easy step, Sartre argues, from a position that assumes that Man is nothing but matter, that there is no spirit but only physicality, to one that therefore sees no purpose in hard work, in social advancement, even of the rational bourgeois kind. Why not fully recognize the sheer materiality of human beings and see all projects—bourgeois and aristocratic alike—as lies? Between two sets of exams for the law school he doesn't want to go to, Flaubert has a seizure and falls to the ground. He emerges from his sickbed as someone destined to be a scabrous writer, not a good bourgeois. And Sartre suggests that there may have been something of Flaubert in many of the young clerks, young professionals, of nineteenth-century France—of the *capables,* as they were called.

Sartre indeed imagines nineteenth-century dominant society as one whose dominance is fictive. The society is riven in its very heart by a double nature in its most seemingly upright citizens. At work, the *capable* is all obedience and diligence; but his fantasies are of overthrow, negation, and violence, and in many cases, in the back drawer behind the "important" documents of his bourgeois work, the *capable* has a scabrous novel or poetry collection of his own that he works on in secret delight in his leisure time. The infamous sexual double standard of the nineteenth century may be only another version of this splitting between a surface capability/diligence and a subterranean longing for impropriety, for scandal. As tradition has it, the nineteenth-century bourgeois alternates between the asexual haven of the home and the sexualized realm of the brothel and underground pornography industries. And yet we may have to acknowledge that the duplicity of bourgeois society is not so much a clear opposition of two impulses as a confused complication of them (for example, the *capable* who fantasizes violence against the boss he considers stupid and inefficient also fantasizes that this violence could put him in the place of the boss—the fantasy is simultaneously bourgeois and antibourgeois, subversive and supportive of order). Indeed, a number of writers have challenged the whore/madonna image of the nineteenth century and the ways it is often tied to distinctions of anticapital/capital. These critics suggest instead that nineteenth-century capitalism often operated by a sexualization of economy and an economization of sexuality. As capitalism became as concerned with consumption (finding new markets, giving an erotic charge to items newly displayed in the innovative steel and glass structures of the department store) as with production, sex itself became a form of commodity, rather than a scandalous subversion of commodification.[5]

Screwball comedy bears the traces of confusions and contradictions in a later moment of capital when this commodification of desire reaches new extremes. The screwball allows capital to work while emphasizing the sensual attractiveness of much of its world. Ted Sennett's terming of one subtradition the "Cinderella" film aptly catches the ways in which the films work not by offering simple myths (the people, the rich) but by holding several mythologies together. The films establish a pluralist situation in which different viewpoints and different strata of the society can all seem to have their role. In *It Happened One Night*, the rich, the people, and, between them, the capable professional (Peter as wisecracking reporter, man from the people, but no longer completely one of them) all come together. *Mr. and Mrs. Smith* and other films focused on well-off professionals who have the time for wacky adventures seem to present a more complicated case: is there nothing but social irresponsibility in works that during the Depression so luxuriate in the wasteful antics of the idle rich? If a film such as *My Man Godfrey* (1936) begins with the unproductive activities of the aristocracy (a scavenger hunt), other screwballs (for example, *Bringing Up Baby*) can seem like nothing but endless scavenger hunts, endless quests for pure fun. For Ted Sennett, indeed, the only social function of the films is, in their avoidance of social responsibility, to offer an escapism from the problems of economic crisis: "They all [the "foolish, scatterbrained, and laughably fallible, but also good-natured, honest, and likeable" characters in such films] seemed to be saying: If nothing makes sense in a crisis-ridden, dangerous world, then why behave sensibly? Why not confront life's problems—a broken love affair, a crumbling marriage, a murder—with cheerful impudence and occasionally a wide streak of lunacy?" (14)

At the beginning of *Mr. and Mrs. Smith*, the couple has just spent three days in the bedroom (playing silly games the film tells us) as a way of resolving a marital dispute. Interrupted by an office worker who has brought a document for Mr. Smith, a lawyer, to sign, the couple quickly and easily retreats back into the intimacy of its private space. The three-day binge will end with the recitation by Mr. Smith, at his wife's behest, of rules that they are to follow if their marriage is to continue to be a success. Several themes come together here: life as endless (sexual) play, work as an interruption of play but one that can easily be accommodated, play as a submitting to a carefully reasoned, carefully analyzed set of strictures. Far from representing an alternative to the system of capital, an escape from it, the film represents the very triumph of late capital, the dream of a state in which the endless saving of a nineteenth-century Protestant ethic can give way to the endless spending (in both the sexual and economic senses of the terms) of a twentieth century newly devoted to pragmatic expenditure.

As a number of scholars (such as Stuart Ewen) have shown, the twentieth century gives rise to an intense consumerist ideology (for Ewen, this comes as an attempt to resolve crises of overproduction). As important as the efficient making of products is the efficient selling of products and of a way of life based on the promise of products. The screwball comedy operates as consumerist art, imagining not that one relaxes in order to work but that one works in order to relax (or, at the same time, that relaxation is a form of work, to be enjoyed but also to be carefully codified, submitted to rules, like the sexology that will come in during the war to tell soldiers how to systematize their sexual activity). The commonality of the film's title, *Mr. and Mrs. Smith,* is not an impossible and weird affectation—could these two spoiled, privileged brats really be representatives of ordinary American people?—but part of its very promises. To be an ordinary American is to want to go against conservative strictures of thrift and economy for the benefits of play, desire, and endless production of sexuality.

Immediately by means of his name, Mr. Smith is in contrast with the old aristocrat, Jefferson. The film plays Gothic mythologies of the South as the true site of unsupportable, improper waste against the hustle-and-bustle, productive efficiency of New York, where capitalism resembles neither the inefficient decadence of an anachronistic aristocracy (Jeff, unable to be enough of a man to fight for Ann's love) nor the cold efficiency of the antiseptic, repressive factory system. (This system is elided in this film but is quickly called into play in the next few years as the needs of the war require that films sexualize the factory, render it a glamorous site where women can realize an essential beauty and allure.) We are neither in the aristocratic world of plantation production nor in the world of factory production; we are in a world of production where sex and production, work and play all appear as one. (In this respect, the recent film *An Officer and a Gentleman* (1982) is an interesting return to the Cinderella myth, the woman romantically saved in the very site of factory production as ex-rad of the 1960s Joe Cocker sings "Love lifts you up where you belong.") It seems not insignificant in *Mr. and Mrs. Smith* that when Jeff takes Ann out for a date, he fails in two ways, both connected to his inefficiency in a new consumer world (the film never suggests he is inefficient in work, just in play): his attempt to take Ann on a Coney Island ride is a disaster (the ride breaks down; they are struck at the top in a torrential downpour) and his revelation on the return home that he doesn't know how to drink. Even though the law firm partnership of David and Jefferson suggests that both are equally efficient workers, only David is the true capitalist, able to combine work and play, fun and production.

In such a context, Stanley Cavell's notion of the romance in the screwball being a form of *re*marriage seems both right and wrong. Cavell is right to suggest that the emphasis on a bringing together of characters who have already been together, who have already known sexuality, adds a level of wiseness and experience to otherwise innocent proceedings. The world of the screwball is a sexualized world. But the assumption that characters can have sexual intimacy only in marriage is an assumption that the 1930s and 1940s are beginning to challenge. At most, marriage is not the goal of romance but an expedient to allow that romance to occur; there is the sense in many of the films that to engage in romance one must marry because that's the law, but one is marrying only because it's the law and not out of any romantic belief in the strictures of the system.

Indeed, *Mr. and Mrs. Smith* ends not with remarriage but with the formation of the couple nonetheless, their coming together in a sexual moment (locking her skis around him, Ann pulls David down to her, out of frame as the film ends). The film's explicit solution to the nonmarriage—a throw-away mention very early in the film that Ann and David do have common-law status—is both trivial (because neither Ann nor David seems to give it much credence) and subversive. It suggests that marriage is a fictive act. Rather than marriage allowing lots of sex with one person during the course of years, lots of sex with one person during a course of years allows one to claim one is married. As America moves toward war, *Mr. and Mrs. Smith* announces the fictionality of marriage, its potential inappropriateness to the new demands of the modern world.

A war service comedy from the same moment, *You'll Never Get Rich* (1941), even gives explicit representation of the idea of marriage as fiction: having been rejected by the woman he loves (Rita Hayward) but who is obliged contractually to appear in his stage show, the hero (Fred Astaire) uses this contract to impose another as he hires a real preacher to perform the on-stage marriage ceremony that he and she will act out. As I've suggested in an article on 1940s film and speech-act theory (a theory that studies, among other things, how we give enough credence to words to allow them to accomplish things), it is precisely the marriage ceremony performed against one of the participant's knowledge of the reality of the ceremony that is for speech-act theorist John Austin one of the supreme examples of a nonbinding, improper speech act. But *You'll Never Get Rich* suggests the potential effectivity of the fiction: a stage marriage comes to be a real marriage. If one follows Cavell, it is easy to imagine that this fiction is the film's own; screwball's optimism that the resistance of the world will always come under the sway of romance leads the film to fictions that it never recognizes. But one could be more cynical (or more wisecracking, to adopt the tone of the screwballs themselves) and suggest that the film is aware of its subterfuge: whether legal or not, the marriage gives back to the woman the chance to be with her man, and for the screwball that's all that matters. The war years will intensify this sense of fictionality and suggest that marriage is an expediency that solves problems but has little value in and of itself. The film *The Miracle of Morgan's Creek* (1944) may be the wartime paradigm of this new trajectory: marriage comes after a woman's pregnancy; a husband is created so that the proprieties can be maintained.

To understand Hitchcock's appropriateness for screwball comedy, we first have to realize that his work is more romantic than comic, in the classic sense of the terms. Hitchcock's films are not about the people, the anonymous masses joining together in festive ceremony, but about the couple, a special twosome, often posed against the vulgarity of the masses, who triumphs over the world through love. But the films treat romance within a pragmatist framework in which what one feels or desires comes as a result of the ways one acts. In Hitchcock, gesture or speech often creates belief, rather than the other way around. In *The 39 Steps* (1935), for example, Richard Hannay is endlessly theatricalizing (to crowds in conference halls, to the woman in his life); finding that no one believes the truth, he fabricates and finds that the more seductive he makes his fabrications, the more credence they garner. The couple forms here not because both members love each other but because circumstances force them to act as if they are in love: handcuffed together, the man and woman check into an inn whose owners mistake physical intimacy for romantic intimacy; the innkeepers' delight at love will rub off on the woman, who comes to trust the man.

When Hannay first meets the woman, he kisses her with great energy as a way of throwing the police off the trail. Like screwball's narrative of re-"marriage," Hitchcockian romance works to bring characters back to a point where reality can be added to what had previously been only a theatricalized simulacrum of that reality. The characters are endlessly put in situations that mimic the full sexuality of couple formation but that are not yet sexual. Hence, there is a recurrent emphasis on characters physically bonded together but not yet fully romantically linked. And there is an interest in scenes whose sexual overtones are ambiguous (for example, the lodger outside the door turning the door handle as Daisy takes her bath; Roger Thornhill staying overnight in Eve Kendall's railway apartment but seeming to sleep alone on her floor), but this ambiguity will be answered by end scenes in which theatricality becomes physicality (the lodger moving toward Daisy as the "Tonight—Golden Curls" sign blinks behind them, a reference perhaps to the sexual sight that will become available to the lodger that evening; the train going into the tunnel to end *North by Northwest* [1959]). In a sense, the absurdity of *Mr. and Mrs. Smith*'s opening (can we really believe the Hays Office scripting that has them doing nothing but playing games for three days in the bedroom?) fits: the two characters are foolish enough to have actually been playing games, and the film needs to move them to that end point where, all sham discarded, all theatricality aside, they actually become physical entities with a full sexuality, the man moving down toward the woman.

I intend the previous pages as suggestions only—for further thought, for further research.[6] In particular, I have bracketed out one of the most important aspects of Sartre's investigation: its attempt to account for the singularity of a life. More than anything else, *L'idiot de la famille* is a biography, one that enlists psychoanalysis and sociology in a quest to understand one person's project. At a moment when a rethinking of authorship seems to have come back onto the agenda of film study, *L'idiot de la famille* may offer some important suggestions to biography and career analysis. (David Bordwell's argument that "broad social forces are warped, refracted, or transformed by the dynamics specific to these mediating factors" [that is, "such forces as Ozu's working situation, the film industry, and the proximate historical circumstances of his milieu"] [17] may bear useful comparison to Sartre's understanding of the individual life as a personalized reworking of social and familial influences.) In the case of Hitchcock, some of Sartre's suggestions about the ways individuals turn to art to escape the analytic pressures of their age may be applicable given Hitchcock's turn to filmmaking as a more exciting alternative to the engineering career to which his own psychology had seemed to destine him (the timid man who seems to avoid participation in life by obsessive fascination with calculation—for example, memorization as a child of railroad time schedules in faraway countries).

But in the case of the Hollywood director, we are still far from being able theoretically and factually to answer the questions that open *L'idiot de la famille* and that seem easier for the case of the solitary writer: "What can one know of a man, today?" "Don't we risk coming up with heterogeneous and irreducible levels of signification?" (1: 7). Sartre himself has to endlessly fictionalize moments of his account, forcing his imagination of Flaubert's life to correspond to what psychoanalysis suggests that life could have been like (in the most famous example, Sartre follows a discussion of Flaubert's mother's attitude toward her infant son with the declaration, "I admit it: this is a fable. Nothing proves that it was like this. And, worse yet, the absence of proofs—which would necessarily be singular facts—pushes us, even when we fabulate, to schematism, to generality: my story fits infants in general, not Gustave in particular" [1: 139]).

In the case of the classical mode of Hollywood production, it may well be that too much of an emphasis on the singularities of a career may lead us to overvalue the individual director as someone special, a figure outside the dominant paradigms. (Even the study of literary authorship runs a similar risk, assuming that because the writer is literally alone when he or she writes, writing is an activity apart from the social. One of Hazel Barnes's criticisms of *L'idiot de la famille* is that Sartre may overemphasize Flaubert's isolation, his supposed lack of friendship, to fuel a virtually auteurist notion of the artist as special sufferer [411–412].) Returning to our opening question, we may have to rephrase it: what might it mean to treat *Mr. and Mrs. Smith* as a Hitchcock film *while treating it as screwball comedy and as part of the Hollywood system?* From the singularities of a life to the regularities of an art and its society, such a question may take a place on film study's critical agenda.

Notes

1. If failure of laughter there be: for whatever this is worth, I have found *Mr. and Mrs. Smith* to elicit much laughter in classes in which I've taught it. One of the evidently most riotous moments comes in the nightclub when David Smith finds himself caught in an impossible blind date, the agony of the situation registered through an intense move of point of view (emotional and literal) into the subjective. As I'll suggest in a moment, this scene fits the definition of Hitchcockian cinema as one in which actions occur at the expense of the characters.

2. See, for example, Tania Modleski's (1987) discussion (using Sartre's *Being and Nothingness*) of food in *Frenzy*.

3. For a useful introduction to *L'idiot de la famille*, see Hazel Barnes (109–116 are specifically on Sartre's discussion of comedy).

4. I also suggest the contemporary pertinence of *L'idiot de la famille* for an analysis of our society of the spectacle in "A Vertigo of Displacement."

5. Stephen Heath offers an excellent discussion of nineteenth-century confusions of sex and capital in the British context.

6. In a book that appeared just as I finished this chapter, *The Hitchcock Romance*, Lesley Brill anticipates many of the points of my approach to Hitchcock by emphasizing the director's place in a tradition of romance, of quest fantasies governed by an ideology of heterosexual love (174–183 discuss romance and irony in *Mr. and Mrs. Smith*). Brill clearly suggests the aggressive-possessive view of love that the film presents—"Egotistical desire no longer opposes emotional generosity but replaces it. . . . Love is not separated, as in the romances, from ownership or control" (177–178). I differ slightly in arguing that the film is nevertheless not that ironic and critical of dominant drives. Rather, in the new capitalism of the twentieth century, it suggests a catching up of irony within dominant structures: if the film disavows older models of romance, it is because they don't work for capitalism. Where Brill sees the childish irresponsibility of the characters as a stultifying quality that they must outgrow, I argue that the film's only criticism of infantilism is that it is not irresponsible enough: the move of the film is toward a liberal situation in which one can be childishly playful and sexually playful at the same time.

References and Additional Reading

Bakhtin, Mikhail. 1968. *Rabelais and His World*, trans. Helene Iswolksy. Cambridge, Mass.: MIT Press.

Barnes, Hazel. 1981. *Sartre and Flaubert*. Ithaca, N.Y.: Cornell University Press.

Bergson, Henri. 1956. "Laughter." In Wylie Sypher, ed., *Comedy*. Garden City, N.Y.: Doubleday Anchor.

Bordwell, David. 1988. *Ozu and the Poetics of Cinema*. Princeton: BFI/Princeton University Press.

Brill, Lesley. 1988. *The Hitchcock Romance: Love and Irony in Hitchcock's Films*. Princeton: Princeton University Press.

Cahiers du cinéma. 1976. "Interview with Howard Hawks." Trans. in Andrew Sarris, ed., *Interviews with Film Directors*. New York: Bobbs-Merrill.

Cavell, Stanley. 1981. *Pursuits of Happiness: The Hollywood Comedy of Remarriage*. Cambridge, Mass.: Harvard University Press.

Ewen, Stuart. 1976. *Captains of Consciousness: Advertising and the Social Roots of Consumer Culture*. New York: McGraw-Hill.

Frye, Northrop. 1961. *A Natural Perspective*. New York: Columbia University Press.

Gehring, Wes. 1983. *Screwball Comedy: Defining a Film Genre*. Muncie, Ind.: Ball State University Press.

Heath, Stephen. 1981. "Le corps victorien anthologiquement." *Critique*, 405–406: 152–165.

Jameson, Fredric. 1981. "Sartre in Search of Flaubert." *New York Times Book Review*, December 27, pp. 5, 16, 18.

Mast, Gerald. 1982. *Howard Hawks, Storyteller*. New York: Oxford University Press.

Modleski, Tania. 1982. *Loving with a Vengeance: Mass-Produced Fantasies for Women*. Hamden, Conn.: Shoe String Press.

———. 1987. *The Women Who Knew Too Much: Hitchcock and Feminism*. New York: Methuen.

Nowell-Smith, Geoffrey. 1978. "Minnelli and Melodrama." *Screen* 18, no. 2: 113–118.

Polan, Dana. 1984. "A Vertigo of Displacement: The Sartrean Spectacle of *L'idiot de la famille*." *Dalhousie Review* 64, no. 2: 354–375.

———. 1985. "The Felicity of Ideology: Speech-Acts and the 'Happy Ending' in American Films of the 1940s." *Iris* 3, no. 1: 35–44.

Rohmer, Eric, and Claude Chabrol. 1979. *Hitchcock: The First Forty-Four Films*, trans. Stanley Hochman. New York: Frederick Ungar.

Sartre, Jean-Paul. 1971, 1972. *L'idiot de la famille: Gustave Flaubert de 1821 à 1857*, 3 vol. Paris: Editions Gallimard.

Sennett, Ted. 1973. *Lunatics and Lovers*. New Rochelle, N.Y.: Arlington House.

Williams, Raymond. 1983. *Problems in Materialism and Culture*. New York: Verso Press.

Wood, Robin. 1969. "An Introduction to the American Horror Film." In Andrew Britton, ed., *The American Nightmare: Essays on the Horror Film*. Toronto: Festival of Festivals.

———. 1979. "The American Family Comedy: From *Meet Me in St. Louis* to *The Texas Chainsaw Massacre*." *Wide Angle* 3, no. 2: 5–11.

Cartoon and Narrative in the Films of Frank Tashlin and Preston Sturges

Brian Henderson

He was a fat, pink and grey pig of a man. . . . He did not have a skull on the top of his neck, only a face; his head was all face—a face without side, back or top, like a mask.

Nathanael West, *The Dream Life of Balso Snell*
(1931, 18)

Harry, like many actors, had very little back or top to his head. It was almost all face, like a mask, with deep furrows between the eyes, across the forehead and on either side of the nose and mouth, plowed there by years of broad grinning and heavy frowning. Because of them, he could never express anything either subtly or exactly. They wouldn't permit degrees of feeling, only the furthest degree.

Nathanael West, *The Day of the Locust*
(1939, 67)

A number of filmmakers practiced caricature before they turned to cinema and frequently continued to do so afterward: Emile Cohl, Sergei Eisenstein, Alexander Dovshenko, Jean Cocteau, and Federico Fellini, among others. But Frank Tashlin (1913–1972), as far as I know, was the only film director of note with an extensive background in commercial animation. Tashlin worked as an animator and director on the Merry Melodies and Looney Tunes, released by Warner Brothers, on and off from 1933 to 1945. (*Brother Brat,* a Porky Pig cartoon directed by Tashlin in 1944, has Porky baby-sitting a sour, card-playing infant of precocious sexual interests—surely the model for Baby Herman in *Who Framed Roger Rabbit?* [1988].) During this period Tashlin also created animation for MGM and Columbia, drew cartoons for magazines, and wrote several cartoon books for children. During and after this period he also moved gradually into gag and screenwriting for live-action features and directed his first film, *The First Time,* in 1951. In all, he directed twenty-four films in eighteen years, the last, *The Private Navy of Sgt. O'Farrell,* in 1968. Among these were two with Dean Martin and Jerry Lewis, *Artists and*

Models (1955) and *Hollywood or Bust* (1956), and six with Jerry Lewis alone: *Rock-a-Bye Baby* (1958), *The Geisha Boy* (1958), *Cinderfella* (1960), *It's Only Money* (1963), *Who's Minding the Store?* (1963), and *The Disorderly Orderly* (1964). Interspersed with these eight films, all for Paramount, were three for Fox: *The Lieutenant Wore Skirts* (1955), *The Girl Can't Help It* (1956), and *Will Success Spoil Rock Hunter?* (1957).

In a chapter on Frank Tashlin and Jerry Lewis in a 1969 book on Hollywood comedy, Raymond Durgnaut writes that "gagology, despite all our efforts, is still the most anaesthetized aspect of aesthetic theory" (236). But in the slim body of criticism on Tashlin—several interviews, a handful of articles—his gags are the one thing that everyone writes about; sometimes it seems that is all they write about. Critics Ian Cameron, Roger Talleur, Peter Bogdanovich, Robert Mundy, and Paul Willemen have all addressed themselves, from their respective points of view, to Tashlin's distinctive gags, which each relates to his background as a cartoonist. (Their articles are collected in the 1973 Edinburgh Film Festival catalogue on Tashlin, edited by Claire Johnston and Paul Willemen.)

Precisely what is cartoonlike in Tashlin's gags? There is no adequate answer to this question in the critical literature. Most critics seem to assume, via the biographic assumptions of auteurism, that there must be a connection between these two phases of their subject's work; examples are cited, the case is made, but its point remains somewhat fuzzy. The subject is, to be sure, a difficult one, requiring as it does a prior theoretical analysis of cartoons and, indeed, of live-action cinema itself. Such a satisfactory analysis of cartoons does not exist; whether one of live-action cinema does is a matter of current debate. Short of such a theoretical effort, the most complete survey of Tashlin's gags is to be found in Ian Cameron's 1963 article, in which he says, "Characteristic Tashlin cartoon gag(s) . . . use cinematic trickery to transform his essentially real world into an exciting place where, unrestricted by the laws of thermodynamics, anything is possible" (in Johnston & Willemen, 68).

Thermodynamics are involved when ice melts and milk bottles burst open as Jayne Mansfield walks by in *The Girl Can't Help It* and when a watercooler boils as Shirley MacLaine kisses Jerry Lewis in *Artists and Models*. More often, however, it is laws of biology and anatomy that are contravened, as in the masseuse's impossible bending and stretching of Lewis's body in *Artists and Models,* variations of which occur in the Lewis-directed films *The Nutty Professor* (1963) and *The Big Mouth* (1967). The laws of mechanics are frequently set aside as well, as in the impossible course of the runaway golf ball and other object behavior in *Who's Minding the Store?* and other films.

Commenting further on the cartoon–live action frontier, Cameron notes that "Tashlin's human heroes have pronounced animal characteristics" (in Johnston & Willemen, 70). Most of the examples he cites are verbal gags and visual gags of uncertain animality—such as children biting adults in *The First Time* and *Artists and Models*. (The baby that Porky minds in *Brother Brat* bites his hand and won't let go; when Porky frees himself at last, the baby bites Porky's other hand.) Comparing animals to humans by a kind of graphic assimilation has been fundamental to caricature since its first appearance in the late sixteenth century (Gombrich). The equation of animals with humans is also fundamental to many cartoons, to be sure, but one must be careful. Bugs Bunny, Daffy Duck, Donald Duck, and Mickey Mouse do embody human characteristics, but they do so in a fixed, unchanging way. They also retain aspects of their animal nature—Bugs lives in a rabbit hole and loves carrots; Bugs, Donald, and Mickey are attracted only to females of their own animal group; and so on. The bite of caricature is further reduced, moreover, not only because these characters do not resemble specific humans but also because they themselves became stars and their human attributes became conventions in such a way that the "shock of recognition" of animal-human resemblance became considerably dulled.

Gags of physical impossibility and of human-animal assimilation—cartoonlike gags—are plentiful in Tashlin's films but still constitute a minority of his gags overall. (Jean-Luc Godard was the first to stress—by quoting Tashlin himself—the density of gags in Tashlin's films.[1]) But gags, however plentiful, are not the only things going on in Tashlin's films. There are also songs, romantic plots and scenes, and frequent parodies of film genres and of television. The gags, parodies, and other elements occur within scenes, of course, and these in turn are arranged in some way to make up a whole film. What has not been examined in Tashlin's films, in short, are their narratives. But attention to narrative in Tashlin's work is necessary if only to account for his characteristic gags and for the reciprocal relationship between them and the other elements in his work. Such attention might also shed light on the cartoonlike dimension of his films.

Is there such as a thing as a cartoon narrative? It is hard to say because the question has not been posed before and the subject has not been studied. There seem to be some characteristic cartoon subjects and themes—not absolutes, to be sure, but recurring patterns. The "reversibility of violence" theme and situation apply to Sylvester and Tweety, Tom and Jerry, and the Coyote and the Roadrunner, among many others. Sylvester, Tom, and the Coyote cook up scheme after scheme and try again and again to capture their diminutive preys, only to have their instruments of assault backfire and injure themselves instead. In these cases and others, cartoon narratives proceed by repeating a basic situation with variations rather than by moving progressively toward a narrative resolution. Rather than resolving themselves, cartoon narratives are often simply suspended at some point and given a more or less arbitrary ending. Sometimes this is in the form of a kind of epilogue that involves a reversion to a previous state or a jumping ahead to some new point. In the case of well-known cartoon characters, needless to say, the endings of particular films usually leave open the possibility of revival in later works.

What all this means in narratological terms is that cartoon narratives make considerable use of ellipsis. There are ellipses first of all between the main part of the narrative and what I have called the epilogue. There are also ellipses between the variations of a cartoon's basic situation—those indeterminate intervals of time in which the Coyote or Tom or Sylvester pulls himself together, physically and psychologically, after his last debacle and outfits himself for a new attempt on the Roadrunner, Jerry, or Tweety. It is impossible to say how long such intervals are—a week, a day, an hour?—particularly because night never falls and the weather never changes in such cartoons, unless such change is part of a particular variation.

What about the narratives of Tashlin's films? The principal difference between any cartoon narrative and that of live-action features is that cartoons are short and features are long, which is a qualitative as well as a quantitative difference. Nevertheless, several Tashlin films end with a cartoonlike suspension of the narrative, usually accomplished by a jumping ahead to a new point in the future of the characters. This new point is not completely arbitrary, but neither is it the inevitable result of the film's narrative and other processes—this point occupies an uneasy, and quite modern, place between the arbitrary and the necessary, as do the endings of many of Godard's films. In *The Lieutenant Wore Skirts, The Girl Can't Help It,* and *Rock-a-Bye Baby,* the epilogue set in the future evidences the birth of one or more children born to the film's central couple after the main narrative of the film. In *Will Success Spoil Rock Hunter?* there is a cut to a future sometime beyond the main time frame of the story in which Tony Randall has dropped out of the advertising business in order to work, accompanied by Betsy Drake, now his wife, and his niece, as a farmer. In the case of *Artists and Models,* there are at least three endings. Martin and Lewis sing, dance, and cut up at a spectacular artists-and-models ball but have to leave it because of a ludicrous and sketchy spy plot that is in turn simply dropped, without resolution or explanation, as Martin and Lewis hurry back to the ball for a happy singing finale onstage with Dorothy Malone and Shirley MacLaine. Suddenly, by virtue of a straight cut, the ball outfits of the four principals—still onstage—are transformed into bride and groom costumes, just before the fadeout. This is a cartoonlike transformation and serves as an epilogue even though, apparently, no story time has been omitted between the main narrative and it.

The use of ellipsis in the narratives of Tashlin's films is not limited to their epilogue-endings. Virtually all filmmakers use ellipsis, even Agnes Varda in *Cleo from Five to Seven* (1962), which is sometimes said to cover two continuous hours in the life of its heroine—the film is ninety minutes long. As Seymour Chatman says, "Ellipsis is as old as *The Iliad.*" But, he continues, "ellipsis of a particularly broad and abrupt sort is characteristic of modern narratives" (71). The sheer magnitude of the time period(s) elided is not by itself a test of modernity, however. Ellipses comprising years were common, for instance, in 1930s biographical films and in family epics such as *How Green Was My Valley* (1941), which covered entire lifetimes or eras. Ellipses in such cases were expected by audiences and were often naturalized by a voice-over narration summarizing the periods omitted.

Modern ellipses include those not expected by audiences and not providing immediate clues to orient them. Several Tashlin ellipses lie somewhere between the classical and the modern. As a result, like Tashlin's work generally, they can be dismissed by classicists and dogmatic champions of modernism and valued by makers of cinematic modernism (Godard) and those as much interested in the becoming of a movement as in its achievement (right-thinking critics). By the standards of high constructionism—Preston Sturges, Samson Raphaelson et al.—Tashlin's films are a mess. But Tashlin's deviations from such standards and what such deviations make possible are precisely what make his films interesting in themselves and crucial for understanding what came later. (Godard's narrative liberties were assailed much more forcefully than his visual innovations.) A flexible criticism need not choose among competing principles and methods, it can seek to understand all of them.

Consider *Rock-a-Bye Baby,* which is a remake of sorts of Sturges's *The Miracle of Morgan's Creek* (1944). (The script credit reads: "Story and Screenplay by Frank Tashlin, Based on a Story by Preston Sturges.") The film begins with sex symbol film star Carla Naples (Marilyn Maxwell) disclosing to her agent (Reginald Gardiner) that she is pregnant. On a trip to Mexico she met and married a bullfighter, who was killed the next day, whereupon she tore up their marriage license. In order to take a part in a movie, she decides to leave her child for six months with her childhood friend and devoted admirer Clayton Poole (Jerry Lewis), who still lives in the small town in which she grew up. To avoid local gossip, however, she cannot tell him of her request in advance. Several scenes follow that show Clayton's misadventures as a TV repairman and the unsuccessful pursuit of his affections by Carla's younger sister Sandy (Connie Stevens). Carla, who has had in the meantime not one child but triplets, drives to Midvale and finds Clayton at the stream where they used to meet.

The audience expects at this point the big scene between Carla and Clayton that the film has promised since its beginning by cutting back and forth between them. Clayton tells Carla, as Norval tells Trudy in Sturges's film, that he would like her to be in trouble so that he could help her. Carla says he can help her—she would like him to be the father of her children. Clayton's response is to look horrified and run away, as the Jerry character always does when faced with what he thinks is a direct sexual invitation (even if it is what he has fantasized). At this point—to the viewer's astonishment—the scene just ends. Carla does not ask Clayton to take care of her children or explain how they came to be or why she is asking him to take care of them; and Clayton does not respond to any of these things. We do not see how the characters feel about each other by virtue of their interaction in this crucial scene.

We learn from the next scene, as Clayton talks to himself while preparing to "find" a child on his doorstep, that Carla has told him everything in the elided scene—except that she has had triplets. (A brief scene between Carla and her agent as they drive away informs us that she could not bear to tell Clayton this.) This gap in Clayton's knowledge allows Lewis to build a characteristic comic routine as he finds first one, than a second, then a third child outside his door.

Sturges of course presents every stage of Trudy's painful revelations and of Norval's stunned responses. With his great skill, Sturges turns these obligatory scenes into comic set pieces. The important point, however, is that every Hollywood writer and director, at least until the late 1950s, would have had to confront this material and present these scenes—there was no shirking this responsibility. Tashlin's omission of most of this scene is something new and stands as a gateway to the modern cinema. This omission is also cartoonlike in skipping a painful scene between two people in favor of a stylized and exaggerated comic solo.

Lateral ellipsis, or paralipsis, is what narratologist Gérard Genette (52) calls an ellipsis that is parallel or to the side of an action that is shown. In *Rock-a-Bye Baby,* for example, Clayton's misadventures in work and romance are shown while Carla's pregnancy, delivery (except for a brief scene afterward), and early care of her infants—all of which are occurring at the same time—are elided.

Artists and Models has instances of paralipsis as well as the other topics we have discussed and shows how they may be interwoven in an extended film passage. Unemployed painter Rick (Dean Martin) and children's story writer Eugene (Jerry Lewis) have gone to the office of a publisher of comic books to ask their neighbor Abigail (Dorothy Malone), who works as an artist there, to help them get jobs. Abigail is inside with the publisher when they arrive—in fact she is being fired for not drawing violent strips. While waiting, Rick manages to enter his name on a list of artists the publisher has asked his secretary to bring in. When Abigail comes out, Rick follows her—first to seek her help, which she refuses, then for sexual interest, which she resists. Instead of returning to the office, Rick follows her out of the building and down the street. This is a surprise because we

had expected Rick to wait in the office in pursuit of a job he badly needs—
he had gone to bed hungry the night before. Rick follows Abigail to an
agency where she is seeking models for another assignment. Rick volun-
teers to model and she accepts. At the end of the session he presses his advances; she resists, but after he leaves begins to respond.

In the next scene Rick gets a call from the publisher asking him to meet
for lunch. As in cartoons, we have no idea when this event occurs in relation to earlier events—is it the same day as his adventures with Abigail, a
day or two later, a week later? At lunch Rick is quizzed by the publisher
about his character the Vulture and he replies that he will have to sleep on
it—that is, monitor Eugene's talking in his sleep about his comic book
dreams—and the scene stops. In the next scene a very happy Rick strides
down the street singing "The Lucky Song" (Harry Warren and Jack
Brooks); he dances with neighborhood children and passes out money. It is
evident that he has gotten the job and an advance; once again Tashlin
prefers to abbreviate a crucial scene and let the omitted information come
out gradually, sometimes explicitly, sometimes by implication, in the
scene or scenes that follow. Once again Tashlin omits a (relatively) serious
scene, so that Rick's happy response is shown not through facial expression in the scene itself but in the more cartoonlike manner of a stylized
song and dance. Musical comedy conventions would have required showing the scene of "getting the job" and then extending the character's happy
response through song and dance.

As Rick continues toward home, he passes a television set in a store
on which Eugene, a life-long addict of comic books, is speaking against
them. He has been invited by Abigail, who was herself invited as someone
who lost her job for refusing to draw violent comic books. When Rick sees
Eugene's face on the television set, he says, "Hi, Eugene!" and keeps on
going, reacting to what he has seen only after a substantial pause—a routine that Tashlin uses frequently. Rick returns to watch the program and realizes that his comic book job threatens his friendship with Eugene and his
romance with Abigail. (The spy plot replaces this dilemma, which is never
returned to.)

The film had left Eugene stranded in the publisher's office in order to
follow Rick's adventures in romance and job hunting. Eugene's activities
during the time period of Rick's adventures, which is itself indeterminate,
is a paralipsis. We never learn what Eugene did during this period—the ellipsis is never filled in—but his appearance on the television program implies that certain events or processes have occurred: (1) he has met Abigail; (2) she has gotten to know him sufficiently well to discover that he is
a lifelong addict of comic books; (3) she has convinced him that his love of
comic books is wrong, a difficult task made more so by the fact that he is in
love with a woman he glimpsed in costume as "the Bat Lady," a comic

book character. We have no idea how these events occurred or during how long a period. Nor can we use what is shown (Rick's adventures) to gauge the time of what is elided (Eugene's activities), nor can we do the opposite. Because there is no way to align them, the two indeterminate temporalities cannot really be perceived as parallel. Because each is free-floating in itself, trying to consider them in relation to each other gives one a sensation of vertigo, of unanchored relativity.

Ellipses of a largely indeterminate sort become the rule in the Martin and Lewis characters' car journey from New York to Hollywood in *Hollywood or Bust*—so much so that the narrative takes on a remarkably flowing quality in which time and space coordinates are set permanently, irrecoverably adrift. To take one example: Tashlin condenses the journey from Chicago to Las Vegas by cutting to various background locations behind (and around) the characters as they drive and sing a song, "You're in the Wild and Wooly West" (Sammy Fain and Paul Francis Webster). This remarkable passage resorts to cartoon technique—the dissociation of character and background—but carries it further than all but the most experimental cartoons. Indeed, it recalls in this respect Chuck Jones's remarkable *Duck Amuck* (1953), in which the backgrounds keep changing behind an increasingly frustrated Daffy Duck. (Godard's multiple cuts to Jean Seberg against ever-changing backgrounds in a car trip across Paris in *Breathless* is both cartoonlike in technique and a specific evocation of *Hollywood or Bust*, which Godard reviewed [57–59].)

The cartoonlike elements in Sturges are more subtle and generalized than those discussed apropos Tashlin. Several exceptions are the animated passages that Sturges includes in two of his films: the opening credits of *The Lady Eve* (1941), which features a coiling screwball snake, and the Disney cartoon that the chained convicts watch at the invitation of the black congregation in *Sullivan's Travels* (1941). Also, the names of Tom (Joel McCrea) and Gerry (Claudette Colbert), the squabbling couple of *The Palm Beach Story* (1942), distinctly evoke the cat and mouse of MGM's Tom and Jerry cartoon series, particularly because Gerry spends most of the film trying to elude Tom while he furiously pursues, seeking again and again to trap her and bring her home.[2]

The animated credits of *The Lady Eve* are discussed below. The cartoon shown in *Sullivan's Travels* is *Playful Pluto*, a black-and-white Disney cartoon released in March 1934. The choice of this title was determined by the fact that because *Sullivan's Travels* was shot in black and white, the interpolated cartoon had to be in black and white also. *Flowers and Trees*, a Silly Symphony released in July 1932, was the first Disney short in color. From that point on all but one of the Silly Symphonies were in color, but the Mickey Mouse cartoons, in which Pluto, Mickey's dog, appeared, remained in black and white until *The Band Concert*, released in February

1935. This was followed by two more black-and-white Mickey Mouses, the second of which—*Mickey's Kangaroo,* released in April 1935—was the last black-and-white short that Disney made. Thus, *Playful Pluto* was among the last black-and-white cartoons but looked sufficiently modern not to seem glaringly out of date in 1941. This was due to the rapid development of animation techniques from 1928, the date of the first Mickey Mouse, to 1934 and to the fact that Mickey and Pluto, like many cartoon characters before and after them, had gone through a long visual and characterological evolution before arriving at their final form—achieved for both characters by 1934. Particularly interesting for the present discussion is that Pluto made his first appearance in *The Chain Gang,* a Mickey Mouse cartoon released in August 1930.

Another factor in Sturges's choice of *Playful Pluto* for *Sullivan's Travels* was that Pluto's antics provoked laughter without benefit of dialogue. Disney cartoons were never as talky as Warner Brothers cartoons, but Mickey, Minnie, and Donald do speak lines in most of their films. The church movie scene in *Sullivan's Travels* required alternating brief bits of screen business with gales of laughter in the audience, a tide of mirth that Sullivan finds puzzling at first, then understands and resists, then gives way to. A cartoon scene that achieved its effects through dialogue would have initiated a logic that detracted from the logic of Sturges's own scene and would have required a montage at crosscurrents with the scene's montage. It is also true that the individual lines in a dialogue scene are rarely equally funny, whereas Sturges wanted on his screen-within-a-screen a plausibly building hilarity that the *Sullivan's Travels* audience would not question. Showing Pluto trying to extricate himself from flypaper only to get ever more entangled fitted the bill perfectly.

Much more difficult to define than such a direct use of animation is a cartooning approach that Sturges sometimes brings to the narratives and characters of his films. First, to begin negatively, Sturges does not use gags of physical impossibility. The apparent exceptions—Wormy and Harold swinging from a lion's leash in *The Sin of Harold Diddlebock* (1947) and the whippet tank-land yacht chase in *Sullivan's Travels*—are slapstick-improbable rather than cartoon-impossible. Second, as noted, Sturges's scripts are well constructed even when they are chaotic and digressive in story line, as in *The Palm Beach Story.* His ellipses are also classical: carefully built up to and returned from, never disrupting the viewer, as in Norval's elided search for Ratskiwatski, which is also the elision of most of Trudy's pregnancy, in *The Miracle of Morgan's Creek.* Sturges also never resorts to an abrupt cartoonlike epilogue-after-ellipsis to end a film; the banana republic epilogue of *The Great McGinty* (1940) has been thoroughly prepared by the film's framing story, which is already set there.

What might be called cartoonlike in Sturges is not absolute but relative, a matter of more and less, varying not only from film to film but even from scene to scene within a single film; it is also less often clear in outline than mixed, in varying proportions, with other comic elements. The cartoon-like in Sturges has to do with the distance at which a character or situation is placed in relation to the viewer; generally speaking, the greater the distance, the more cartoonlike, although there are important exceptions. It also has to do with the modeling of characters and situations themselves. This issue has been discussed by E. M. Forster:

> We may divide characters into flat and round. Flat characters were called "humorous" in the seventeenth century, and are sometimes called types, and sometimes caricatures. In their purest form, they are constructed round a single idea or quality; when there is more than one factor in them, we get the beginning of a curve towards the round. (67) . . . The test of a round character is whether it is capable of surprising in a convincing way. If it never surprises, it is flat. If it does not convince, it is a flat pretending to be round. (78)

> It is a convenience for an author when he can strike with his full force at once, and flat characters are very useful to him, since they never need reintroducing, never run away, have not to be watched for development, and provide their own atmosphere—little luminous disks of prearranged size, pushed hither and thither like counters across the void or between the stars. (69)

Forster understands flat characters as foils, props, or background to round characters, whose creation is the main business of the novel: "For we must admit that flat people are not in themselves as big achievements as round ones, and also that they are best when they are comic" (72–73). When he discusses Dickens, however, Forster glimpses a fictional world beyond his hierarchical dichotomy of flat and round.

> Dicken's people are nearly all flat. . . . Nearly every one can be summed up in a single sentence, and yet there is this wonderful feeling of human depth. Probably the immense vitality of Dickens causes his characters to vibrate a little, so that they borrow his life and appear to lead one of their own. It is a conjuring trick; at any moment we may look at Mr. Pickwick edgeways and find him no thicker than a gramophone record. But we never get the sideway view. Mr. Pickwick is far too adroit and well-trained. He always has the air of weighing something. . . . Part of the genius of Dickens is that he does use types and caricatures, people whom we recognize the instant they reenter, and yet achieves effects that are not mechanical and a vision of humanity that is not shallow. Those who dislike Dickens have an excellent case. He ought to be bad. He is actually one of our big writers, and his immense success with types suggests that there may be more in flatness than the severer critics admit. (71–72)

Sturges's most cartoonlike films by far come toward the end of his career: *The Sin of Harold Diddlebock* and *The Beautiful Blonde from Bashful*

Bend (1949). *Diddlebock,* starring Harold Lloyd, opens with the last reel of Lloyd's 1925 film *The Freshman,* in which a water boy becomes the hero of his school's big football game. Harold is offered a job in Horatio Alger fashion by E. J. Waggleberry (Raymond Walburn), a thrilled spectator at the game. Harold accepts and is assigned to the lowly bookkeeping department in order to work his way up, but twenty-two years later he is still in the same job, and even after he is fired, Harold still spouts the same hard-work-leads-to-success clichés that he did as a just-graduated eager beaver on his first day with the company. Harold resembles a cartoon character not only in not changing but also in mechanically repeating the same behavior patterns despite experience that invalidates them. (Likewise, Elmer Fudd goes hunting for Bugs Bunny despite countless prior failures.)

Harold's fixity is finally broken, or blasted, by a drink, created in his honor, that is stronger than a Texas Tornado. Harold alternates saying he feels nothing with howling like a wild man, a sound his sane self hears but cannot connect with himself. Such a reaction to a strong substance, often called Tabasco or red hot sauce, is familiar from cartoons—Roger Rabbit's paroxysms at the taste of strong drink quotes a long-standing cartoon tradition. We see the postdrink Harold being fitted for a loud suit and betting all his money on a horse race, which he wins. We see a brief shot of his cavorting at a wild party—we find out later it is Tuesday night—and then see him waking up in his old persona on Thursday morning: the most abrupt, cartoonlike ellipsis in all of Sturges. Harold does not find out all that he did on his lost Wednesday until the end of the film. The first revelations—that he bought not only a carriage and a driver but also a circus—come early. The animals are hungry and Harold has no money for food: to the challenge of this dilemma he does what he has not done thus far in his life—he begins to think. He concocts and successfully executes a plan to sell his circus for a tidy sum, and the Horatio Alger satire takes on a cartoon ending. (The ending that turns failure, or indeed utter desolation, into success is familiar both to cartoons and to many Sturges films.)

A crucial test for tracing the cartoon element in any Sturges film has to do with his treatment of the obligatory romance. As Harold cleans out his desk after being fired, he finds a jeweler's box and seeks out Miss Otis in the art department; she agrees to meet him by the file cabinets. Over the years, Harold tells her, he had fallen in love with each of her sisters, who had successively worked at the company: Hortense, Irma, Harriet, Margie, Claire, and Rosemary. Various complications prevented his marrying any of them. He tells the youngest, Miss Otis, that of course he is in love with her, too, but that he is leaving the company and wishes her to have the engagement ring he has finally paid for that he had intended to give to each of her sisters in turn, and then her, when proposing marriage. There is some pathos in the scene, but it is almost entirely undermined by the cartoon version of romance that the dialogue conveys. Harold's final revelation of his lost day, which still remains a blank, the pure suppression of libido, is that he carried off Miss Otis and married her. After much disbelief and stammering ("I . . . I . . . I . . . my dear child") and offers to annul the marriage—this is the film's last scene—Miss Otis tells him she loves him and they kiss:

> Harold comes dreamily out of the kiss, then looks rigidly straight into the lens. Now he turns back to Miss Otis.
>
> *Harold:*   (Yelling)
>   *That* must be what I was doing all day Wednesday!
>
> He takes an enormous breath and gives the Tarzan Yell. (Sturges 1945, 151)

The Beautiful Blonde from Bashful Bend is a comic western whose parody or travesty of the genre also includes a cartoonlike plot and cartoonlike gags. A saloon singer named Freddie (Betty Grable), who is also a deadly shot, tries to shoot her faithless lover Blackie (Cesar Romero) and instead shoots, in the rear end, a judge who happens to be staying at the same hotel. At her trial she accidentally shoots the judge in the same place again and, escaping on a train, assumes the identity of a dead school teacher named Hilda Swandumper, who was going to the town of Snake City. Freddie is accepted by the townspeople and subdues her unruly class, notably the Basserman brothers (Sterling Holloway and Danny Jackson)— two howling adolescents who dress like Indians and act like wild animals, "two Cro-Magnon boys" (Sturges 1948, 48), as the script calls them. Her impersonation is jeopardized by the untimely arrival of Blackie, whose apparent killing of the Basserman boys sets off a shootout between the respectable townspeople and the wrong-side-of-the-tracks father of the Bassermans and his friends. Freddie displays her accuracy of shot in the battle and thereby gives herself away. Taken back to Rimpau City, she stands trial again; Blackie escorts a French woman into the court but leaves her to speak up for Freddie, saying they plan to marry and raise a family. The judge gradually softens and agrees to marry them; Blackie asks his French floozie for the ring he gave her to use in the ceremony and she graciously accedes. Freddie, however, is outraged once again at Blackie's infidelity and grabs a pistol to try to shoot him but hits the judge for a third time "right in the caboose."

Cartoonlike repetition is not limited to the film's plot but structures many of its gags as well, particularly in the climactic town battle. The last begins with the respectable townspeople, including Freddie, throwing crockery (instead of pies) at the Basserman gang: twenty or thirty pieces are thrown, all making the same stylized smashing sound. Once the shooting starts between the two groups, identical stock rifle and pistol sounds are heard again and again, poking fun at the dull repetition of such sounds in conventional westerns. Several actions are repeated almost exactly again and again: a man shooting from a roof is shot, falls off, and climbs back onto the roof, shoots again and is shot off the roof again, climbs back on again, and so on—four times in all. Another man kneeling in front of a water trough gets a face full of water every time he shoots; after this happens four times, he holds his pistol higher, and the splash, which he seems to have avoided, is merely delayed. After this he shoots into the water itself and gets a huge water jet in the face, after which he throws his gun away and gives up. Another gag has a nearly bald man ready to shoot a rifle, only to have his hat blown away by an incoming shot. He leaves his post to retrieve his hat, returns, gets ready to shoot, and has his hat blown away again. This happens three times; on the fourth attempt, he gets off his shot, and then his hat is blown away. A onetime cartoon gag has a man aiming and firing a shotgun only to have it blow up in his face—we see his shotgun in black radiating shards and his face black, just like Elmer Fudd's shotgun and face after Bugs Bunny has put his finger or a cork in the barrel or has twisted the barrel in a knot just before Elmer fires.

In the midst of the shootout, who should stick their heads around a corner but the Basserman boys themselves? "What's the shootin' fer?" howls one. "Can we shoot too?" howls the other. Freddie says why not, then realizes who they are and asks what happened. They pretended to be dead, says one, the other then continuing the story stuttering like Porky Pig: "When that big B-B-B-Blackie tried to kill us." (The stuttering Basserman is played by Sterling Holloway, who "has probably done voices for more Disney cartoons than anyone else" [Maltin 1973, 52].) Earlier, when the Basserman boys learn Freddie's true identity—overhearing her exchange with Blackie—their eyes, seen just above the window sill, turn and look at each other in the way that cartoon characters sometimes do, Heckle and Jeckle, for instance.[3]

In Sturges's other films, there are elements that might be called cartoonlike. But, they are so thoroughly mixed with other elements, comic and dramatic, that the term loses whatever clarity it has had in the foregoing discussion. It may simply not be a useful term for the complex issues involved. In what follows, then, the term and notion of cartoonlike are used rather more loosely than heretofore and with far less assurance. They function in the discussion perhaps as a kind of x, the designation of an unknown, to be solved by subsequent writers in this area.

The opening credits of *The Lady Eve* feature an animated snake coiling down a tree in a cartoon Garden of Eden. The tilted, slightly battered top hat on the snake's head and his besotted grin tell us that the film we are about to see is a screwball comedy. The message is necessary perhaps because the film has a somewhat uncertain relation to the genre, veering toward cartoon in the beginning, straight romance in the middle, and revenge drama in later parts.

The jungle scene that follows the credits is perhaps the most cartoonlike of the film and not merely because of its link with the snake of the credits. The clichéd jungle foliage behind the characters is cartoonlike in its thick, patently artificial overlay of plants and underbrush, its animal sounds, and so on. The dialogue of the scene is also cartoonish—the professor who heads the expedition speaks with undue formality to his co-workers, extolling his own achievements. He says to the departing Charles (Henry Fonda), "Tell Dr. Marzditz I have named her [the rare snake Charles is bringing with him] especially in his honor: Columbrina Marzditzia, and that this is only the beginning of what I am bringing out . . . when I come out." Charles responds with cartoon seriousness, "I'll do that, Professor, and I want to tell you—all of you—how much I've enjoyed being on this expedition with you. If I had my way, believe me, this is the way I'd like to spend all my time . . . in the company of men like yourselves . . . in the pursuit of knowledge."

After a brief chorus of good-byes, the scene shifts to the railing of the *SS Southern Queen* as the camera pans various passengers, including Jean (Barbara Stanwyck) and Colonel Harrington (Charles Coburn), as they all observe the boarding from a launch of Charles Pike and his bodyguard-valet Mugsy. The dialogue of Jean and her father, licking their chops over the rich pigeon they've been delivered and Jean's dropping an apple on Charles's head, seems to sustain a cartoon spirit. What follows the railing scene, however, is cartoon in a purer sense—Charles sitting along in the dining room reading *Are Snakes Necessary?* by Hugo Marzditz. The scene, including the book's title, might be put into a cartoon with no alterations but graphic ones.

Once Charles and Jean meet, however, cartoon in a pure sense, perhaps in any sense, goes out of the film altogether, at least until Jean masquerades as Lady Eve Sedgwick in the Pike mansion, causing Charles to fall over the furniture, upset food trays, and so on. The cartoonlike aspect resurfaces to some degree in these scenes, later when Eve's horse nuzzles Charles as he attempts to propose, and of course on the honeymoon train when Eve sketches a number of erotic balloons the details of which Charles fills in against his will as he struggles to maintain an attitude of "sweet forgiveness." These scenes are funny but also painful; once the intimate feelings of Jean and Charles have been established, the audience cannot forget them—there is no going back to the uncomplicated cartoon of the opening scene in the jungle.

Joel McCrea as Sullivan and Veronica Lake in Preston Sturges's Sullivan's Travels
(1941)

Sullivan's Travels differs from earlier Sturges films in a number of respects. For one thing, it has eleven sequences, an unusually high number for a Sturges script, reflecting the story's picaresque subject. *Sullivan* is a journey film and, as such, far more episodic than anything Sturges has done before. Like Miguel de Cervantes's *Don Quixote,* Henrik Ibsen's *Peer Gynt,* or Louis Feuillade's serials, Sullivan's adventures on the road could in principle go on forever. The other side of the picture is that *Sullivan* lacks the narrative cohesion and the tightly integrated dramatic structure of Sturges's first three films, particularly *Christmas in July* and *Eve.* The Miz Zeffie sequence is an example. On his first journey, Sullivan ends up doing yard work for a lecherous country widow and her sister; later he goes to the movies with them, avoids the widow's advances, and escapes out of a window. The entire sequence, including many jokes about the widow's dead husband, has little connection to the rest of the film. Its beginning serves to get Sullivan away from the studio crowd, and its ending sets up his meeting The Girl (Veronica Lake) in the owl wagon—when he hitches a ride that takes him, unknowingly, back to Hollywood—but many other kinds of sequence would have served these functions as well.

No scene, let alone sequence, in *Christmas in July* or *Eve* is comparably flat in itself or irrelevant to the film as a whole—each scene, and no other, seems necessary in these films.

The flaws of *Sullivan*, however, go hand in hand with what is new in the film, including many kinds of scenes and humor that the earlier films did not permit. Take, for instance, *Sullivan*'s uncharacteristic treatment of some of its character actors, notably the studio employees ordered to follow Sullivan on his journey. These "eight stooges," as one of their number calls them, include some of Sturges's most distinctive supporting players—William Demarest, Frank Moran, Torben Meyer, Charles Moore, and Vic Potel. In the earlier films each would have had one or more "star turns" and would have been given distinctive dialogue to speak throughout. Here the studio people are introduced all at once—a squabbling gaggle—and are never much differentiated at any later point either. The impression they give, in fact, is that of a *Mad* magazine cluster of press agents, chauffeurs, photographers, doctors, radiomen, and secretaries. Even the way the secretary's underwear shows in her ungainly sprawls in the tank-yacht chase has a *Mad* magazine aspect. This is only one respect in which *Sullivan* is ahead of its time, opening the way not only to the free-wheeling style of Sturges's own later comedies, but to much of the best postwar comedy as well, including the cartoon style of Frank Tashlin and the bold departures from narrative of Jerry Lewis in *The Bellboy* (1960) and *The Errand Boy* (1961). Equally ahead of its time is the boy whippet-tank commander who gets Sullivan away from the studio crowd. He is the infernal child of the day's technology, not only abreast of it but coequal with it, therefore a monster. He walks from *Sullivan's Travels*, by way of *Mad* magazine and *The National Lampoon*, into *The Loved One* (1965), by which time the speed-demon driver has become a homemade-rocket engineer (Paul Williams).

The cartoon effects and other exaggerations of *Sullivan* imply a greater distance from its characters and plot than we find in the earlier films, and this affects the film's romance, too. *Eve* and *Sullivan*, made back to back, are a natural pair for comparison on this point, even though they seem to belong to different universes of cinema. I have examined elsewhere Sturges's careful rewrites of the Charles-Jean romance in *Eve* and the increasing seriousness of the affair that resulted. Without ceasing to be a comedy, the film treats the romance with surprising tenderness: its inner dimension is emphasized as much as is its social and satirical aspect.

None of this is true of the romance in *Sullivan*, which seems arbitrary and not very believable by comparison. The affections of The Girl—she has no other name in script or film—seem puppyish, and Sullivan stolidly refuses them until his unlikely marriage proposal, shouted in a hectic crowd scene, at the end of the film. The romantic sections of *Sullivan* were

written once and not much changed later. When Sturges had less time—
and wrote more freely?—the result was perhaps a more externalized, even
cartooned version of romance or simply a posited or conventional romantic attachment, usually ridiculed in one way or other. (Buster Keaton, like
Sturges a nonsentimentalist, also resorted to cartoon, as in *Seven Chances*
(1925), or parodied convention, as in *Sherlock, Jr.* (1924) and many other
films, in presenting the obligatory romance.)

Transitional works such as *Sullivan's Travels* often reveal tensions and
difficulties. Its episodic, to some degree unconnected narrative form and
its treatment of some of its characters indicate the transitional character of
the film. From the perspective of the earlier films, *Sullivan* represents a
falling off in dramatic-narrative cohesion, in character differentiation, perhaps even in dialogue. From the perspective of later Sturges and, indeed,
of later comedy, these "failures" are the portals to a new kind of comedy—to structures and effects that could not have been achieved within
Sturges's older, "classical" forms.

The Palm Beach Story seems the complete antithesis of "the well-made
play" or screenplay but achieves cohesion on the new ground that *Sullivan's Travels* opened up but did not master, stranded as it was between old
and new modes, the well-made tradition and its ill-made modern opposite.
The Palm Beach Story goes all the way over to the side of disintegration—
it seems to be simultaneously falling apart and reinventing itself continually. On the other hand, the romance between Tom and Gerry, troubled as
it is, provides the film with an emotional cohesion, if not a dramatic-
narrative one, that the film's digressions never quite overcome.

The Palm Beach Story is also picaresque, a kind of female version of
Sullivan's Travels. Here it is Gerry who sets out on a journey, meets a variety of strange characters, and has a number of diverse adventures. The
open structure of journey films permits the introduction of different kinds
of elements, including the cartoon elements I have been examining; but the
central situation of such films must be well launched and sustained if they
are not to fall apart completely. This was a special challenge for Sturges
because he tended to pose his premises and explode them into action at the
same time—usually in the first scene. *Sullivan*'s opening in a screening
room and adjoining producer's office is perhaps the best example—when
the fast talk between Sullivan and two producers is over, he is already on
his way.

Getting Gerry out the door took a great deal more rewriting—and
screen time—than launching Sullivan had, however. As a screwball comedy, the interaction of male and female leading characters is paramount in
The Palm Beach Story. In this sense the film is a kind of synthesis of *The
Lady Eve* and *Sullivan's Travels*. In *The Palm Beach Story*, however, the
couple's breakup comes at the beginning of the film, so that Sturges had to

show simultaneously the causes of the breakup and the bond between the characters that will eventually bring them back together. Indeed, most of his work on all versions of the script had to do with the dynamics of Tom and Gerry's interaction. What everyone remembers about the film—its cartoon elements—Sturgès wrote rather quickly: The Ale and Quail Society, Rudy Vallee as John D. Hackensacker, Mary Astor as his much-married sister the Princess Centimilla, and her hanger-on Toto, whose name identifies him as a lap dog.

In *The Lady Eve*, I noted, cartoon gives way to a concern with feelings when Charles and Jean fall in love. In *The Palm Beach Story*, the central relationship is in place when the film begins so that the cartoon elements have to be included within the narrative of that relationship. The construction problem here is not only how to sustain a sense of the relationship through the separation caused by Gerry's departure but also how to sustain a concern with feelings through the cartoon sequences. One aspect of the solution is to include scenes of the separated lovers thinking of each other at various points. Another involves a differentiated treatment of the film's cartoon elements, depending upon which elements, each of which appears initially as a digression, is to be included in the film's main action.

In a screwball comedy the criterion for such inclusion is the capacity for romantic feeling. The Ale and Quailers are unassimilable cartoon elements—hence they are carefully relegated to one portion of the film only. When their mayhem has reached its peak, their dog-led rampage through the train in search of Gerry, the conductor detaches their car and strands it on a sidetrack, and they are seen no more in the film. John D. Hackensacker, on the other hand, begins as a cartoon, in any case as a caricature, and continues in that mode for quite a while. When his caring for Gerry is seen to be genuine, however, and deeply felt, he ceases to be a cartoon. This never quite happens in the case of the princess, although her wistful regret over Tom is a step in that direction. Toto of course never ceases to be a cartoon, a somewhat wearing one because he hangs on in scene after scene and is not particularly amusing in the first place.

The Miracle of Morgan's Creek is perhaps the most outrageous comedy ever made in classical Hollywood, a genuinely black comedy, worthy to stand with William Faulkner's *Sanctuary* (1931) and Nathanael West's *The Dream Life of Balso Snell* (1931), *Miss Lonelyhearts* (1933), *A Cool Million* (1934), and *The Day of the Locust* (1939). André Bazin says correctly, "Sturges delights in forcing upon his characters—who are totally unfit to deal with these situations—the entire weight of the prejudices, social conventions, and social imperatives that could exist in a small American town in wartime" (40). More disturbing, however, is that Trudy and Norval seem unprepared for life itself. Adulthood seems hopelessly beyond them, and there are no models or traditions in view to help them.

In regard to structure and tone, *Morgan's Creek* reflects the lessons of *Sullivan* and *Palm Beach* and applies them in new ways. *Sullivan* introduces new kinds of comedy and comic characterization at the edges of Sullivan's journey, in certain of those who accompany him and others whom he meets on the way. They stand alongside more traditional Sturges figures such as The Girl, Sullivan's butler and valet, and the producers. *Palm Beach* intensifies this tendency; all the characters whom Gerry meets—the Weenie King, the Ale and Quail Society, John D. Hackensacker, the princess, Toto—are living cartoons. Gerry and Tom, or at least their love for each other, are presented seriously. (The film's surrealist framing footage, however, puts the plot as a whole, including their relationship, in brackets.) In *Morgan's Creek* the cartoon stylization reaches to the heart of the film; it is now the main characters themselves, played by Eddie Bracken and Betty Hutton, who are cartoons.[4] Placing cartoon characters at the center of the work, however, obliges Sturges to take them seriously—a paradox, but one that became fundamental to comic art in the postwar period—Joseph Heller, Terry Southern, Stanley Kubrick, and so on. The cartoon status of the characters in these works is not only a new mode of rendering, however. It reflects those gigantic social forces—determining and stereotyping our lives—that were brought into being by the total mobilization of World War II and that persist in the postwar period.

Notes

1. In the August–September 1957 issue of *Cahiers du cinéma*, Godard quotes with approval a letter Tashlin sent him: "*Son of Paleface* contained 2,857 gags at a conservative estimate, there were only 1,538 in *Artists and Models* and 743 in *The Girl Can't Help It*. As for *Will Success Spoil Rock Hunter?*, it will have barely 50. Don't worry, it will still be the funniest film of the year" (61).

2. The connection of Tom and Gerry in *The Palm Beach Story* to MGM's Tom and Jerry cartoons seems too obvious to belabor. There is a slight problem with dates, however. William Hanna and Joseph Barbera joined MGM separately in the late 1930s and later teamed to make the first of what was to be their Tom and Jerry series, *Puss Gets the Boot,* released on February 10, 1940. The cat in this first effort was called Jasper, and the mouse was unnamed. To the surprise of MGM, which had reassigned Hanna and Barbera to other projects, *Puss Gets the Boot* turned out to be an enormous commercial success and was nominated for an Academy Award. *Midnight Snack,* their second film, released on July 19, 1941, identifies the characters for the first time as Tom and Jerry. Sturges began taking notes on *The Palm Beach Story* on September 1, 1941, referring to his couple immediately as Tom and Gerry. (*Puss Gets the Boot* is an excellent description of what happens to Tom in *The Palm Beach Story*.) Sturges finished his script, in which Tom and Gerry get back together, on November 21, 1941. *The Night Before Christmas,* the second Tom and Jerry cartoon, in which they make peace for the holiday, was released on December 6, 1941.

3. The first Heckle and Jeckle cartoon, *The Talking Magpies,* was released by Paul Terry's Terrytoons Studio early in 1946; in November of that year, a second Heckle and Jeckle was released (*The Uninvited Pests*) and an official series begun. The last Heckle and Jeckle, *Messed Up Movie Makers,* was released in March 1966. The birds had been supplanted by two Ralph Bakshi series, "Sad Cat" and "James Hound," which dominated the studio's last years of production for theatrical release (1965–1968). Conceived as twins or lookalikes, Heckle and Jeckle were visually identical; they were differentiated by their voices, however, "one New Yorkese, one slightly British falsetto" (Maltin, 1980, 140). The Basserman boys bear a family resemblance, but because they are played by live actors, they cannot be visually identical. They are intertwined, however, by behavior and dress and by similar vocal rhythms—a kind of frontier hooting-falsetto—and their tendency to finish each other's sentences.

4. The other characters in *The Miracle of Morgan's Creek* seem, interestingly, less cartoonish than the principals. The lawyer (Al Bridge), the doctor (Torben Meyer), Mr. Rafferty (Julius Tannen), and the editor (Vic Potel) are serious, sympathetic characters; Mr. Twerk (Emery Parnell), president of the bank, is serious and unsympathetic. Officer Kockenlocker (William Demerest) and Emmy (Diana Lynn) are borderline cases.

References and Additional Reading

Bazin, André. 1982. *The Cinema of Cruelty: From Buñuel to Hitchcock,* ed. François Truffaut. New York: Seaver.

Chatman, Seymour. 1978. *Story and Discourse: Narrative Structure in Fiction and Film.* Ithaca, N.Y.: Cornell University Press.

Durgnaut, Raymond. 1969. *The Crazy Mirror: Hollywood Comedy and the American Image.* New York: Delta.

Faulkner, William. 1985. *Sanctuary.* In *Novels, 1930–1935.* New York: Library of America.

Forster, E. M. 1927. *Aspects of the Novel.* New York: Harcourt, Brace.

Genette, Gérard. 1980. *Narrative Discourse: An Essay in Method,* trans. Jane E. Lewin. Ithaca, N.Y.: Cornell University Press.

Godard, Jean-Luc. 1972. *Godard on Godard,* trans. Tom Milne. New York: Viking.

Gombrich, E. H. 1960. *Art and Illusion: A Study in the Psychology of Representation.* Princeton: Princeton University Press.

Johnston, Claire, and Paul Willemen, eds. 1973. *Frank Tashlin.* London: Edinburgh Film Festival.

Maltin, Leonard. 1973. *The Disney Films.* New York: Bonanza Book.

———. 1980. *Of Mice and Magic: A History of American Animated Cartoons.* New York: New American Library.

Sturges, Preston. 1945. *The Sin of Harold Diddlebock* (May 2, 1945, version, the shooting script). An original screenplay by Preston Sturges. Preston Sturges Collection, UCLA Library.

————. 1948. *The Beautiful Blonde from Bashful Bend* (September 23, 1948, version, the shooting script). A screenplay by Preston Sturges, based on a story by Earl Felton. Preston Sturges Collection, UCLA Library.

————. *Five Screenplays by Preston Sturges,* edited with an introduction by Brian Henderson. Berkeley: University of California Press.

West, Nathaniel. 1962. *Miss Lonelyhearts* and *The Day of the Locust*. New York: New Directions.

————. 1988. *The Dream Life of Balso Snell* and *A Cool Million*. New York: Farrar, Straus and Giroux.

The Three Stooges and the (Anti-)Narrative of Violence

De(con)structive Comedy

Peter Brunette

The earth also was corrupt before God, and the earth was filled with violence. And God looked upon the earth, and, behold, it was corrupt; for all flesh had corrupted his way upon the earth. And God said unto Noah, the end of all flesh is come before me; for the earth is filled with violence through them; and, behold, I will destroy them with the earth.

Genesis 6: 11–13

What follows is not meant to be, strictly speaking, a *study* of the Three Stooges' films. In other words, the goal will not be to arrive at certain overarching generalizations that give meaning to their films by organizing them or delineating an essence. Nor will I be interested in tracing their development chronologically, the goal of much traditional criticism, for such attempts invariably bring with them a host of assumptions and models imported unconsciously from developmental psychology and a discredited organicist aesthetics. In any case, there will be little here that can be empirically verified, and I make no claim to have seen all or even most of their two hundred plus films. Rather, I want to *play* with these texts, to tease out some of the patterns they seem to give rise to, even if, as constrained by the rules of academic discourse, such play will be rather moderate and circumspect. For if they can be said to represent anything, the Stooges represent a kind of excess that should be respected and preserved. In short, I will be irresponsible, like my subjects.

Or at least as irresponsible as the institution of film studies allows. In this regard, the Stooges provide an interesting nexus in which to examine such questions of the institutionally permissible and the "proper" (with its attendant question of boundaries, frames, limits and so on[1]), for the excess that they represent is obviously transgressive, like all excess, and it leaks out, infiltrating everything. On the most immediate level, this fear of the excessive is what accounts for the general dismay that is registered when the critic sheepishly admits to his colleagues that he is writing an essay on the Three Stooges. "The Three Stooges?!" is the baffled and sometimes outraged reply, a reply usually covered by a kind of nervous, protective laughter. "Are you serious?"

The Stooges are transgressive because their films, quite simply, are about violence. Violence is celebrated, continuously and joyously reinvented, even reveled in. This is of course why children, in whom the proclivity to violent self-expression always remains to some extent unrepressed, like the Three Stooges' films so much and why many parents forbid their children to watch these films, as was the case even back in the 1930s and 1940s. In the responsible adult, however, a certain reluctance is evident when it comes to thinking this violence. For example, a well-meaning critic such as Leonard Maltin earnestly complains of the Stooges' "artlessness": "There are no nuances, no layers of interpretation, no smatterings of genius in their films" (163). Of course, whatever smattering of genius they do possess is a genius for violence, and it is this unconscious realization, I think, that disturbs Maltin and that must be denied. Yet he, too, must eventually deal with the violence because it continues to assert itself so forcefully, rending the fabric of acceptable humor. He therefore objects that the Stooges' violence sometimes "obliterates any possible humor except, perhaps, that of sheer outrageousness. Often a funny Stooges short is marred by this kind of startling violence" (167).[2] In another attempt to quarantine the threat of the transgressive, he further complains that they didn't really "need" the violence because they were such good comedians (even though this assessment contradicts the earlier one concerning their "artlessness"). The violence is thus rendered marginal and is put "outside" the essence of their own comic skills. Watching the films quickly convinces one, however, that while it may be unpalatable, their violence is them.

This violence may first be considered in narrative terms. In each Stooges' short, the violence always has a life and trajectory of its own. It is anticipated, set up, and provided for, and it always follows its own painful logic, the logic of the *surenchère*, of the ever-increasing stakes of one-upmanship. Thus, each violent outburst contains its own mininarration, its own plot; like Roland Barthes' proairetic code, each episode offers its own tiny logical narration of escalated event: one slap leads to an eye gouging, which leads to a hair pulling, which leads to a multiple slap or some other baroque combination of professionally administered pain. The violence goes off like a string of ever-larger firecrackers, building and complicating itself as the verbal does in the Marx Brothers. Constituting its own narrative, the violence offers a kind of play-within-the-play.

What, then, is the relation of that narrative to the surrounding, ostensibly mastering narrative, the narrative of the film, of which it is a part? First, it is difficult to decide whether in fact such violence is diegetic or extradiegetic—is it an essential part of the film's narrative or, because it

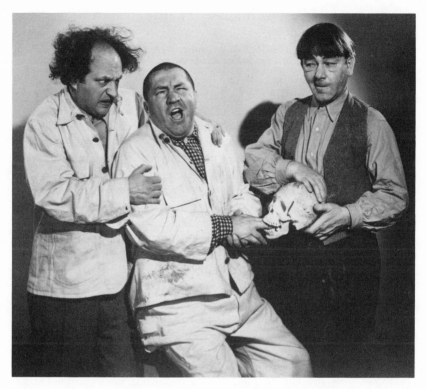

In each Stooges short, the violence always has a life and trajectory of its own

rarely has anything to do with the plot, merely a supplement to the narrative? But is it not true that the putative "larger" narrative is really there
only to provide a frame for the narrative of violence, a place for it to take
place? Since the violent narrative is the one we have come to watch, in
what way can it legitimately be said to be a "part" of, and thus subsidiary
to, the other? Then which one *is* the play "within" the play? This violence,
in other words, also does a certain violence to the structures that attempt
to contain it and within which we try to think it.

In another sense, this narrative of violence—the slapping, the poking,
the pinching—occurs rhythmically, at regular intervals, and thus acts as a
kind of punctuation, a system of commas, periods, and paragraph breaks,
for the syntax of the ostensibly plotted, "larger" narrative. This is especially true given that the violence is almost always accompanied by a variety of special-effects enhancements on the soundtrack.[3] Yet it is a linguistic system in which the punctuation is, once again, more important than
the syntax it supposedly serves and clarifies. In this way, the violence is

similar to those nonphonetic elements of language, in Jacques Derrida's account, without which the phonetic cannot signify and that thus paradoxically "create" meaning.

The relation of the two "narratives" has a chronological dimension as well. Naturally, the mastering, conventional plot lines of the feature-length films done in the late 1950s and early 1960s, after the Stooges were rediscovered through the television syndication of their earlier shorts—films such as *The Three Stooges in Orbit* (1962) or *The Three Stooges Go Around the World in a Daze* (1963)—are much more involved.[4] Because of the story requirements of these longer films, the narrative of violence exists as only a small part of each film's overall trajectory and can seem to be an awkward, unfortunate afterthought—a lame attempt of men well into their sixties to keep up with a certain violent reputation.[5] The earlier short films, on the contrary, are filled with a great deal more anarchic energy—for one thing, the Stooges were a lot younger. In narrative terms, this energy works itself out in different ways. Sometimes the "main" narratives in the shorts—such as they are, or can be, in films that are usually sixteen minutes long—are thin but relatively coherent. At other times, however, the "principal" narratives simply seem to explode and disappear without leaving a trace once the text of violence and crazy obsession has been introduced and put into motion. In "Restless Knights" (1935), for example, a short that is set vaguely in the Middle Ages, the plot, never really properly begun, goes virtually nowhere. When the film's allotted sixteen minutes are up and the requisite expenditure of energy has been accomplished, the Stooges—with absolutely no narrative motivation—simply knock out the queen, and each other, and the film ends.

Although it is in many ways true that narrative is the great motor of film, the great systematizer and restrainer of the order of the signifier—reducing it always and immediately to a signified of story, of meaningful narrative—in these films "both" narratives are often treated as simply additional sites for the joyous freeplay of a writing, in Derrida's sense of the word, that respects no rules. It is thus no accident that Derrida relates "the power of writing" to "the exercise of violence" (1976, 106), as they both mark the eruption of the irrational into the realm of the rational, the ostensibly whole and self-present, the realm of Logos and meaning. In fact, violence, usually seen as a disturbance of a prior order, can be considered as "first" or "originary" in the sense that writing comes before speech:

> There is no ethics without the presence of the other but also, and consequently, without absence, dissimulation, detour, differance, writing. The arche-writing is the origin of morality as of immorality. The nonethical opening of ethics. A violent opening. As in the case of the vulgar concept of writing, the ethical instance of violence must be rigorously suspended in order to repeat the genealogy of morals. (Derrida, 1976, 139–140)

In other words, it is precisely this "originary" violence, as differance, as the trace, that comes "before" a nonviolent order, "before" meaning can be constituted as something whole and consistent. In that sense violence *creates* or allows for meaning, rather than something that befalls nonviolence or meaning from the "outside." It is the narrative of violence in the Stooges that is the difference, the spacing, that allows us to perpetuate a certain conception of nonviolence as its opposite and thus a certain idea of meaning.

This free play of a violent writing comes to its own climax, or *jouissance,* in a final moment of pain and destruction that always ends the film, even providing a kind of ironic, contradictory closure to the "surrounding" narrative that it also destroys in the process. It puts an end to that narrative. It is in this sense, of course, that the narrative of violence is really not a narrative at all, for to remain within this logocentric category is still to submit to a system of rules that regulate meaning. In the refusal to have meaning, to *make* sense, the Stooges' violence in fact constitutes an anti-narrative. It is precisely their violence, as an "originary" writing, that both allows for and destroys narrative and thus allows for and destroys meaning itself.[6]

Beyond the violence, this element of free play, of writing,[7] can most immediately be seen in the Stooges' penchant for various insignificant details of stage business that also do their part to wreck the "legitimate" narrative. Thus, in "Restless Knights," for example, the Stooges get involved in various moments of hand clapping and head scratching that cause them to lose sight of whatever goal they happened to begin with. They start doing one thing, that particular activity reminds them of something else, and that in turn reminds them of something else again, even though the progression makes no sense in logocentric terms. This process resembles an overt collective free association[8] and is always something very childish indeed. Willfully maintaining themselves in the realm of the signifier, refusing meaning, they act out the drama of the Lacanian metonymic chain of signification, signifiers relentlessly leading to each other, motivated solely by proximity, never to a signified. Fully involved in puns, chance, and the writing of the body, they celebrate all that works against logocentrism and toward the kind of "grammatology" that Derrida has been attempting to practice in his theoretical writing, at least since *Glas* (1974).[9] Very postmodern comics, indeed.

The violence that the (anti-)narrative of violence wreaks upon the main narrative of the shorts is doubled "extratextually," as it were. As mentioned earlier, the Stooges seem impossible to recuperate, let alone master, through the imposition of an intellectual discourse (including this one). It is this instability, this failure of mastery, that threatens the distinctions between high and low culture that remain operative despite the exis-

tence of journals of popular culture and other evidence of an institutional-
ization of the forbidden. As with the relation discussed previously between
violence and nonviolence, it is precisely the fact of "lower" forms such as
the Stooges that reflexively allows for or even creates such "higher" forms
of cultural expression as philosophy, literature, and criticism. The privilege and very existence as a definable entity of the latter are established
and guaranteed by the existence of the former through the workings of difference. Yet this Other must always be kept at arm's length, and any
"serious" study of the former by the latter threatens the hierarchy through
contamination, especially when mastery of the lower form can never be
achieved. Yet as Peter Stallybrass and Allon White point out, in such an
economy interest for the lower form always remains unabated, despite (or
because of) the effects of repression:

> Repugnance and fascination are the twin poles of the process in which a *po-
> litical* imperative to reject and eliminate the debasing "low" conflicts power-
> fully and unpredictably with a desire for this Other. (4–5)

It is precisely this duality that accounts for the avoidance/interest behavior regarding all forms of the lower, especially as embodied in what
Mikhail Bakhtin calls the carnivalesque, where all restraints are exceeded:

> A recurrent pattern emerges: the "top" attempts to reject and eliminate the
> "bottom" for reasons of prestige and status, only to discover, not only that it
> is in some way frequently dependent upon that low-Other . . . but also that
> the top *includes* that low symbolically, as a primary eroticized constituent of
> its own fantasy life. (Stallybrass & White, 5)

Here, I think, a kind of Derridean perspective emerges from Bakhtin's
notion of the carnivalesque, a perspective that suggests that the high is always already irradiated with the trace of the low (although neither can ever
be conceived as the whole entities or presences that such a formulation
suggests). This dynamic of top and bottom also has a physical correlation,
and the Stooges seem clearly relatable to the Bakhtinian-derived category
of the "grotesque body," with its distinctive discursive norms:

> Impurity (both in the sense of dirt and mixed categories), heterogeneity,
> masking, protuberant distension, disproportion, exorbitancy, clamour, de-
> centred or eccentric arrangements, a focus upon gaps, orifices and symbolic
> filth . . . physical needs and pleasures of the "lower bodily stratum," materi-
> ality and parody. (Stallybrass & White, 23)

This imagery correlates with that presented by the Stooges in many of
their shorts, especially their persistent identification with animals, a category that maintains the animation and apparent volition of the human

yet removes it from rationality, which is the obvious target here. In *Have Rocket Will Travel* (1959), the Stooges become birds in a cage and even begin eating birdseed. After the late 1930s virtually all their films have the "Three Blind Mice" theme playing under the credits, thus associating them with animals traditionally connected with filth. Curly's various outcries, such as "whoop, whoop, whoop!" clearly recall animal noises, and in "We Want Our Mummy," he shakes the water off him like a dog, then whoops; in "Restless Knights" he is explicitly associated with a dog and begins barking. In *Have Rocket Will Travel* he talks to a monkey in a monkey voice. In "Calling All Curs" (1939), the Stooges operate a pet hospital and sit down for a joint dinner with all the resident dogs; in the same film, Curly later acts like a mule, kicking with his back feet. And on and on. (In an interesting and consistent reversal, in "An Ache in Every Stake" [1941], it is the horse pulling the ice wagon who knows how to read street signs, where to deliver the ice, and so on, rather than the Stooges, who are asleep in the back.)

These various Bakhtinian associations find an echo in what Georges Bataille has called "heterogeneous matter." He is concerned with the transgressive potential of various forms of violence, as well as with animals, flies, excrement, in much the same way that the Stooges are—although of course only up to the point of what was allowed on the screen.[10] This peculiar fascination is focused on Bataille's continuing obsession with the symbolic value of the eye, especially the ruptured eye. Given the Stooges' predilection for eye gouging (arguably their most notorious form of violence), we can see in their assault on the eye a more general assault, outlined by Bataille, on all that the eye can represent—the reason, the mind, vision, the father, and meaning itself.[11] In this scenario, the Stooges constitute an ongoing affront to the maintenance of logocentrism and all the forces that want, always, to make sense, to deny the unregulatable, disseminative effects of writing, to move to the transcendental signified. From this perspective we can perhaps better understand the Stooges' continual attack on the eye and, more important, our continuing fascination with this attack; for as Bataille points out, with characteristic Bakhtinian duality, the eye is very seductive "but extreme seductiveness is probably at the boundary of horror" (17). We may even be able to read the Stooges into Bataille's discussion of the eye-slitting scene in Luis Buñuel's *Andalusian Dog* (1928). For Bataille, this scene is liberating precisely because it is so horrible:

> If Buñuel himself, after the filming of the slit-open eye, remained sick for a week . . . how then can one not see to what extent horror becomes fascinating, and how it alone is brutal enough to break everything that stifles? (19, note 1)

We may not want to go along with Bataille in his celebration of the brutal and the horrible, not even in order "to break everything that stifles." Yet his analysis also makes it clear that our morbid fascination with the Stooges' eye gouging can never be entirely innocent either.

The suggestive meanings that surround the ruptured eye can be generalized to include the entire head. Hair pulling is a central feature of the Stooges' films, of course, and constitutes a favorite method of striking against the head and all that it symbolically represents. The face is also clearly important. Consider, for example, the way in which Curly keeps violently "wiping" his face, as part of his repertory of reactions, as though he were trying to obliterate it, to remove all of its features. Similarly, the films are filled with multiple pie-and-cake-throwing scenes, with the camera always lingering on the astonished, smeared faces that have lost all of their familiar human markings and become little more than masks. (In *Have Rocket Will Travel,* Moe disfigures Curly Joe's face by painting it with shaving cream; in other films, faces and entire heads are drenched in flour, eggs, oil, and so on.) Slapping is another key gesture of their violent repertoire against the face, at times even developing into a bravura performance culminating in the multiple slap, when a father figure (Moe, or, for example, the father-noble in "Restless Knights") slaps all three of them in a single, smoothly efficient gesture.

It is the face, the head—again, the seat of reason, truth, control, the Logos—that must be punished, banished, made to disappear in the general celebration of the nether regions of the body.[12] Reason and truth are also associated, by Derrida and others, with the "naturalness" and power of the voice, of speech—products of the head and the face—and thus many films (for example, *Have Rocket Will Travel*) begin with an authoritative Voice of Science and Knowledge voice-over, a rational discourse that is wrecked within minutes by the Stooges' mayhem. Similarly, many of the shorts concern the complete fouling up of things in books—those repositories of the Logos that, although written, represent the highest form of the truth of speech—things that require expert knowledge that the Stooges always claim to have but never do, such as cooking a fancy meal in "An Ache in Every Stake" (1941), making rocket fuel in *Have Rocket,* and mixing chemicals in "Hold That Lion" (1947).

This accent on the body also puts the Stooges firmly in the realm of the material signifier, in an area of free play that cannot finally be tamed and that will also resist what Derrida calls "the theological gesture" of moving toward the transcendent. But the language of the lower body does not simply replace that of the upper body either, for this would merely reverse the hierarchy. Thus, some of the bodily terms in play are also themselves internally divided. Hair, for example, when pulled can be seen as an assault on the site of reason. Yet it can also have the opposite sense; thus, as befits the (virile) father figure of the group, Moe has the most hair. But because his helmet of hair most closely recalls Louise Brooks's in *Lulu* or, as is often pointed out, a child's hair, it also makes him the most feminine or childish of the three. Curly is not curly at all; in fact, he has no hair. It is as though signifiers cannot be trusted to move smartly to their signifieds in this topsy-turvy world, for they at times name their opposite. This confusion in signification is related to a certain free play of language that is found in virtually all the titles of their shorts ("The Yoke's on Me" [1944], "Boobs in Arms" [1940], and so on) and that also occupies many of these films, as, for example, the running use of pig Latin in "Tassels in the Air" (1938). Puns and language games by their very nature insist on remaining on the level of the signifier and thus resist a centering discourse. This is also true of the fake medieval English of "Restless Knights" and is most gloriously in evidence in "Woman Haters" (1934), in which the entire dialogue is in rhyme. In "Tassels" the minimal narrative in fact arises because the Stooges have misapplied all the labels to the doors in an office building, again pointing to the unstable signifier.

Language thus becomes crucial here and represents another kind of violence. Curly, especially in the early shorts—for example, "Pop Goes the Easel" (1935)—is sheer verbal exuberance and is constantly given to making jokes, puns, and so on, always refusing "proper" signification ("I have an uncle in Cairo—he's a chiropractor") or even the minimal sense-making that other comedians usually seek.[13] He is always punished for this pleasure by Moe, on one level the father figure and thus ostensibly the representative of reason, truth, and meaning. It is as though Moe knows that the infliction of pain is the most efficient way to stop language, as described by Elaine Scarry in *The Body in Pain:*

> Physical pain does not simply resist language but actively destroys it, bringing about an immediate reversion to a state anterior to language, to the sounds and cries a human being makes before language is learned. (4)

Although Scarry clearly means language here as an instrument of reason and meaning, the infliction of pain is capable of stifling language in any form. But the kind of language that Curly uses is at least in a sense already the equivalent of "the sounds and cries a human makes before language is learned" and has as much (or as little) meaning as does pain. Curly's language is of the same order as Moe's violence. Thus, whereas Moe employs violence precisely to *stop* the free play of the (verbal) signifier, his violence always reinscribes its own form of free play at the same time, thus accomplishing the same thing as Curly's language originally set out to do.

Such play, of course, is particularly associated with children, those archenemies of the forces of reason and the Logos, and it is no accident that many of the Stooges' associations with animals also relate them to children. The Stooges act like children, they dress and gesture like children, they are children in fact, and they stand in for the children watching them. Endlessly repeating verbal tics and various bits of slapstick business, they drive their humor into the ground, as children are also wont to do. Yet they are old men at the same time, and it is perhaps this chronological confusion that appeals to children, themselves chronologically confused, and also because this is one more thing that doesn't add up, doesn't make sense. There is also a certain collapse of the space of representation here as well, for the Three Stooges are known precisely as that and only secondarily as individuals with names. But they don't have last names either, like children, and their first names always remain the same. Curly, Moe, and Larry, they always play themselves and erase the space between them and their characters, another assault on narrative. Representation, and the doubling or otherness it always requires, is thus threatened because the difference here, necessary for representation, is elided; the signifier does not point inevitably to a signified, an elsewhere of meaning, but only to itself.

The Stooges authorize childish violence, childish activity of all sorts, in the world of the adults, especially the general carnivalesque attack launched against the "responsible adults," the men (usually) who are in charge; over and over, revenge is wreaked upon them, presumably to the delight of all the children watching.[14] This is especially conveyed through the size of the "adults" who surround them. In many of the shorts, they are immense figures, Titans and Amazons, who accentuate the childish stature and being of the Stooges—a good example is the gigantic saloon owner in "Yes, We Have No Bonanza" (1939); another is the women in "An Ache in Every Stake." In many of these films—for example, "Woman Haters"—the "girls" who are to be interpreted as being sexually attractive are the appropriate size, while those who occupy positions of power, both male and female, are immense. (They are, of course, often the same actors used over and over.) But such sexuality is itself unstable, and sexual roles, themselves a function of a binary logocentrism, also become oddly confused as part of this dynamic. In the 1930s shorts, Curly is portrayed as a skirt-chasing maniac, clearly a function of the celebration of the lower body, yet there is also a great deal of cross-dressing, as in "Pop Goes the Easel"; and in "Woman Haters," Larry spends his wedding night cuddled up with Moe and Curly. In the later films, of course, as older men in a Hollywood film, they cannot aspire to any overt sexuality, especially not with the leading lady, whoever she happens to be. Yet in the fairly late short "Muscle Up a Little Closer" (1956), they are provided with "girlfriends," but all of their girlfriends are immensely bigger and stronger than they are and in fact lift weights.

The childishness of the Stooges and their clinging to the signifier are also continually inflected as part of another nexus, that of social class. For the adult world is also the world of logocentric rules and conventions, and these are perhaps nowhere more obviously embodied than in class distinctions. This again relates the Stooges' films to the celebration of carnival that in Bakhtin's formulation "marks the suspension of all hierarchical rank, privileges, norms and prohibitions" (Bakhtin, 109). "An Ache in Every Stake" revolves around the horror that results when polite society is intruded upon by gross elements from the lower classes. In "Restless Knights," the Stooges perform the same intrusive function at court among the nobles; in "Three Little Beers" (1935), they invade a golf course, historically marked as a clear signifier for privilege, and the humor comes completely from the fact that they do not know the appropriate social rules connected with golf. From the very opening credits of *Snow White and the Three Stooges* (1961), Larry's nasal Brooklyn accent is made to clash humorously with the toney British-accented voice-over with which the film begins. In psychoanalytic terms, what the Stooges represent is the pure, unbridled lawlessness of id. They do not know the rules; they don't even know that there are rules. Their outwardly directed violence is thus often about the classic American desire to deflate social pretensions (especially in "Tassels," where the plot concerns the nouveau riche wife of a former postman). More than that, however, the Stooges refuse the symbolic order completely and thus refuse the strictures of the Oedipal complex that are supposed to usher us into society, culture, and meaning through repression. The Stooges will not be repressed; hence they remain above (or below) any notion of language as consistently meaningful. Their anarchy is not about "freedom" or any other such bounded, logocentric notion; rather, it is completely without rhyme or reason, wild, like Freud's seething unconscious, on the one hand, and like Lacan's very different unconscious, with its endless chain of signifiers, on the other. The Stooges remain instead within the love-hate, simple identifications of Lacan's imaginary. Their (non-)narratives of violence make so little sense because narrative structure is itself a function of the symbolic, of the Oedipal.

At the same time, *inside* their little "family," they reenact the family struggle themselves with Moe, "moi," as the ego, the controlling figure, the father, the one who pretends to rationality and the Logos. (Although seen in the larger terms of the society, of course, this little family is very silly indeed.) This is also why the narratives of violence always retain at least some modicum of sense, for there is a kind of ersatz symbolic present through the machinations of Moe as the punishing father, a symbolic that appears to lend a certain structure to the violent events. But of course Moe is really only another one of the children himself, as he constantly demonstrates. This is therefore only a parody of the symbolic, a parody of the Oedipal drama. No meaning results here either.

But the violence of the Stooges is, finally, a parody as well. In discussing their violence, in celebrating it as a kind of anarchic free play of writing, we must always keep this in mind. No one really gets hurt in their films because theirs is the violence of cartoon figures, a kind of counter-mimesis that curiously reverses the usual direction and relation of visual signifier to signified. Their violence is not real; it is a trope, a figure. Although their use of their own names threatens always to collapse the space of representation, nevertheless, because we watch them on film, we must always watch them as characters, even as characters who represent themselves, rather than as themselves. The spacing of representation, however minute, can never be fully effaced. The same is true of their violence. Filmed, it will always be a represented violence, and that dynamic, that space of representation, turns the real slap into a fake slap, even if they are the same, even if the slap has caused real pain. Which is not to say that real pain is not itself always also a representation, always spaced from itself. But that is another story altogether, another narrative of violence for another time.

Notes

1. For a full discussion of the question of boundaries and frames as it applies to film, see Peter Brunette and David Wills.

2. He maintains that the level of violence in any given Three Stooges film depends upon which director they happened to be working with. For Maltin, the archvillain is Jules White, who "leaned heavily on violence," Maltin implies, as a way out of plot difficulties. In the films I have seen, I have been unable to detect any pattern of violence that correlates with specific directors.

3. Interestingly, in their first independent short, "Woman Haters"—subtitled "A Musical Novelty"—which contains singing and whose recitative lines as well are all in verse, the violence is sparing. This may be because the musical aspects of the short present such a strong rhythm of their own, such a strong punctuation, that they leave no space for the orchestration of violence. By the end of the film, however, the two rhythms have become much more fully integrated.

4. Throughout this chapter, titles of the Stooges' short films are indicated by quotation marks, and titles of the features are italicized.

5. Distinctions must be made, however. Thus, whereas *Snow White and the Three Stooges,* a color, Cinemascope extravaganza made for Twentieth Century–Fox in 1961, is almost completely uninteresting, *The Three Stooges Go Around the World in a Daze* (black and white, Columbia, 1963), is witty, politically topical, and self-reflexive all at once. The high point of the film comes when an attempt is made to "brainwash" the Stooges in China; after a closed-door session with them, the three Chinese psychiatrists emerge doing all the Stooges' routines—with the

exception of the eye gouging, which, as Moe comments, is not part of their act any longer. (It is clear that this film is superior because it is, in fact, merely five or six shorts that have been strung together.) *Have Rocket Will Travel* (1959), another black-and-white Columbia feature, is similarly filled with self-reflexive metacommentary.

6. This perspective on the Stooges' violence as antinarrative because it is senseless and without any goal or meaning contrasts with other forms of the narrative representation of violence that purport to offer meaning. In the context of an insightful discussion of Pier Paolo Pasolini's *Salò* (1975), Leo Bersani and Ulysse Dutoit make the following point:

> Narrativity sustains the glamour of historical violence. Narratives create violence as an isolated, identifiable topic or subject. We have all been trained to locate violence historically—that is, as a certain type of eruption against a background of generally non-violent human experience. From this perspective, violence can be accounted for through historical accounts of the circumstances in which it occurs. Violence is thus reduced to the level of a plot; it can be isolated, understood, perhaps mastered and eliminated. And, having been conditioned to think of violence within narrative frameworks, we expect this mastery to take place as a result of the pacifying power of such narrative conventions as beginnings, explanatory middles, and climactic endings, and in art we are therefore suspicious of works which reject those conventions.

This project of giving meaning to violence through its narrativization, and explanatory power to its representation, is exactly the reverse of what the Stooges attempt.

7. The graphic mark of writing is also literally inscribed in their films, as a clue to the arche-writing that can be seen at work in many different aspects of the image, broadly conceived. (See Brunette and Wills, Chaps. 3 and 4, for a general discussion of this problematic.) Thus, the shorts often accomplish a great deal of exposition through a sign or label of some sort or another—a mark of the *material* eruption of writing into the visual text—which replaces, for obvious reasons of narrative economy, the establishing visual shot of most films.

8. The collective also extends beyond the Stooges themselves. No hard-and-fast boundaries are ever established between them and the straight characters, for the excessive play of the signifier leaks out into the main narrative as well. Thus, a certain playfulness is evident as well on the "adult" narrative level that these films halfheartedly posit, as when the serious scholar in the first minute or so of "We Want Our Mummy" (1939) identifies, within the "straight" narrative, the object of the search as the tomb of "King Rootintootin." In their first independent short, "Woman Haters," made presumably before things were stabilized, one of the "straight" characters (although these distinctions break down) gouges *their* eyes.

9. See Gregory Ulmer's important work in this context.

10. One can easily imagine the Stooges playing with excrement, as children do, even if one cannot imagine ever seeing this on film.

11. Bataille gives this Bakhtinian insight a political spin that relates it to bourgeois sexual anxiety: "Communist workers appear to the bourgeois to be as ugly and dirty as hairy sexual organs, or lower parts: sooner or later there will be a

scandalous eruption in the course of which the asexual noble heads of the bourgeois will be chopped off" (8).

12. Perhaps the most violent visual representation of this reversal can be found in René Magritte's painting *Le Viol* (The Rape), in which the eyes and mouth of a woman's portrait are replaced by her breasts and genitals.

13. Interestingly, the Stooges' verbal jokes are most often one-liners, not built upon as they usually are with the Marx Brothers; the Stooges, instead, build upon physical violence.

14. This is sometimes elided, or even overtly negated, however, as when in "Three Little Beers" (1935), the Stooges comment that golf "looks like a kid's game; they're wearing short pants"—which is presumably the way kids would look at golf as well.

References and Additional Reading

Bakhtin, Mikhail. 1968. *Rabelais and His World*, trans. Helene Iswolsky. Cambridge, Mass.: MIT Press.

Bataille, Georges. 1985. *Visions of Excess: Selected Writings, 1927–1939*, ed. Allan Stoekl. Minneapolis: University of Minnesota Press.

Bersani, Leo, and Ulysse Dutoit. 1982. "Merde Alors." In *Pier Paolo Pasolini: The Poetics of Heresy*, ed. Beverly Allen. Saratoga, Calif.: Anma Libri.

Brunette, Peter, and David Wills. 1989. *Screen/Play: Derrida and Film Theory*. Princeton: Princeton University Press.

Derrida, Jacques. 1976. *Of Grammatology*, trans. Gayatri Spivak. Baltimore: Johns Hopkins University Press.

———. 1986. *Glas*, trans. John P. Leavey and Richard Rand. Lincoln: University of Nebraska Press. Originally appeared in French in 1974.

Maltin, Leonard. 1982. *The Great Movie Comedians*. New York: Harmony Books.

Scarry, Elaine. 1987. *The Body in Pain: The Making and Unmaking of the World*. New York: Oxford University Press.

Stallybrass, Peter, and Allon White. 1986. *The Politics and Poetics of Transgression*. Ithaca, N.Y.: Cornell University Press.

Ulmer, Gregory. 1985. *Applied Grammatology*. Baltimore: Johns Hopkins University Press.

Paralysis in Motion

Jerry Lewis's Life as a Man

Scott Bukatman

Jerry Lewis: the disorderly orderly, the delicate delinquent, the ladies man, the nutty professor. Jerry Lewis: oxymoron, idiot savant. In *Cracking Up* (d. Lewis, 1983), Jerry slips, trips, slides and glides his way across a polished floor toward the psychiatrist's couch. He reclines, prepared to speak, and tumbles to the floor. An extended moment of paralysis in motion, of articulation delayed and denied. A stutter that structures the phenomenon of the filmmaker as a discursive metaphor. Jerry explicitly defined as a pathological case: a patient producing, and not producing, a discourse of the self. Not, of course, the fictive stability of the self as it "really" exists, but the schismed, unresolved, and contradictory formations of the self produced through the analytic discourse:[1] in this instance, the self constructed through the films produced by, written by, directed by, and starring (in a multiplicity of roles) . . . Jerry Lewis. These works, like the speech of the patient on the couch, turn upon the figuration and displacement of sexual desire, a struggle for control that is externalized into the struggle to control both world and self. This fiction of control finally yields the inscription of a male subject position that demolishes any prospect of a coherent masculine subjectivity.

Lewis the filmmaker controls and produces Jerry the character: a symbiosis cum rupture that is crucial to any critical understanding. There exists an isomorphism between creator and creation that structures this complex enunciation, which produces its own enunciating subject. Lewis has always taken credit for teaming up with Dean Martin, and perhaps this analytic work ought to begin with a historical excursus. The pairing with Dean dominates American interest: questions about the team's demise continue to echo among fans of that generation, which made them the most successful comedy act of the 1950s on stage, screen, and television. In Europe, conversely, it is the moment of solo production that inaugurates the fascination with the case of Jerry Lewis. In its earliest, and crudest forms, the auteurist configuration that dominated French critical thought in the late 1950s and early 1960s defined film as an art form by reinstantiating the figure of the solo artist/creator/author (for more on auteurism and Lewis, see Polan, 1984). Within this definition there exists no significant role to be occupied by other figures involved in the production process, be they writers, producers, or other halves of comedy teams. The French definition of Lewis as an artist, then, depended upon the banishment of Dean Martin (to whom ample homage is also paid as a solo performer) and even, to some extent, Frank Tashlin (although here there exists a rare willingness to acknowledge a dual auteur).

I argue that there is no moment of "ontological break" around the end of the Martin and Lewis partnership; rather a continuity exists between these two phases of Lewis's career.[2] Although this is consistent with the French position, it pushes the moment of significant control back to Lewis's precinematic, and presolo, career.

Another reason for the French devaluation of the Martin and Lewis era is the emphasis on Lewis as a purely cinematic figure: a formulation that slights the importance of the television work. It is crucial to remember that throughout the 1950s and into the early 1960s, the American public was exposed not only to the biannual release of a Lewis or Martin and Lewis comedy but to almost monthly appearances on live television (this in addition to radio and stage performances). To fully assess the Lewis persona and output, the TV work must be granted a critical viewing. Such a viewing, however, amounts to much more than a dreary documentary task; rather, the consistently high quality of so much of this work provides a constant source of delight, although any critical emphasis must necessarily be placed entirely on the specifics of *performance,* rather than on the intricate ruptures of cinematic or narrative structures that will finally define the Lewis cinematic text (as I hope to demonstrate).

Following several appearances by Martin and Lewis on the "Welcome Aboard" show in 1948, as well as on "The Texaco Star Theatre" in 1949, NBC agreed to star them as rotating hosts of the new "Colgate Comedy Hour."[3] The Martin and Lewis "Colgates," aired live between 1951 and 1956, demonstrate better than any other forum the team's astonishing improvisational abilities. Whereas the films of this era lock Lewis into a single character, the television skits, with their climate of spontaneity, permit him to surge through a range of performance modes. The "Colgate Comedy Hour" also permits a new understanding of the Martin and Lewis team with regard to their mode of interaction.

In the context of the television work, most of the Martin and Lewis films reveal a glaring inability to exploit their appeal: the two stars are usually filmed in separate shots, destroying any sense of interplay. The films also miss the strengths of Martin's performance style, based as it is on an easy informality. In the "Colgate" episodes, on the other hand, Martin reveals an ability to follow and respond to Lewis, providing a measure of control while sharing in the delights of comic anarchy. The warmth of the partnership and the evident affection of the two for each other are in evidence here to a much greater degree than in *any* of their films as a team. An understanding of this predirectorial portion of Lewis's career has been inadequately represented by the studio product the team appeared in, and hence the value of Dean Martin to the team has been broadly misunderstood or even lost entirely. The television work encourages a more accurate view and permits a recognition of the value of the team to both Lewis's and Martin's later performance styles.

Jerry Lewis has always claimed credit for the Martin and Lewis teamup; he is its auteur. In an interview, Lewis recalled proposing a new form of comedy team. " 'Dean and Jerry' was my baby," he said. "I even called my father as a research source. 'Dad, was there ever a two-act that was not a two-act?' " After noting that all teamups, or two-acts, were based upon a doubling—two characters from the same class, with the same dress and/or the same profession—Lewis said, "I have an idea of making a team out of the handsomest guy in the world and a monkey."[4] From the outset of the career of Martin and Lewis, then, the notion of a split or division is fundamental to the comic premise, as two assuredly different representations of masculinity coexist.

Following his split with Dean in 1958, Lewis successively takes on the writing, production, and direction of his own films and television specials. In contrast to the increasing public resistance displayed toward Lewis's solo productions, the Martin and Lewis era is fondly remembered—Jerry is less "self-indulgent," less "pathetic." The works of the Martin and Lewis era are indeed, for the most part, a sunnier lot than those of Lewis alone. The final scene frequently presents a song that serves as an ode to stability ("Pardners," for example, or "We Belong Together"), perhaps culminating in the curtain calls of *The Caddy* (d. Taurog, 1953), *Artists and Models* (d. Tashlin, 1955), or *Hollywood or Bust* (d. Tashlin, 1956). This final two-shot, which appears in so many of their films and television shows, is itself a most potent image of resolution: the two constructions of masculinity linked and united in a nonparadoxical vision of harmony—too bad it takes two to tango.[5]

Dean Martin and Jerry Lewis in a "potent image of resolution" from Frank Tash-lin's Hollywood or Bust *(1956)*

The pairing of Dean and Jerry remains thoroughly commensurate with the concerns in evidence through the later films: the displacement of the control function onto the adult figure of "sexy," "virile" Dean Martin serves to disguise the sexual conflicts that remain latent in spastic, juvenile Jerry. Small wonder, then, that after the departure of Dean's balancing force, Jerry's quest for the resolution of a stable identity becomes ever more provisional and ever less convincing.

The trajectory of Lewis's career is marked by this quest, which is first revealed in a continual struggle for control and finds its echo and confirmation in the title of his 1971 "textbook," *The Total Filmmaker*. The films within this totalistic discourse are consistently organized around

Jerry's struggle for self-control and for a stable position within the socially constructed definitions of masculine behavior and desire, to a degree that transcends the usual structures of film comedy. The career of Jerry Lewis is therefore doubly marked by a continuing struggle for control: control over the production of the comedic discourse and the complementary comic struggles enacted by that Jerry character, that alter ego, or perhaps we should call it the alter *id*.

Before proceeding to an analysis of Lewis's cinematic productions, I wish to note the various dramatic works in which Lewis participated during the years, two of which seem especially relevant to any reconsideration. Both are concerned with career aspirations and with the conflicting pressures that interfere with personal goals, a theme that also structures the comedies *The Disorderly Orderly* (d. Tashlin, 1964), *The Errand Boy* (d. Lewis, 1962), and even the Lewis homage, Martin Scorsese's *The King of Comedy* (1982).

The Jazz Singer (d. Ralph Nelson, 1959)[6] is distinguished by an unaffected performance as well as by an audacious finale that perfectly captured the unresolved conflicts of identity that characterize so many of Lewis's works. Lewis, as the cantor turned vaudevillian, hastens to his father's deathbed made up as a clown for his television special and later leads his father's congregation in the "Kol Nidre" while remaining in clownface. Here, typically, Lewis presents a resolution that is in fact a contradiction, and the critical dissatisfaction with the work may have been a response to the glaringly unresolved paradoxes of selfishness versus selflessness, of career versus family, of religious identity versus American assimilation.

The openly Oedipal themes of *The Jazz Singer* find their echo in the episode of "Ben Casey" starring and directed by Lewis, "A Little Fun to Match the Sorrow" (1965). Here Lewis's selfless aspiring surgeon, working under (and against) the authority of Dr. Casey, is incapable of dealing with the pain around him. His comic compensations arouse the ire of Drs. Casey and Zorba, who regard the younger figure as frivolous and arrogant (complaints so often leveled against Jerry Lewis the performer). Here comedic arrogance operates as only a defensive formation, an isolating strategy of protection against agony. Again and again in Lewis's work we find the reluctance to grow up, to accept the responsibilities of adulthood: from the little-boy masquerade in *You're Never Too Young* (d. Taurog, 1955) to the refusal of the reality of pain that dominates the "Ben Casey" episode, the self fractures and splits beneath the contradictory pressures under which it labors.

Although Lewis has acknowledged in an interview the autobiographical component at work in the "Ben Casey" episode, he is slower to recognize its echo in his own comedic performances and filmic works (this is extraordinary for two reasons: first, *The Disorderly Orderly*, released the year before, is oddly identical to the "Ben Casey" episode in many ways;

and, second, Lewis's comedy frequently contains dramatic components, as is the case with *The Nutty Professor* [d. Lewis, 1963]). Perhaps comedy operates as a defensive formation against pain for Jerry Lewis himself, although such an interrogation approaches the intimacy of a purely biographical analysis, which risks limiting the understanding of the work's broader value. Such analysis becomes difficult to avoid, however, in the face of Lewis's MDA work and marathon/telethon, in which an ultimate, and even ritualistic, confrontation with the pain of human suffering is staged in a continual and endless fashion. The isomorphism between creator and creation begins to appear frighteningly exact, the boundaries between them more difficult to discern.

Lewis's work—with and without Dean Martin—is fascinating, then, in its continual play around the fragmentation of self-identity. As in psychoanalysis, the battle is waged upon the field of language, and it is in the total films of the total filmmaker, Jerry Lewis, that the disruption of language is most constant. In these works it is not only natural language but the entire articulations of narrative and cinematic structure that are agitated and unsettled through the pirouettes around the tropes of broken syntax, shifting tonalities, and free association.

In verbal as well as cinematic enunciations, these disruptions inscribe the literal incoherence of the speaking subject and in a manner that might specifically invoke, perhaps surprisingly, the position of the nineteenth-century female hysteric. The failure of Anna O. to comprehend her native German while suffering her hysterical symptoms has been described by Charles Bernheimer as a "disruptive polylingualism" in which a refusal of a coherent subject-position is inscribed. What Mary Ann Doane has called "the desire to desire," whereby female desire is thwarted and repressed through the absence of a legitimate figuration system for the expression and legitimation of that desire, might be perversely adapted to describe the disruptive polylingualism of the Lewis text (an adaptation performed by Thyrza Goodeve [1989]). Jerry, taking on the persona of the female hysteric, acts out his own ambivalence toward an inscribed and proscribed social position (masculinity).

As houseboy and stepson in *Cinderfella* (d. Tashlin, 1964), Jerry is granted an actual compliment:

Stepmother:	And Fella, the prime rib was delicious.
Fella:	The prime . . . you loved it. The prime rib? You loved the prime rib? (Gasps) My ribs? Was good? I'm gonna faint! Did you really love the prime rib? Really—didja—didja—was it—Did you like it a lot, or just a little-lot? Oh I'm gl—Ohhh-ho! I worked very to my bones—fingers? I'm glad you liked my meat prime. Oh I c—Oh thank you mother for enjoying my prime meat of ribs. I'm so grateful to you all.

The resistance to an ambivalent and emasculated social role is performed through a simultaneous excess and failure of linguistic function. And if a film such as *The Nutty Professor* reveals a resistance to fixed subjectivity and the cultural inscription of the codes of masculine behavior, then this resistance is first evidenced linguistically, in the alternation between the nasal intonations of Professor Kelp and the crooning tones of his alter ego, Buddy Love. Indeed, *The Errand Boy* is strikingly organized around the sound of the human voice, and vocal repetitions and misrepetitions determine the structure of its comedy.

The language of the filmmaker is equally culpable in this resistance to a coherent and delimited order. In the films of Lewis, the carefully delineated narrative situations and conflicts that constitute the logic of the syntagmatic chain inevitably fall victim to a degeneration into a series of isolated sketches unrelated to the main narrative. The discursive operations of these films are dominated by digression and repetition, rather than by causal logic and narrative closure, and are thus more easily linked to the associational language of the patient than to the telos of the narrator. This tendency is most emergent in Lewis's most "total" productions: the carefully prepared scenario of *The Ladies Man* (d. Lewis, 1961), with gradually introduced characters, settings, and conflicts, disintegrates into a series of blackout sketches unrelated either through chains of causality or the impetus of narrative functions. In *The Ladies Man,* architectural structure replaces narrative structure, as the massive cutaway house (which is simultaneously open and closed) operates as the merest gesture of containment toward the multitude of frenetic actions taking place within.

Dana Polan (1988) cites critic Claude-Jean Philippe, who writes that

> to be logical with himself, Lewis should eliminate gags from his comedy. That's what he has already done in part. Since *The Patsy* [1965], he has constructed his gags in utter disdain for effectiveness. He barely sketches in the gags or, quite the contrary, he prolongs them, dilates them while diluting them. Laughter gives way to the lyricism of derision. (10)

Polan notes that Lewis's later films evoke

> the fascination with duration in minimalist ventures in avant-garde film; for example, the seemingly endless repetition of a gag way after any comic effect has been reached might well be compared to the deliberate cultivation of ennui in such experimental films as Michael Snow's *Wavelength* [1968].

As Jerry fumbles from chair to chair in *The Patsy,* slipping first from one and then another, the constant return to the reaction shots of others constructs a temporal distension; the narrative literally halts to permit this creeping and incessant lassitude. Vases fall, only to be snatched from disaster at the last moment—quite simply, *nothing happens* in this prolonged

Jerry Lewis directing on the elaborate multiple set of The Ladies' Man

gesture of paralysis in motion. In the context of such an experience of *longue durée,* one might add to Polan's citation of Snow the domestic nightmare of duration suffered by both the character and the viewer in Chantal Akerman's *Jeanne Dielmann* (1975). Akerman's film is recalled, for example, as Jerry darts from one end of the monstrous dinner table in *Cinderfella* to the other, over and over and over again. The feeling of entrapment and of the impossibility of action or change arises agonizingly. Within such spatiotemporal distension, the physical dominates character, as the individual is reduced to automaton—but a malfunctioning automaton, a marionette with severed strings.

The looseness of narrative structures is applicable to performance as well. *Cracking Up* features a flashback with Jerry as a Frenchman, yet suddenly his dialect swerves toward the Oriental ("I'm talkin' Japanese here!" he says and continues with the scene). A scene with Jerry driving along a highway metonymizes into Jerry as a Southern sheriff on patrol. These elements of the random most strongly parallel the activity of the psychiatric patient. As the patient must verbalize freely to permit the psyche to follow its associative pathways, regardless of the seeming incoherence of the discourse, so is the Lewis corpus permeated by a dizzying array of slips, elisions, and repetitions. It is as though the creator of this discourse lacks the capacity for secondary revision: the mechanism through which the dream's apparent absurdity and incoherence are eliminated. Revision, of course, is an act of censorship, a smoothing of the areas of anxiety, and a repression of trauma. The film works, by contrast, stand with all contradictions and incoherences intact. Jerry Lewis dreams on film.

The results of this "dream work" are singular. The insistent retardation of Jerry's motor and linguistic skills achingly transmits the experience of an inhibited development, and the character is so obsessively involved in spills and explosions that it becomes difficult to avoid linking these failures of physical coordination with deeper, psychosexual levels of failure (incompetence gives way to incontinence). The narrative that might best introduce such an interpretive level is *The Disorderly Orderly* (1964), produced by Lewis and directed by Frank Tashlin. Jerry, a hospital orderly, suffers from a "neurotic identification empathy," as he calls it, which leads him to suffer from the symptoms endured by his (only female) patients and which blocks his emulation of his father, a brilliant surgeon. In his menial position, Jerry finds ample opportunity to disrupt the normal operations of the hospital and impose a continuing chaos. Only by overcoming his identification with women (and Goodeve notes that women are defined throughout this film as physically or hysterically "ill") can he fill his father's stethoscope and thus "succeed."

A deliriously Oedipal scenario such as this makes manifest what remains latent in so many films by Jerry Lewis and relates strongly to what Freud notes as the "repudiation of femininity": one of two obstacles to the successful completion of psychoanalysis. The interrelated phenomena are the experience of penis envy in women and the corresponding struggle in men, "against their passive or feminine attitude towards other men" (Freud, 1963b, 268). The problem is generated in both instances by the anxiety regarding castration, and the inevitable result is a resistance or hostility directed toward the figure of the analyst: "negative transference." Alfred Adler's appellation for such behavior, "masculine protest," is accepted by Freud, although he also offers the alternate label of "repudiation of femininity." This resistance to the passivity of the feminine (passivity, of course, in the face of the threat of castration) results in its massive suppression, and, writes Freud, "often the only indications of its existence are exaggerated over-compensations" (1963b, 269).

Thyrza Goodeve's analysis of *The Disorderly Orderly* poses the crucial question of the (vanishing) position of the woman within this film, which culminates in a literal displacement of the female. In Lewis's temporary appropriation of the hysterical position of the woman in film after film, women are themselves marginalized, absented, or fetishistically multiplied. This last is perhaps the most common: in *You're Never Too Young* (d. Taurog, 1955), *Hollywood or Bust,* and especially *The Ladies Man,* Jerry is surrounded by a plurality of interchangeable objects of threat/desire

("30 of Filmdom's Fabulous Females," proclaims the trailer for *The Ladies Man*). This multiplicity fails to fully disguise the sense that there is literally *no place* for these women in a universe that operates only as a projection of a hysterical male psyche that repudiates their very existence.[7]

The phenomenon of "masculine protest," directed against the controlling figure of the psychoanalyst, has urgent consequences. The construction of a coherent subject-position by the patient becomes suspect, based as it is upon an external and falsely perceived threat. Whereas *The Disorderly Orderly* presents a ridiculously clear example of the refusal of the (inherently ailing) feminine, it is in *The Nutty Professor* that the overcompensation of masculine behavior is most explicitly and hilariously (hysterically?) pronounced through a narrative that is explicitly centered, or decentered, around a suspect and shifting subjectivity.

The Nutty Professor is entirely devoted to Professor Julius Kelp's attempts to surmount his deficiencies as a man. Unable to contend with his own desires, the inadequate professor develops a potion that transforms him into a swinger, the significantly named Buddy Love. The film is a fantasy of metamorphosis: where the nasal-toned and easily cowed Kelp is colorless and bland, constantly attired in a white lab coat, hair combed forward over his face, Love is the embodiment of cool with his flashy jackets, slicked-up hair, throaty voice, insouciant attitude. Love clearly represents a macho Kelp, a Kelp in control of situations, of others, and especially of women. Kelp need never acknowledge the disparity between his sexual desire and his sexual competency because desire is displaced onto another character who performs in his stead. Love desires and can ostensibly achieve satisfaction, while Kelp neither admits desire nor attains fulfillment.

Professor Kelp is easily bullied, not merely by his superiors but by his students. In a reversal of accepted power relations, one aging footballplayer type resists Kelp's authority by interpellating him as a child ("Naughty, naughty, naughty") and stuffing him into a closet.[8] Whatever damage is sustained by the ego can only be exacerbated by the wellintentioned words offered by Stella, student and love (Love) interest: "He's a typical bully that loves picking on a small man." Kelp's first attempt at self-transformation at a local gymnasium is marked by his utter inability to master the simplest piece of equipment, and his weakness, myopia, and dysfunction are evident to all. The presentation of Kelp continually involves the humiliations that follow upon his incapacity to perform as a strong and commanding figure of masculine competence.

Following his failure at body*building*, Kelp retreats into the rational abstractions of formulas and scientific analysis, finally to produce his metamorphic and metonymic potion. The substitute ego thereby constructed, the regrettable Buddy Love, is a model of "masculine protest" and overcompensatory behavior. Kelp's transformation, presented as a technicolor excess of masochistic self-victimization, does more than affect him physically: it alters his entire subjective experience. The first appearance of Love is perceived through an exaggeratedly extended subjective tracking shot foregrounding the central perspective of the self-centered Buddy Love. Love's gaze is duplicated by Lewis's camera work, and thus character and filmmaker seize overt control of the space, the gaze, and the spectators, both diegetically and within the space of the theater itself. A two-shot trajectory is thus traced from Kelp's position of passive and even masochistic repose, the camera craning upward in a cold movement of abandonment, to a new sadistic power immediately signified by Love's clear domination of the cinematic apparatus as well as those around him. The transition is also marked linguistically, as Love reappropriates the position of the adult that was stripped from the ineffectual Kelp: "You're all very, very nice little boys and girls," Love tells his enthusiastic fans.

It represents only the smallest act of will to recognize *The Nutty Professor* for what it is: a phallic allegory in which Love represents Kelp in an erect, active, and threatening state. When Kelp is summoned to meet with the dean of the university, he is swallowed by the chair into which he slowly but inexorably sinks; in a later scene Love perches on the back of this same chair, upright and faintly shocking. One theory of psychosexual development clarifies the conflict embodied by this split persona: "based upon the fact of the bisexual constitution of human beings, it asserts that the motive force of repression in each individual is a struggle between the two sexual characters" (Freud, 1963a, 129)—in this case, the passive Kelp and the hypermasculine Love.

The repression of the passive/feminine and the consequent exaggeration of the active/masculine is clearest in the relationship with Stella. Where Kelp expressed embarrassment, Love is overbearingly confident:

Love: Just a minute, sweetheart. I don't remember dismissing you.

Stella: You, rude, discourteous ego-maniac!

Love: You're crazy about me, right?

Overcompensation takes the form of an aggressively active controlling force. "Here you are, baby," he tells Stella. "Take this, wipe the lipstick off, slide over here next to me, and let's get started." There are no niceties here to disguise the hostility directed toward the figure of "feminine passivity": Stella.

The Nutty Professor is acknowledged to be a profoundly personal work; its roots, however, are clearly evident in Lewis's earlier career. Speaking of the success of Martin and Lewis while acknowledging their lack of originality, Lewis said, "Now, the psychologist would say, 'No, there's more to it; there's some stuff underneath.' And the stuff underneath was the key. These were two guys who were in love with one another. They adored one another. One that could show it, and one that couldn't." Thus, the same passive male/hypermale dialectic operates from the beginning, in the very teamup with his hypermale partner, the handsomest guy in the world, Dean Martin. (Jerry here is "the monkey," his very vulnerability rendering him literally subhuman.) Although critics and audiences in 1963 perceived Buddy Love as a parody of ex-partner Dino, it is clearly more accurate to say that Dean's character was *always* representative of the hypermale side of Jerry.

The patient in analysis constructs a self-centered discourse in an attempt to produce, center, and analyze the repressive mechanisms at work within the psyche, but repression continues to function within the analysis, of course, and is displaced onto the analyst, who is imagined to be objective and therefore possibly threatening. The subject resists this recognized authority to protect the fiction of psychic coherence and control. Lewis positions his characters within a similar model of simultaneous submission and resistance (*Cracking Up:* Jerry lies on the couch but slips to the floor). This is demonstrated in *The Nutty Professor,* the most linear and most confessional of his films. The self-love and self-loathing attached to both Kelp and Love suggest the ambivalence involved in the act of constructing a satisfying subject position, and the resemblance between Buddy Love and Jerry Lewis is striking and undeniable.[9] And yet the disintegration of narrative structure is present even in this most structured of Lewis films and results in a failure to explore the numerous ramifications of the Kelp/Love dichotomy in favor of an incessant repetition of the basic situation of metamorphosis and regression. Considered as a confession, *The Nutty Professor* alludes to much more than it actually reveals: the digressions, repetitions, and circuitous paths of association continually enact the fact of resistance within the text. This discursive structure, combined with thematic material organized around desire, sublimation, and masculinity, suggests the film as a text involving the concurrence of confession and repression that characterizes the psychoanalytic situation.

The Nutty Professor is interesting, however, not simply for its clinical perfection as an illustration of the masculine protest but for its analysis of the status of the male in culture, which points to the inadequacy of the *definition* of the masculine, not the inadequacy of the male characters. This is demonstrated through the failure of the alter ego. Kelp's transformation to Buddy Love is temporary: the effects of his potion do not last even a single night. Love/Kelp is repeatedly forced to abandon Stella, in the first instance at the very moment of conquest (their kiss). The climactic scene depicts the regression of Love to Kelp on stage and in performance. Kelp's ardor thus remains ultimately unfulfilled, even through the substitute figure of Buddy Love, and the text thus stages a metonymy of desire: that which is always approached, never attained.

The spectator awaiting the promised resolution of this narrative will finally be presented with three endings in succession: Kelp and Stella embrace, each happy with the other as he or she is; Kelp is presented wearing braces and neatly groomed hair, while Stella carries two bottles of potion; the characters group for a cinematic curtain call, and Lewis appears with Kelp's hair, teeth, and demeanor and Love's flashy clothing. The endings first present the status quo; then Kelp as Love; and finally Love as Kelp. The surfeit of resolutions of the Kelp/Love dichotomy unsuccessfully masks the fact that there is no resolution at all: the passive male and the hypermale cannot find a stable balance within a single subject. Language masks its own inability to produce the object of desire, but, the mask being imperfect, the elision is fleetingly revealed.

The Lewis narrative thus makes problematic the social construction of masculinity, but even this does not exhaust the vertiginous experience of these works. The resistance to the masculine ultimately extends to a refusal to occupy any rigidly fixed subject position. As Lewis has Kelp transform to Buddy Love and back again, finally settling on two different hybrids by the finale, so the Jerry character constantly manifests multiple personae. This multiplicative tendency begins when his partnership with Dean Martin ends: in other words, when Dean splits, Jerry *splits*. *The Nutty Professor*, *The Big Mouth* (d. Lewis, 1967), *The Family Jewels* (d. Lewis, 1965), *Cracking Up, Cinderfella,* and *Which Way to the Front* (d. Lewis, 1970) all feature Jerry either disguised or transformed into different characters. If, as is well documented, Lewis has moved to fill multiple roles behind the camera (as producer, director, editor, cinematographer, and writer), then so does he fill multiple roles before it: a phantasmagoria of Jerrys. The filmmaker and the performer, locked in an isomorphic repetition, continually overlap. In *The Bellboy* (d. Lewis, 1960), Jerry plays Stanley the bellboy at a hotel visited by Jerry Lewis (a "guest star" appearance credited to Joe Levitch, Lewis's real name, which adds another referential level). *The Errand Boy* begins with Jerry pasting up a diegetic billboard that reads, "Jerry Lewis Is The Errand Boy." Later, as a successful comedian, he encounters another inept paperhanger—also portrayed by Lewis. At the end of *The Patsy,* Jerry/Lewis falls from a balcony, reappears to assure all concerned that he's not really hurt, that it's only a set, that he can't die because he's the star, and then he breaks the production for lunch. *Cracking Up* ends with Jerry exiting a theater where that very film has been playing. And finally, in all instances, the protagonist of these films—whether hospital orderly, bellboy, paperhanger, or professor—is always seen wearing the same elaborate jewelry, which could belong only to the wealthy and famous Jerry Lewis.

Repeatedly, then, the character is revealed as a diegetic convenience, with only the reality of the filmmaking milieu behind it. Yet if this is the case, if Stanley the bellboy is "really" Jerry Lewis, then what of the fact that Jerry Lewis is "really" Joseph Levitch? If the identity of Levitch is rejected to become Lewis to become Stanley who is visited by Levitch, then from where in this morass of self-referentiality can a fixed "reality" emerge? The answer, clearly, is that no reality does emerge. Identity stands revealed as a construction, frequently willful but often not, rather than an already existing condition to be inhabited. The multiplicity of identities in the world of Jerry Lewis belies the existence of identity as anything other than a necessary but unworkable fiction.

On another level, of course, the constant slippage of identity serves mostly to reinscribe Jerry Lewis, filmmaker, Jerry Lewis, auteur, at the center of all this tumult. Jerry Lewis is not to be confused with the schlemiel on screen; he is instead the star and the creator, the figure responsible for the elaborate mise-en-scène and elegantly craning camerawork.[10] Far from stabilizing this dispersed subjectivity, however, the fact of authorship only displaces the problem of identity even further: he is *not* who he *is* (or is he?).

Tania Modleski has noted the generic conventions within which Lewis's work may be situated, in opposition to such "auteurist" posturings as my own (77). It is certainly true that comedy serves as a privileged site for the return of repressed anxieties and fears, including the rampant reflexivity of cinematic technique and character formation that I have positioned at the center of Lewis's filmmaking. I nevertheless argue that something unique is staged through the productions of Jerry Lewis. It is not the task of the critic to simply isolate or define Lewis as an auteur (why bother?), but rather to recognize the degree to which this filmmaker may be characterized by his continual aspiration to auteurhood. The status of auteur thus becomes yet another part of the problematic inscription of identity that dominates so many aspects of the Lewis text, rather than an arbitrarily chosen (and somewhat romantic) critical concept. It would certainly be profitable to examine Lewis in the context of other actor-directors such as Orson Welles or Clint Eastwood (who work outside the genre of comedy), all of whom are engaged in the production of what might be called a projected self.

To return to this elusive and elided self, it must be noted that the ambivalence toward the stability of subjectivity does have its positive side. In the "Colgate" episodes, Lewis's improvisational range operates in counterpoint to a film such as *The Nutty Professor,* which acts out the difficulty of maintaining a stable identity in a brilliantly agonized manner. The "Colgates" allow for a similar experience of the slippage of identity, but this is presented instead as a joyous and liberating expression. Again, the gigantic house of *The Ladies Man* provides an effective analogue: particolored and partitioned, the camera at such a distant remove that to see the entire set is to see it *as* a set, Lewis celebrates its very artifice and the phenomenon of false containment. As the camera pulls back, each room is subsumed by the gorgeous entirety, and if that wholeness is finally defined as provisional and explicitly fictive, it is no less gorgeous for that. Subjectivity becomes mercurial, its very fictiveness a cause for celebration.

If, however, this proliferation of Jerrys is evidence of a narcissism, as so many of his critics contend, then it is hardly the passive scene of a Narcissus poised gracefully above a limpid reflecting pool; it is instead a scene set in a Wellesian hall of mirrors, each glass reflecting back a different image. Beneath the struggle to control body, speech, and desire, there exists in Lewis's work an ongoing but finally failing struggle to control identity itself. Here lies the interest of the career of Jerry Lewis, in both its successes and failures. If the characteristic banality of Lewis's rhetoric on "love" and "being a somebody" suggests the presence of a recuperative function (which perhaps reaches its apotheosis in Lewis's role as a healing and uniting force on his annual telethon broadcast along the Love Network), a positivistic attempt to contain and define the subject, then the maze of internal contradictions, displacements, and transformations that crosses these texts continually subverts such a function in a deeply and successfully ambivalent manner.

I wish to conclude this meditation on the functions, both liberating and repressive, of the Jerry Lewis text by noting the one arena that allows for a temporary resolution of the tortured paradoxes, the one site where the struggle for self-control is tentatively won. To watch Jerry Lewis dance is a most particular pleasure. The dance is where the character's uncoordination is transcended as grace and control emerge in fantastic balance. Movements that first seem spastic become instead signals of emancipation: the normally repressive tendencies of the Jerry character and the freedom represented by the act of dance stabilize in a precarious but exhilarating equilibrium. These moments, brief as they are in *The Nutty Professor* and *Cracking Up,* and especially in *Cinderfella* and *You're Never Too Young* (a sequence appropriated by Rainer Werner Fassbinder in his *In a Year with 13 Moons* [1976]), represent a settling, albeit temporary, of the internal conflicts riddling the character. These moments are at the center of nearly every Lewis film and produce a movement of sublime excess. Here is that instant of activated resolution, the emergence of a contradictory but functional self that lies poised at an uneasy intersection of order and chaos. These sequences, and not the final speeches on "being a somebody," constitute the climaxes of the films in their fulfillment of a tantalizing promise of unity.

But it is important that these moments are so often literal illusions: the astonishing dance in *Cinderfella* follows Fella's magical transformation; the pas de deux with Miss Cartilege in *The Ladies Man* may, or may not, be a dream. At the center of his work, then, Jerry Lewis produces an illusory and temporary transcendence that is to be recognized as such and nothing more. And although this transcendence is the promise of the Lewis text, it very rarely is the ending.

It is now a staple of cinematic theorization that the movie screen serves as a Lacanian mirror, providing the spectator with an ego-ideal. Our experience before this mirror reassures and resituates us at the perfect center of a stable world. The Lewis film, it should now be clear, often presents something quite different, and perhaps it is here that the American resistance to Lewis (text and figure) has its genesis. Jerry, far from the idealized and coherent self we are encouraged to see, is instead more closely aligned with the image of the infant, as Lacan put it, "still sunk in his motor incapacity and nursling dependence" (Lacan, 1977, 2). An image of motor incapacity, sexual ambiguity, and unfixed identity: surely these are the precise phenomena that must be denied by the ego craving reinforcement. And so the spectators are placed in the radical position of searching into the mirror's depths, only to find reflected back the incoherent and fragmented, multiplied yet elusive image of Jerry Lewis.[11]

Notes

1. "What happens in an analysis is that the subject is, strictly speaking, constituted through a discourse" (Lacan, 1985, 93).

2. At the same time, it must be acknowledged that within an assessment of Dean Martin's career, a break certainly does exist, and a liberating one at that.

3. The other hosts included Eddie Cantor, Bud Abbott and Lou Costello, and Donald O'Connor.

4. Interview with the author, Las Vegas, June 27, 1988.

5. On the other hand, whereas the films schematically produce a dual version of masculinity to be played through before the final curtain, the "Colgates" permit a seemingly direct engagement with the genuine affection of these two men. This is a privileged view of a male interdependence that could be seen as an alternative to the traditional, and fully patriarchal, buddy-buddy structure founded upon an exclusion not only of women but of the feminine by definition.

6. This adaptation was prepared by Ralph Nelson and Ernest Glucksman (Lewis's television producer), scripted by Oliver Crawford, and directed by Ralph Nelson.

7. It should also be noted that many of the novels of Philip Roth bear upon these issues in a provocative way and within a similar pathology. For a text that intriguingly parallels *The Nutty Professor,* see Roth's 1974 work, *My Life as a Man.*

8. A fascinating outtake from the production suggests another interpretation. Instead of saying to the overbearing football player, "Perhaps I was stupid," Lewis ad-libs, "Perhaps I was a stupid Jew." *The Nutty Professor* is, of course, easily understood as a discourse of Jewish self-hatred (in which Jerry Lewis is literally transformed into the Italian Dean Martin). The parallel between Lewis and Philip Roth is maintained.

9. Although many critics saw the character as a parody of Dean Martin, the tuxedoed and Brylcreemed figure of Jerry Lewis was familiar to television audiences through his frequent television appearances, including his live 1963 telecasts for ABC.

10. My thanks to the nameless participant who attended "Jerry Lewis: A Film and Television Retrospective" at the American Museum of the Moving Image in New York for pointing this out.

11. A substantially shorter version of this chapter originally appeared in an issue of *Camera Obscura* devoted to the theme of "Male Trouble." Considered in the context of the other articles, as well as the publishing project of the Camera Obscura Collective, I finally became aware of the difficulties that inhere in my appropriation of a primarily feminist discourse on the cinema to locate a site of male "resistance" to partriarchal structures. It occurs to me that I am in a position analogous to Jerry's assumption and introjection of the "hysterical" female position. By claiming the territory of feminism as a legitimate terrain from which to begin to understand my own sexuality and subjectivity, I unwittingly participate in further marginalizing the female by broadening the province of the male. It is here that Goodeve's chapter becomes a valuable corrective to my own by returning us to the presence of the woman in the picture and reminding us of the larger political context that always conditions the process of subject construction. My thanks to Caitlin Kelch for directing my attention to this problem.

References and Additional Reading

Bernheimer, C. 1985. "Introduction, Part 1." In *In Dora's Case: Freud-Hysteria-Feminism,* ed. C. Bernheimer and C. Kahane, pp. 1–18. New York: Columbia University Press.

Doane, Mary Ann. 1987. *The Desire to Desire: The Woman's Film of the 1940s.* Bloomington: Indiana University Press.

Freud, S. 1963a. "A Child Is Being Beaten." In *The Psychology of Love,* ed. P. Rieff, pp. 107–132. New York: Collier Books.

———. 1963b. "Analysis Terminable and Interminable." In *Therapy and Technique,* ed. P. Rieff, pp. 233–271. New York: Collier Books.

Goodeve, T. 1987. "The Female Man: Hysterical Jerry Professes Desire." Unpublished ms.

Lacan, J. 1977. "The Mirror Stage as Formative of the Function of the I." *Écrits,* pp. 1–7. New York: Norton.

———. 1985. "Intervention on Transference." In *In Dora's Case: Freud-Hysteria-Feminism,* ed. C. Bernheimer and C. Kahane, pp. 92–104. New York: Columbia University Press.

Lewis, J. 1971. *The Total Filmmaker*. New York: Random House.
Modleski, T. 1988. "Three Men and Baby M." *Camera Obscura* 17: 69–81.
Polan, D. 1984. "Being and Nuttiness: Jerry Lewis and the French." *Journal of Popular Film* (Spring): 42–46.
———. 1988. "L'idiot de la famille: Jerry Lewis." Unpublished ms.
Roth, Philip. 1974. *My Life as a Man*. New York: Penguin Books.

Woody Allen's *Zelig*

An American Jewish Parody

Ruth Perlmutter

Parody as a pervasive postmodern theory and practice was reinforced in the 1980s by the translation and publication of the works of Mikhail Bakhtin, Russian literary theorist. With weighty terms such as heteroglossia, hybridization, dialogization, double-voicing, auto-critique, the heroic ordeal, refraction, and reaccentuation, Bakhtin elucidates parody's primary target: the disruption of accepted social dicta.[1]

According to Bakhtin, parody is accomplished when contending "voices" are dialogized—that is, when a counterpoint of multiple discourses (language, ideologies, and individual belief systems) dismantle the class-oriented speech of apparent "truth-bearing" characters, those who speak "official languages" (of class, occupation, or geographical region).[2] For Bakhtin, the parodic method of exposing the deceptions of long-held inflated verities serves to demythicize the novel's "most fundamental organizing idea"—the testing of heroes for fidelity, martyrdom, valor. In parodic novels, the heroic discourse itself is on trial.[3] This line of reasoning leads Bakhtin to the conclusion that the most effective parody occurs when the very heart of the novel, the reality of its characters, is transgressed. In what he calls "auto-critique," a character either lives "according to literature" (Don Quixote and Madame Bovary) or, like Marcel Proust, is writing a novel within a novel, thus exposing both the process of making fiction and the reality pretensions of single-line fiction.[4] As an interrogation of the mirror/window realism of the traditional novel, auto-critique is eminently served by the two-voiced conditions of parody—the mimed appropriation of other texts/modes and a critique of sacredness.

Zelig (1983) is a pivotal film for an understanding of Woody Allen's parodic style.[5] From his first film, *What's Up, Tiger Lily?* (1966), he flirted with two primary parodic elements: a play with language that defuses the serious (noncomedic) intentions of an original work and a play with image that interrogates the nature of film. From these flow other parodic concerns, which become even more pronounced in later films and reach fruition in *Zelig:* specifically, his mockery of the movies' promotion of fandom, imitation, and fantasy and a preoccupation with his status as an American Jew inserted into and engulfed by a problematic culture.

More than any other Allen film, *Zelig* exemplifies the elements endemic to Bakhtin's notions of auto-critique as they are applied to cinema: an appropriation of other movies, a transgression of their sacred intent, and a demythification of the Hollywood star syndrome. In no other film is there as emphatic an interaction between a modernist strategy of author-to-character-to-viewer relationships and the cultural criticism inherent in Allen's obsession with movies and with being Jewish. More than a critique of Hollywood and stardom or a demonstration of Allen's stance as master-baiter of that media "monster," the Medusan viewer, *Zelig* is also the essence of "hysterical" parody: mode and character, real life and movies are inextricable from a messianic denunciation of the mediocre coinage of both American and Jewish cultures.

The Insertion of the Author

Zelig is *within* and *about* movie mythology. Nowhere else in Allen's work do we witness as clearly the intentional counterpoint of multiple systems of discourse: that is, the audience's need for heroes (read: stars) and for transparent filmic "as if" reality; the interpolation of author into character (Allen plays the central protagonist, Leonard Zelig);[6] the expectations of comic style and persona from previous films—his gag structures, inside jokes, and erudite intellectual jargon; his ideological framework as a New York Jew converted to psychoanalysis; and, particularly, his self-consciousness about movies *and* comedy. Allen's protagonists (mostly played by himself) are also typically from showbiz and/or movies. Thus, as a comic star, author, or agent and always an insatiable movie buff who plunders previous comics, he is forever playing with the tension between star status and his own self-berating position as the typical schlemiel—that is, the bumbling inferior Jew who both aspires to and mocks the class-conscious world of Gentile gentrification.

Both in method and metaphor, *Zelig* represents Allen's most exhaustive transgression of American Gentile culture by a Jew, a "star," and a comic. A media freak and a nobody, Leonard Zelig becomes a somebody (a star) through the mechanisms of film comedy's primary strategy, metamorphosis, which permits him to be anybody (no matter the minority, ethnicity, professional, or class rank). Besides, the ability to parody himself and real events through different styles and voices, which is the essence of parody,[7] reveals Allen's struggle with author as character as star. As a film about a media freak, *Zelig*'s comic transformations and doublings exist within an intertextual framework of revitalized modes, like newsreels, home movies, the documentary, Hollywood melodrama, movie-fan crazes, and the 1920s-style song-and-dance clichés of vaudeville and musical theater.[8]

The narrative structure, plot, comic action, and editing principle of *Zelig* rest on the changeability of its principal (imaginary) figure, Leonard Zelig. As a "schlemieleon," Zelig moves facilely among numerous voice and image zones. He is not just the auteur playing an ordinary fictional character; he is an insert into actual events and accounts of the 1920s. F. Scott Fitzgerald writes about him; contemporary cultural moguls such as Susan Sontag, Saul Bellow, and Bruno Bettelheim recall him as a familiar icon of that age. Zelig is integrated into popular songs ("You're the tops, you're Leonard Zelig," by Cole Porter) and dances (the "Chameleon" dance), is edited into actual newsreels, and, parodying the crazes associated with Charlie Chaplin, is the inspiration for lunatic fads and paternity/ libel suits.[9] Zelig's body accommodates to different belief systems and societal hierarchies. He can change color, time, space, and dialect, thus personifying the comic's ability to defy natural and physical laws with his body distortions. Zelig can swell, dislocate, and forever adapt.[10]

Zelig's changes stem from two aspects that are always present in the film: the narrative function—Leonard's pandemic (Jewish) sexual anxieties, which first prompt his contortions; and the character function—the subtextual acknowledgment of the transgression of the Hollywood convention of the main character as a single-line central narrative motivation. Thus, to prove masculinity, Leonard must surmount his single-voiced state, hysteria-ridden narcissism, and onanistic sexual preoccupations (note all the references to masturbation in the film) by becoming multiple *male* subjects.[11] In a way characteristic of Allen and therefore a mockery of Hollywood convention, when Zelig finally falls in love with his psychiatrist, he sheds his many incarnations and free-floating (mal)adaptability and moves toward the dominant culture's affirmation of "normalcy"—a single identity involved in a heterosexual romance. In other words, the guilts and moral consciousness that promote Zelig's multiple personalities and male crisis are resolved when he achieves the Hollywood happy end-

Woody Allen as Zelig the "schlemieleon" with Eugene O'Neill in Zelig *(1983)*

ing; that is, when he marries the shiksa who is also, handily, his psychiatrist, there is both narrative harmony (the voices of Zelig are stilled into a single-voiced unity) and sexual resolution, which presumably defuses both his masturbatory inclinations and the ethnic guilt of assimilation.[12]

Thus, *Zelig* is a further extrapolation of Allen's literalizations of himself as the Jew in the WASPish world (consider: his fantasy as a Hasid at Annie Hall's family table). If he can change himself into a goy and marry the oxymoron, the non-Jewish female psychiatrist, he has resolved his own sexual inadequacies (which seem always tied to his Jewishness) while retaining the American dream of assimilation promulgated by the Jewish Hollywood moguls.

The Parody of Speech-types

A primary parodic principle of *Zelig* rests on its accumulation of irreverent language styles, such as the exposure of the ceremonious and pompous tones of the "professional" (academic and medical jargon). The unreal Zelig is authenticated by interviews with real intellectuals such as Saul Bellow and Susan Sontag. These scholars represent Allen's pantheon of household gods, his personal Sanhedrin, called from Mount Zion to witness Zelig's authenticity. As is their wont, they deliver problematic testimony. They describe him by parodying their own scholarly predelictions. Sontag, a noted modernist, characteristically describes him as an aesthetic triumph, whereas Irving Howe, a scholar of Jewish life, considers him an "extreme product of assimilation in the American Jewish experience."

Medical terminology is ridiculed as well in interviews with pompous doctors who examine Zelig, especially the doctor who announces that Zelig will die of a brain tumor and is himself subsequently struck down by one. Zelig adopts the mannerisms of psychiatry so successfully that Dr. Eudora Fletcher, his psychiatrist (played by Mia Farrow), mistakes him for a doctor. "He had such a professional demeanor," she states. Thus, Zelig appropriates institutional discourse while critiquing its conventionality and duplicity.

While the ideological voices throughout the film paradoxically document the existence of a fantasy, they undermine the traditional mechanisms for the authentication of real events and people. The use of an off-screen commentator in the style of a Movietone News narration and the mixture of actual newsreels and interviews with staged interviews that span the 1920s to the 1980s call into question the authority and the ideological premises of the "truth" genres—the talk show interview, the "documentation" of history on film, the authenticity of newsreel footage. In effect, with a restaging of the audacious "invention" of a public personality by the conventional talk show interview, Allen is reexamining the entire realm of the artifice of cinema/TV. The preinvented characters in *Zelig* are interviewed—in color—in 1983 looking back at the days when they made "news" in the 1920s—in grainy black-and-white newsreel format. In an interview with Dr. Fletcher's mother, she badmouths her own husband and daughter, thus reversing celebrity pretensions to a glamorous life-style while exposing the fraudulence of the staged realism of talk show programs—and of *Zelig* itself.

Underlying the critique of multiple modes, professional languages, and hallowed belief systems is a specific parody of Warren Beatty's *Reds* (1981), Hollywood saga of John Reed, the American eyewitness reporter of the Russian Revolution. In the film's one parodic innovation—the appearances of aging leftists as corroborators of Reed's existence—"real" people are talking about a "real" person they knew. The interviewees in *Zelig* dialogically validate Zelig's reality and reputation by talking about an invented character as if real, while also parodying their own rhetorical styles.

Allen's parody of *Reds* reaches virulent proportions in the embedded parody of an overblown Hollywood melodrama that replays Zelig's life. Called *The Changing Man* (Warners Bros., 1935), it mimics the attempt in *Reds*—with its blend of live interviews and melodramatic love story—to make fiction look like history. Moreover, the sequence in *The Changing Man* in which the Dr. Fletcher character scours the world in search of the missing Zelig mocks the excessive nature of Louise Bryant's frantic trek across the ice in Finland in search of John Reed. It could be assumed that Allen's submerged rivalry with Beatty, who appropriated Allen's girlfriend, Diane Keaton, for his own bedmate and costar, and who, with *Reds,* took almost all the Academy Award prizes in 1981 (as *Annie Hall* did in 1977) influenced the conception of *The Changing Man.* The parody of *Reds,* both as fictional documentary and historical melodrama, indicates how much Allen refracts his personal interests "through another's speech in another's language,"[13] thereby exposing the paradox of invention and the "factitious" nature of pretensions to "truth" in movies.

Reaccentuation

Zelig's parodies of the "truth" genres—documentary reporting and the fictionalizing of history in melodrama—reaccentuate the process in classical film construction of creating a plausible "as if" real world.[14] Through an excessive manipulation of continuity editing logic and the passage of a character's voice through multiple registers, *Zelig* both embodies and ironically defies the conventional movie practice of a central consciousness singly carrying and instigating the course of events.

The apparent moral center of the film, moving from self-doubt to self-revelation, and the resolution of his fictive credibility, Zelig exists only by the manipulations of montage. Modally and metaphorically, Zelig slides across the frame as a multiple signifier of the banality of cinematic reconstitution. Literally "built" through editing, Zelig is *the* motivated link, *the* carrier of motion and emotion, *the* example of how a character becomes a metonymic linear structuring device in classical movies (since their inception).

On the one hand, Zelig's uncanny ubiquity challenges the foolish consistency of trapping a central figure within a single-line discourse. The film thus interrogates the classical method of wooing the audience with the logic of sequential flow, progress toward closure, and other structures that propel invested characters along a narrative trajectory.[15] On the other hand, the redistribution of this omniscience not only among posited authors (newscasters, interviewees) who attest to Zelig's magical existence but also in the assumed shapes that he verifies before our eyes reveals an underlying motivation: the use of such distortions as a device for self-protection from betrayal by the fickle idolatry of the viewer. Shedding his own substance in an *apparently* involuntary accommodation to the public's desire for and identification with a hero and/or star, Zelig *becomes* its monstrous product. By assuming all the ridiculous roles dictated by the viewer, he pillories the insidious power of public acclaim. This strikes at the heart of Hollywood's most enduring myth—the Pygmalionesque creation/construction of the hero/star—and thereby interrogates the Frankensteinian nature of viewer involvement in movies: the phenomenon of the monster that is controlled or ultimately destroyed by its creator.

Zelig's passage through stages of angst, self-doubt, and miraculous "heroic" feats—attending a Hitler rally, crossing the Atlantic upside down, using his body magically—epitomizes the way the parodic film repositions the traditional pieties of the heroic ordeal.[16] Cinematically, Zeligism *is* refraction in the sense that a divided and reflected existence restates the star-crazed "hysteria" that underlies the classical text.

Beneath this formal restatement of Hollywood's "dogmatic pretensions to lead a real life"[17] are the syllogistic reversals—stars and viewers are all freaks—that were already evident in the parodic involutions of *Stardust Memories* (1980). Both *Zelig* and *Stardust Memories* revile viewers for their blindness to the magical qualities of film and the sanctity of the Holy Fools that make them.

Long before *Zelig* (even in his first film, *What's Up, Tiger Lily?* where Allen plays a projectionist whose shadow making love on screen interferes with the image track), the idea of Zeligism provided Allen with a major parodic device for escaping fictional containment within the cinematic frame.[18] He yearns to "be" like someone else (Bogey), to be elsewhere

(Kugelmass), to be a revolutionary (*Bananas*), and, literally, to get out of his own skin. *Zelig* itself compounds its Zeligism—in an effort to cure the changing man, Dr. Fletcher pretends to be Leonard's patient, with his ailment. In a public TV interview, a man on the street wistfully says, "I wish I could be Leonard Zelig." Echoing these Zelig-like anxieties in the preface to his autobiographical play *The Floating Light Bulb* (1982), Allen flatly states that the author's "one regret in life is that he is not someone else."[19]

The whimsy of his vicarious longings allows Allen as Zelig to critique cinema from within—as a "filmic" man who is created by the invention of self and film. Zeligism exposes the limitations of character/actor and author/narrator status within a film. A creation of the editing room, Zelig defies spatial logic and continuity as well as his own reality. His changeability is a reflection of the dreamlike quality of film. Like Buster Keaton's *Sherlock, Jr.*, and Dziga Vertov's "Man with a Movie Camera," Zelig's transports into many fantasized selves represent an auto-critical demonstration of the artifice in staging the illusion of reality.

The overdeterminism of Zelig—his presence as the epitome of narrative excess—creates an infinite regression of self-consciousness. Just as in Allen's short story "The Kugelmass Episode," where the protagonist wishes himself into Emma Bovary's salon, Zelig's interventions reveal the deception of fictional logic.[20] In the shifts between Zelig as a comic performer (read: freak) and as a literalization of Allen's envy of the "Other"—the American, the non-Jew—Allen's views are merged with his character's belief system while also reflecting the film's collective voices. This explains why it is significant that long before we hear Zelig's voice even indirectly on a tape, we hear about him in the canonized tones of public opinion.[21] The true filmic man, Zelig has dissolved himself into the text, merged with others, and only lives according to the conventions and artifices of cinema.

The film's putdown of official movie culture reflects how central *Zelig* is to modernist themes: the challenging of authority, both in terms of social hierarchies and textual illusionism; the assertion that the reconstituted self is the only reality; the assumption that citational works are the only texts and irony the only appropriate contemporary posture. *Zelig*'s modernism stems from a tension between the regressive narcissism implicit in self-creation and a distinctly adversarial and antinostalgic tonality. What remains is a text that challenges the spectator with an invented compositional protagonist. If Zelig's self-cancellations turn against celebrity cultism and the spectator's credulity in Hollywood's conquest of reality by fantasy, they also mock the heavy-handed terminology of cultist interpretations. The excoriation of spectatorial competence crosses class lines—

from the inadequacy of popular culture to satisfy the yearnings of the mass audience for stars and their fantasy life to the derision of pronouncements by recognized cultural authorities.

Comic Metamorphosis
and the American Jew

Underlying Zelig's involutional conformities is a condemnation of the insidious results of narcissism and nostalgia, both cinematically and societally. As a formalist exercise in editing, Zelig's endless replacements attack the viewer's gullibilities. As social comment, the film *Zelig* connects self-conscious paranoia with the immorality implicit in accommodation. Zelig's anxiety over the American public's rejection leads him to an outrageous transformation into one of Hitler's claque. Not only is the humor compounded by such an unthinkable role for an American Jew, but the tone of mock seriousness camouflages Allen's messianic impulse. Allen himself has stated that the film is not a "pleasant fantasy of metamorphosis but about the kind of personality that leads to fascism" (James, 25).

Within the film, Saul Bellow, as one of the pundits, interprets Zelig's Nazi switch as a means of satisfying a desire to become "anonymous," to "immerse himself in the mass," even a mass that promises his own destruction. This echoes Allen's implicit attack on the viewer masses that can applaud a "psychotic" act: "It shows you what you can do if you're psychotic"—Zelig addressing the crowd that gives him tickertape adulation upon his return from Germany—with the implication that the crowd that adulates a psychotic is itself suspect.

Zelig's changes and accommodations are also extensions of Allen's ideological framework as an American Jewish comic suffering "the ordeal of civility." As "the changing man," he wanders between masturbatory self-analysis and guilt from abandoning the Jewish "ethic" for the Protestant "etiquette" (Cuddihy). He is the Jew who dares to insert himself into culture and discovers that he also inherits a fictive reality and a morally corrupt world.

The mask of the freak, the exhibitionist, the *apparent* innocent, hides—as Bettelheim suggests in the film—the fact that Zelig is "the ultimate conformist."[22] Underlying his transformations and desire to be like others is Zelig's assimilation anxiety. Eager to be absorbed into the dominant culture, he epitomizes the dilemma of the American Jew who wants to change his or her ethnic envelope in order to be socially integrated. *Zelig*, then, sums up Allen's notions throughout his career: innocence, romance, nostalgia, morality have been betrayed. As an *apparently* self-hating Jewish comic, the loss of America as a locus of values is also laid

Woody Allen as Zelig flanked by Presidents Calvin Coolidge and Herbert Hoover

at the door of ethnic collision with American consumer culture. Heir to the "immigrant culture shock" comics—Charlie Chaplin, the Marx Brothers—Zelig enacts the legacy of rootlessness and loss of patriarchal constraints (domesticity, monogamy, family loyalty) and becomes the victim as well as perceiver of the contending voices that trouble the Western world.[23]

He uses the safety of the comic—vulgar taste, aggression, antisocial behavior, confusion of genre registers, and formal dislocations in order to suggest that the crisis of the maker and the spectator to comedy is also the crisis of Jewishness and American culture. In the spirit of Amos who denounced his self-indulgent people as "the kine of Bashan," Allen is reviling Americans and Jews for their bad taste and capitulation to the superficial.

Never at home anywhere, yet struggling to reinvent a home in other shapes and forms, Zelig/Allen personifies Theodore Herzl's view that an emancipated Jew never leaves the ghetto except through illusion. Ravaged by the pressure to make it in America, obsessed with the need to record truth in art and life, Allen has made *Zelig,* his most radical deconstruction of cinema, into an acomedic lament for the impossibility of his task.

The supreme filmic parodist, Allen has entered the parodic world through Ellis Island. The continual argument underlying the multivoiced contentiousness of his life's *ordeals* has the structure and flavor of his Tal-mudic ancestors, who have always been confined to the ghetto to argue eternal issues with each other.

The Two "Roses": *Broadway Danny Rose* and *The Purple Rose of Cairo*

Allen's work can be considered a working through of two poles of self-categorization. He subverts previous traditions and outmoded conventions of the cinematic canon in order to warn against the real dangers to society of easy accommodations to mediocrity. Yet he incorporates these within a "pleasant fantasy of metamorphosis," accompanied by running gags, movie buffery, and movie buffoonery that reveal his view of the malicious absurdity of reality.

In earlier films, his protagonists are like Keaton's Sherlock, Jr.—inno-cent voluptuaries of Hollywood "romance," either receiving directives from a revered hero as in *Play It Again, Sam* (1972) or as a schlemiel whose exposure of his self-hating worries covertly exposes societal preten-sions, as in *Manhattan* (1979). Since 1980, with *Stardust Memories,* Al-len's growing self-assurance allows him to express his ambivalence about the relationship between his comic muse and the moral turpitude of the public vampire. An investigation into the problematic nature of cinema "magic" interacts with the comic strategies of replacement and Allen's own brand of literalization, his Bovarist wit. Thus, his anachronistic self-insertion into official "sacred cows" blends with cinematic manipulation the comic's ability to become someone else[24] and to question the nature and benevolence of reality itself.

In the two "rose" films that followed *Zelig* (*Broadway Danny Rose* [1984] and *Purple Rose of Cairo* [1985]), Allen contends in a gentler vein with the public's star crazes, which prompt Zeligism in his protagonists.[25] Pedagogically, he valorizes freaks who live in the grotesquerie of so-called normal reality and fantasize a world with "rose"-colored glasses. Instead of pillorying the process that creates public idols in *Zelig* and *Star-dust Memories,* Allen lingers on the more redemptive aspects of literaliza-tion and the conquest of reality by cinema: his protagonists either choose a higher life-style as in *Danny* or an ideal narrative in which to be reborn as in *Purple Rose*. The title of *Broadway Danny Rose* itself embeds a belief in transformation and the possibility for a modern "ascension." Danny "Rose" has bloomed in the spiritual desert of Broadway. As a nurturer of many Zeligs yearning to be stars, he imbues his "nobodies" with his scrip-tural homiletics: "acceptance, forgiveness and love."[26]

Purple Rose makes a more definitive separation between the simpler inadequacies of Hollywood and the gloom of the real world. While morally culpable actors are captured on the screen mouthing cultural pieties, Allen's "real-life" story takes place in a tenement in the slums where a Chaplinesque heroine suffers physical abuse from an unbearable bully.

Only thin disguises for other Allen transplants (stand-up comics, theatrical agents), the character mutations in *Purple Rose* sustain the Allen spirit of the "filmic" comic—movie buff, conjuror, inventor—who entertains the customers while picking the pockets of their accepted culture. Allen's (and Zelig's) presence flirts around the edges of a screen in which is embedded the paradox that not only are movies an escape from failed romance, deceptions, and harsh realities, but they also reveal the sad vicariousness beneath the viewer's narcissistic identification. With a relief born of that sadness, we welcome the heroine's return to the protection of the "magic" movie house.

Zelig's quixotic challenges of societal tyrannies and questioning of the benevolence of reality are harbingers of the redemptive pedagogy of *Danny Rose* and *Purple Rose*. After *Zelig*, we have no choice but to accompany Allen through Joyce's cracked or Alice's magic mirror and enter the spiritual world of Danny or the magic world of early Hollywood movies.

Conclusion

If the persona of Zelig and the essence of Zeligism turn on the irony of accommodation, the film itself reflects on the transformative and ultimately duplicitous nature of film. Zelig, the comic subject, and *Zelig* the film, the metatext, encompass the paradox of parody. Not only are they both self-engendering—Zelig spins identities out of himself like a caterpillar, while the film strives to control the subject (as character/author) *and* the narrative. They are also self-transgressive—humor and irony arise out of Zelig's violation of norms, while he and the text incorporate and adapt to them.

If the author is both omnipresent and absorbed into the text, so is the viewer. *Zelig*'s hyperbolic editing style mocks our mythologies (Hollywood star craze) and the modes/fictional universe that forms our shared belief systems. In the end, the double-voiced parodic text incorporates us by demanding our competence as decoders of its forebears, while its manipulations and transgressions evaluate—indeed, lead us to question—our cultural mystifications.

The humor in *Zelig* arises from the disruption of canonized formal and social forms. Zelig's shifting identity challenges and acts out the institutional modes of representation in social life and in cinema—at once central subject, hero, star, poseur, exemplar, of the crisis of both his masculinity and ethnic assimilation and, most particularly, the self-denigrating anticomic whose animus is finally directed at the impercipient and cannibalistic viewer.

The presumption in this inextricable cinematic embrace between the viewer's distortions and the characters' transformations to escape an unacceptable reality lies in the creation of a character sutured together until whipped into shape in order to survive the culture and the rules of film. Thus, the innate contradiction in Zelig as an adaptive character and as a character who is trying to wrest control of his own narrative acknowledges and challenges the acterly and fictional traditions of a character contained within a continuity.

This character hybridization—Zelig as both a freak (societal deviant, exceptional man with a unique identity) and a conformist (loser of identity) fed to the consuming public—reinforces a view of parody as a modal barometer of the social self. Grounded in a dialogized interrogation of the cinematic mythmaking process—the "framing" of characters in the time and space of a Hollywood romance—*Zelig* exemplifies the parodic link among allusion to primary cinematic texts, formal binding consistencies, and social practices. For one, there is a disruption of the unity of character through temporal disorientations. An involuted critique of the reconstitution of a character within a parody of the *March of Time* parody of the reconstituted life of Citizen Kane, further dialogized in *Zelig* by the reconstitution of "real-life" characters as they would look today (in color) redefining their past relationship to Zelig (in black and white), puts into play the whole notion of the invention of a chronology of a life as-if-real, while it also reflects on the capricious nature of memory, history, and their reconstruction. For another, *Zelig* reaccentuates the viewer-parody of Hollywood romance in *Sherlock, Jr.* (1924; a primary text for Allen's parodies, from *What's Up, Tiger Lily?* through *Purple Rose*). Zelig as an "impossible" character inserted within self-created "impossible" events and situations ends up catching "the girl of his dreams." The narrative is closed not only with the character's restoration to a single identity but also with a final irony: the proverbial happy ending suggests that "escape" has led to fictional conformity à la *Sherlock, Jr.*

The film's epilogue plays with the tradition of Hollywood closure with a double entendre joke about endings. At the beginning of the film, Zelig lies about having read *Moby Dick* and suffers his first transformation (multiple self) and, paradoxically, his first wished-for conformity (single self). At the end of the film, it is stated that on his deathbed he confessed that he was in the middle of the book and his only regret was that he could not live long enough to find out how it ended—thereby reopening the parody of filmic truth and Hollywood endings.

Notes

1. For explanations of Bakhtin's terms as they apply to Allen's parodic style, see notes 6, 7, 8, 13, 14, 15, 16, and 17.
2. Bakhtin (291, 304, 311, 374).
3. Bakhtin (388).
4. Bakhtin (414).
5. Another comedic trend for Allen are the films strung along by gags—such as *Take the Money and Run* (1969)—that owe a great deal to Allen's avowed influence, Bob Hope.
6. Bakhtin calls the mechanism of author insertion and absorption among characters "direct authorial narration" (262).
7. Bakhtin calls this the stylization of oral everyday material (262).
8. Bakhtin calls this the stylization of written narration—that is, letters, diaries, and so on that in cinema extends to modal insertions such as letters, signs, photos, paintings, TV screens, other movies, and performance codes (262). Hutcheon discusses *Zelig*'s "cross-genre play" as a "cinematic parody of the television documentary and movie newsreel" (18). She also points out that *Zelig* is a parody of *They Might Be Giants* (d. Anthony Harvey, 1971), where the protagonist believes he is Sherlock Holmes and is treated by a female psychiatrist named Dr. Watson (110).
9. McCabe describes the Chaplin mania, which includes Chaplin buttons, dances such as the "Chaplin Waddle," and paternity suits leveled against Chaplin (79).
10. According to Durgnat, *Zelig* belongs to this comic tradition: the "trucage" (trickery) of Georges Méliès, the double nature of Chaplin's persona, the defiance of the laws of continuity and spatial logic in the formulaic Hollywood "romance" in *Sherlock, Jr.,* and the verbal anarchy of the Marx Brothers and their forbears have all thrived on the doubling strategies of mime, pose, mask, and self-display that underlie their visual and verbal games of wit. The power of silent comedy derives from comic figures who defy natural and physical laws by virtue of the manipulations of cinema.

According to Hutcheon, the majority of theorists consider parody a subgenre of the comic because it usually holds its model up to ridicule. In Hutcheon's view, irony more than ridicule is a parodic principle, and especially in modernist metaparody, the tendency is to say something serious, positive (rather than just pejorative), and reverential (rather than just mocking). The strategies in *Zelig* certainly produce irony and serious explorations of societal customs and institutions. The reverence comes in the homages to the magic of cinema (51).
11. Zelig can change only into other men. Cross-gendering has not been a parodic device for Allen.
12. Allen is also voicing an autobiographical litany of culpability in succumbing to American culture. He refashions his dependency on psychoanalysis to actual "transference"; he rewrites his real-life love affair; he converts his own intermarriage discomfort into malaise about the false consciousness of Hollywood romance. By the outrageous insertion of a Hollywood romantic reunion at a Nazi rally with Zelig as a Nazi cohort, Allen even assuages his American Jewish guilt

complex about being spared the Holocaust (compare the compulsion to see *The Sorrow and the Pity* (1971) over and over again in *Annie Hall*), while impaling both the Mephistophelian seduction of Hollywood and its grotesque offspring, the American dream.

13. This is Bakhtin's definition of "refraction." (324)

A further personal refraction and parody of the Beatty-Keaton relationship could be in Zelig's settling down with a "better" shiksa than the neurotic Annie Hall (played by Keaton). Therefore, it is significant that Zelig/Allen is cured by a Gentile psychiatrist, who is played by Allen's live-in mate, Mia Farrow. Refraction and the dialogization of author's life and characters go hand in hand.

14. Reaccentuation is a term used by Bakhtin for textual innovation and restatement.

15. Bakhtin terms this "the impulse to continue" and "the impulse to end" (32).

16. This conforms to Bakhtin's notion that the comic novel desacralizes.

17. This is how Bakhtin describes the distortions of the classical novel (414).

18. One wonders if this highly comic device is an inverse reflection of Allen's ethnic discomfort and guilt, as in the scene when he mortifyingly and hilariously sees himself as a Hasid at Annie's grandma's table.

19. Replacement strategies have been constants in Allen's work, and they extend not only to sexual fantasies but to the resolution of Allen's competition with and for women. In *Play It Again, Sam*, he loves his buddy's wife and surrenders her à la *Casablanca* (1943). In *Manhattan*, while excoriating his adulterous buddy's immorality, he plays around with his girlfriend. *Stardust Memories* replays Allen's resentments toward his ex-girlfriend, Diane Keaton. Her persona is recast (by Charlotte Rampling) as an extreme neurotic. In *Broadway Danny Rose*, Danny plays John Alden and wins the girlfriend of his Italian singer client. Even *Hannah and Her Sisters* (1986) plays musical beds with the Allen protagonist. He is replaced in his relationship with Hannah by a male who lusts after one of her sisters, while he (the Allen persona) ends up with the third.

20. See Yacowar for a more extensive discussion of Allen's short story (95).

21. The first time we actually hear his voice is in a taped interview, where he refers to himself as someone else, a psychiatrist. Until then, his character is described—in newsreels, songs, and by others. His voice is not heard directly until half the movie is over, and there again he pretends to be a psychiatrist, making jokes about fees and his course in advanced masturbation.

22. Hutcheon not only connects Zelig's physical changes to his desire "to be loved" and "to fit in"; she points out the ideological connection between his assimilation anxieties and the rise of Hitler and the Holocaust—which was leveled against those who did not "fit" (110).

23. Characteristically, Zelig's first changes reflect his assimilation duplicity. They occur because of his intellectual shame—he had to pretend he had read the great American novel *Moby Dick*—and because he was not wearing green on St. Patrick's Day.

24. With replacement, comics are always becoming someone else—either by changing their body shapes or sexual identity (for example, the infantilized contortions of Jerry Lewis) or by serving as victims of mechanical objects that run

amok (in Buster Keaton's conversion gags, machines overpower him until he uses, indeed, "becomes" them for his survival).

25. *Broadway Danny Rose* and *The Purple Rose of Cairo* also reaffirm the pre-modernist belief in the self-creative power of the imagination to alter reality. Romanticist devices of illumination—the magic lantern in *A Midsummer Night's Sex Comedy* (1982)—and the transmogrifying magic trick in the play *The Floating Light Bulb* actually mediate between grotesque reality and "lovable" freaks.

26. In terms of the comic strategies of replacement and the desire to enter the mainstream, Danny himself is a dialogic character. Conspicuously wearing a giant gold medallion with the Hebrew letter *Chai,* he is the Jewish John Alden. He acts as intermediary in his client's romance, and as a result, he not only gets the Italian shiksa, but he also "converts" her from cynicism to his essentially religious philosophy. As a consequence, the "deli" ("stage" for the affabulation of Danny, its marquee opens and closes the film) where all the comics hang out awards Danny his "Oscar." A symbolic testimony to the rewards of assimilation, a Jewish-Italian sandwich will bear his name.

References and Additional Reading

Bakhtin, M. M. 1981. *The Dialogic Imagination.* Austin: Texas University Press.

Cuddihy, John Murray. 1974. *The Ordeal of Civility.* New York: Dell.

Durgnat, Raymond. 1969. *The Crazy Mirror: Hollywood Comedy and the American Image.* New York: Dell.

Hutcheon, Linda. 1985. *A Theory of Parody.* New York: Methuen.

James, Caryn. 1986. "Auteur! Auteur!" *New York Times Magazine,* January 19, p. 25.

McCabe, John. 1978. *Charlie Chaplin.* Garden City, N.Y.: Doubleday.

Perlmutter, Ruth. 1982. "The Melting Plot and the Humoring of America." *Film Reader* 5: 247–256.

Yacowar, Maurice. 1979. *Loser Takes All.* New York: Ungar.

The Mouse Who Wanted to F—k a Cow

Cinematic Carnival Laughter in Dusan Makavejev's Films

Andrew Horton

The elephant who wanted to stamp out a mosquito eventually came out as the mouse who wanted to fuck a cow.

Dusan Makavejev (69)

Carnival Laughter and Film Comedy: Limits and Potential

Mikhail Bakhtin's multifaceted concept of the carnivalesque as expressed in *Rabelais and His World* and briefly explained in our introduction has at least four implications for the study of film comedy.[1] First, Bakhtin's approach is sociological/contextual. From Bakhtin's perspective we must search beyond the confines of genre and of the aesthetic to see a particular comic text in "dialogue" with a polyphony of voices in any given culture and time period. Second, in terms of film comedy, the initial obvious distinction is between the medieval European culture Bakhtin writes about and our own postindustrial capitalist and Puritan-influenced American society.

Bakhtin defines carnival in part as "the people's second life, organized on the basis of laughter" (1968, 66). Clearly, contemporary American culture has no such analogous recognized and sanctioned embodiment of a "second life" running counter to the perceived norms and hierarchy of society.

This sense of celebration is for the period of carnival one of near total freedom. Carnival was, Bakhtin explains, all encompassing; it embodied speech and act, the head and the "lower bodily stratum." Except for the much tamer version of carnival witnessed in New Orleans's Mardi Gras, such a realm of complete expression has not been part of our American heritage, cultural or cinematic. Clearly there have been various levels of censorship, direct and subtle, that have assured that films (and television) have presented a much more limited view of freedom than that of carnival, especially in the territory of the sexual and scatalogical.

Third, the carnivalesque is not only a celebration but a critique, and often a parody, of the other life: that of the Catholic church, the state, and daily existence. Thus, within such a popular festive framework in the Middle Ages, parodies per se played a major role. In particular, parodies of sacred texts (*parodia sacre*) were especially popular.

Fourth, this observation leads to Bakhtin's emphasis on the ambiguity of carnival as a double vision of existence. As simultaneously a celebration and a critique, carnival (and parody) implies that "the death of the old is linked with regeneration: all the images are connected with the contradictory oneness of the dying and reborn world" (1968, 217). Therefore, it is impossible to label such laughter as progressive or conservative, for it is both at the same time.

In terms of cinema, several points can be made immediately. One is that although American cinema has had no direct relationship with a carnivalesque culture as seen in medieval Europe (and reflected in writers such as François Rabelais), much of silent film comedy was created and performed by vaudevillians—that is, those raised in a "popular," nonliterary art form geared for as broad a public as was possible. The world of physical comedy, which was liberated from the prison house of language, made this silent medium a universal signifying system aimed at and dedicated to laughter. William Paul's chapter earlier in this book, "Charles Chaplin and the Annals of Anality," emphasizes how much "carnivalesque" attention, for instance, Chaplin gives to "the lower bodily stratum," although later critics, unattentive or unsympathetic to such a broadly based concept of comedy, chose to ignore or pass over this important element.

These remarks relate, of course, to content: to what degree do we find a carnivalesque atmosphere or subject matter in film comedy? But Bakhtin's writings encourage us to look beyond subject matter to form and structure as well. How can a comic filmmaker use film to overturn the "everyday" ways of presenting comic narratives on film?

Here again, Hollywood's approach to comedy, particularly since the advent of sound films, has been channeled into "classical" structures and genres. More specifically, the American film comedy tradition has been predominantly that of romantic literary (written/scripted) comedy. As such it is much more closely aligned to William Shakespeare (as Stanley Cavell has cogently detailed) than to Rabelais.

Furthermore, we must acknowledge the modes of production in Holly-

wood as working against an expression of "the people's second life."
Whereas it is the goal of a consumer-driven culture to create a mass audience, it is the nature of capitalism, especially today as megacorporations
swallow other megacorporations, to consolidate power in the hands of a se-
lect few. The application of Bakhtin to American sound comedy, therefore, has by definition a limited direct use, which is perhaps best represented by his discussion of ambiguity in comedy.

If not in Hollywood, then where might the carnivalesque more fruitfully
be seen in film? I wish to suggest that one of the most fertile examples exists in a remarkable series of films made by the Yugoslav director Dusan
Makavejev in the late 1960s and early 1970s.

Makavejev has delighted, disturbed, and puzzled audiences everywhere
for more than two decades. All agree that he is refreshingly original as a
jesting practitioner of a dialectical form of comedy/parody/satire. And yet
no satisfying study of his films has managed to outline or embrace the
complex ambiguity and exhilaration of Makavejev's accomplishment.

Makavejev has been labeled, for instance, the father of a "cinema of collage" (Armes). Through surprising juxtapositioning of shots and equally
incongruous composition within the frame and within the sound track,
he playfully exposes how personal freedom (especially as expressed
through sexuality) is thwarted, repressed, and misdirected by political-
social ideologies. In a strikingly original series of films—*Man Is Not a
Bird* (*Covek ni je tica,* 1965), *The Loves of a Switchboard Operator*
(*Ljubavni slucaj: Ili, tragedija sluzbenice PTT,* 1967), *Innocence Unprotected* (*Nevinost bez zastite,* 1968), and *W.R.: Mysteries of the Organism*
(*WR—misterije organizma,* 1971)—Makavejev emerged as the best-
known director of a talented group of Yugoslav filmmakers in the 1960s
known loosely as "The Black Cinema," a title conferred on them by
Yugoslav officials who found their critical attitude toward all social and
political ideologies uncomfortably "negative."

My suggestion is that we can examine his work, especially his Yugoslav
films, as some of the purest examples we have in world cinema of a wide-
ranging carnivalesque form of parody and comedy. With specific attention
to *Innocence Unprotected* and *W.R.: Mysteries of the Organism,* I wish to
briefly map how Makavejev's early films embody a spirit and form of carnival parody and freedom that celebrate what Mikhail Bakhtin sees as the
essence of the carnivalesque—a state of becoming or, more accurately, of
"unfinalizedness" (Morson, x). Finally, I aim to bring into focus an aspect
of carnivalesque comedy that has been ignored or underplayed in the study
of comedy: that the temporary freedom of carnival laughter sets the stage
for violence and sacrifice, a juncture that suggests the close connection between the comic and the tragic or "serious" (Girard, 1977, 1986).

Carnival Parody
and Innocence Transcended

Real movies do something quite deep.
Dusan Makavejev (Oumano, 253)

Makavejev is most often identified with a postmodernist tradition bounded by the satiric surrealism of Luis Buñuel, on the one hand, and the dialectical play of documentary and illusionist elements found in Dziga Vertov and Jean-Luc Godard (Eagle). Such remarks are not a disservice, but they do not go far enough. For Makavejev is the cinematic heir to a long Serbian tradition of folk parody and humor, which means his films are premodernist as well as postmodernist.

Simply stated, the facts are these. Serbia was under Turkish domination from 1389 until the late nineteenth century. During this occupation, the Serbs preserved their identity through their language and their oral folk epic poetry. The folk epics dating from the fourteenth century fall into several categories, but one of the most popular is known as the "Marko cycle." This group of poems features a hero who is a Serb outlaw ambiguously working for and against the Turks. He is a slave to no one, however, and manages to triumph through deception and guile more often than not, although he is at times the butt of the jokes and abuse of others.

A sense of folk carnivalesque parody and humor expressed in such an "outlaw mentality" has thus long been of immense importance to the Serbian national character. According to Yugoslav scholar Svetozar Koljevic, Serbian folk laughter was clearly a defense mechanism against the despair of life under the Turks. As such, it emerged as a fantasy or carnivalesque triumph over the oppressive enemy. "Laughter thus becomes a kind of power for the helpless," he writes, "and this ancient function of comedy in life and art is nowhere so richly mirrored in Serbo-Croatian epic singing as in the poems about Marko Kraljevic" (209).

In the poem "The Wedding of Marko Kraljevic," for instance, Marko is a complete parody of the traditional epic hero. In his freewheeling speech, this Balkan outlaw mocks the most sacred customs and norms of Serbian patriarchal culture. He cannot find a woman to marry who pleases both him and his mother. But when he finally finds such a bride, he is forced to contend with the lustful ambitions of his best man. When he discovers his trusted friend has attempted to seduce his wife-to-be the night before the wedding, Marko kills his best man in a scene that becomes a parody of a romantic death scene, ending with the ironic line, "And of one body, he made two bodies."

As examples of folk poems, composed anonymously and passed down from generation to generation, these works are clear examples of parody on a carnivalesque level. Furthermore, they are oral folk songs that were sung at festive occasions, including carnivals. Thus, Marko emerges as a double-edged folk hero: he is both irreverent fool and popular hero, a trickster tricked and a triumphant common man able to survive under oppressive circumstances.

Such a double vision reflects the power of the carnivalesque to celebrate the individual's potential while critiquing his or her limitations. Finally, the outlaw mentality of Serbian parody is a statement through laughter against oppression of any persuasion. The outlaw exists happily and gloriously outside all sociopolitical norms. And yet, as in the case of Marko's wedding, the outlaw lends validity to the rituals he parodies by his participation in them.

Obviously there are other forms of carnivalesque humor in Yugoslavia, including a popular surrealistic strain in art and printed literature. Most recently, for instance, Milorad Pavic's innovative novel *Dictionary of the Khazars,* published in "male" and "female" editions, playfully evokes such a tradition as it invites the reader to experience the "narrative" in any order he or she pleases with the least satisfying approach being, according to one reviewer, the straightforward, traditional method (Coover).

Keeping in mind Bakhtin's twin perspective of celebration and critique, we should adopt a double approach to Makavejev as well. On the one hand, as I have already suggested, we should consider the degree to which Makavejev's films are part of a long tradition of carnivalesque culture. It's worth noting, for instance, that Makavejev introduces the carnivalesque into his films beginning with the first scene in his first feature, *Man Is Not a Bird.* At a carnival in a small Serbian town a magician appears who lectures the crowds on "magic," suggesting that under his hypnotic spells, they can learn to liberate themselves from earthly cares and "fly."

I wish also to explore how his films function as metafilms critiquing film language and history while simultaneously celebrating cinema's potential as a form of liberated personal expression (Rose). Finally, and even more significantly, we then will be in a better position to appreciate how such carnivalesque parodies critique the levels of political repression Makavejev exposes as operating within his country and, in *W.R.,* abroad as well.

In *Innocence Unprotected,* Makavejev manipulates six narrative levels to create a critique of an early Serbian film and the dimensions of Nazi destruction and Quisling collaboration as well as a celebration of film as a medium of liberation and self-expression. Briefly told, the film's title is actually that of the first feature sound film made in Serbia. Ironically it was not made by a filmmaker but by a Serbian daredevil entertainer, Dragoljub Aleksic, in 1942 during the German occupation of Yugoslavia.

Makavejev uses a number of sequences from the original black-and-white film, which is a naive romantic melodrama involving Aleksic's love (yes, he stars in the film as well!) for a young beauty, Milica, whom he must protect from a lusting old fellow, Mr. Petrovic.

Employing the original film as his basic text, Makavejev cross-cuts between Aleksic's film, documentary footage of the German occupation at that time (also in black and white) and contemporary (1967) interviews in color with Aleksic and others who worked on the film a quarter century earlier. There are also documentary sequences of Aleksic performing daring feats around Belgrade in the past and as an aging man in the present.

But this is not all. Makavejev's carnivalesque collage goes two steps further: as the film progresses, some twenty years before the American "colorization" process for old films, he begins to hand-paint objects within the frame of Aleksic's film (the overly red lips of the heroine in one scene, the golden wine on the table in another; both with the color splashing out of the confines of the object as in a child's first efforts to "stay within the lines"). And he makes use of the sound track to juxtapose incongruous popular and political songs to add aural as well as visual complexity to his parody.

The effect of such a seemingly random cinematic scrapbook is one of liberating laughter and of unexpected pleasure in the savoring of the multiplicity of incongruous "texts" that emerge in our, the viewers', minds. Such a free-for-all format that is so strongly anti-Aristotelean and counter to classical Hollywood narrative invites us to enter the text wherever we please. As Makavejev has said, "What I smuggle into my films, does not necessarily have to be what you smuggle out of the film for yourself" (Oumano, 254).

Consider Makavejev's presentation of his protagonist, Dragoljub Aleksic, the man and the entertainer (daredevil and filmmaker/actor/performer). Like Marko the outlaw, Aleksic emerges as a popular hero/fool/entertainer. A simple man who has risen to fame on his own merits, Aleksic is obviously an exaggerated reflection and parody of the Serbian people. His strength lies not in politics, poetry, public service, or religion. Rather, he has the ability to hang from airplanes by his teeth (chomping a swing at the end of a rope dangled from the plane), explode sticks of dynamite in his mouth, be shot from canons, or balance various objects on a high wire without a net below. As an actor, of course, he is laughable, but his "innocent" energy and daring rescues cannot help but entertain us and the Yugoslav audiences who first saw the film.

When one adds the 1967 interviews, a portrait of a man with an insatiable ego emerges. Is Makavejev simply satirizing Aleksic using the man's own words and film to create an auto-critique? Certainly we laugh *at* Aleksic throughout the film. He is so completely without a sense of

Dragoljub Aleksic in the "present" (1967) documentary sequence within Dusan Makavejev's Innocence Unprotected *(1968)*

irony himself, so unaware how bizarre his stunts appear to us, particularly because time itself works against him: the 1967 footage shows him pumping iron in a ludicrous attempt to maintain the body that is now long past its prime. But in a spirit similar to the freedom of carnival, Makavejev draws no conclusions, makes no easy judgments. Aleksic—daredevil, youthful actor, and aging man—simply is. And certainly on a level beyond laughter the audience is free to admire this "outlaw-hero" as a survivor and as someone who obviously has enjoyed himself entertaining others.

Makavejev's interjection of history (the Nazi occupation) adds a much darker hue to his carnivalesque collage. He skillfully cuts, for instance, between a shot of the evil Mr. Petrovic lustfully approaching the young heroine and documentary footage of the German entry into a bombed-out Belgrade where countless dead lie strewn in the rubble (20,000 died on the first day of bombing in 1942). Other cuts are to the Quisling Serbian government.

How are we to read such jarring juxtapositions between melodramatic cinema and tragic history? Bakhtin would suggest that the importance of ambiguity in carnivalesque laughter is that it can be read in multiple ways.

In carnival, therefore, ambiguity itself becomes a virtue, a form of freedom from limitations, dogma, didacticism. Such a polyphony is for Bakhtin at the heart of carnival because it means that under the spell of the carnivalesque, the potential for surprise and delight is never lost. Thus, such a multiingredient narrative gumbo as Makavejev serves up keeps alive the possibility of change, of a fresh perspective, of a new experience.

In the case of *Innocence Unprotected,* we can locate at least six layers of possible response:

1. The triviality of Aleksic's film viewed against the horror of history (World War II, the occupation)
2. The surprising similarity between the simplistic "good versus evil" scenario of Aleksic's pop film and Hitler's master plan
3. The "innocence unprotected" of both the Yugoslav people in the wake of the Nazi invasion and the Quisling rule and that of the young heroine, Milica, within the 1942 film text
4. The power of film (art), no matter how silly or trivial, to reflect the desire of a people to transcend (escape) crushing social reality
5. The political implications behind a seemingly unpolitical work of art or entertainment (at one point during the documentary footage of Aleksic's stunts, Makavejev alternates songs of praise written for/about Aleksic—themselves a parody of hero songs in a pop vein—and the Communist Internationale as well as a Soviet hymn, "Wide Is My Native Land")
6. The questionable self-promotional tactics used by those of whatever political ideology, which can be seen as no more sophisticated than Aleksic's more naive and therefore acceptable and honest self-absorption

For those unaware of Yugoslav history and culture, Aleksic appears as a self-parody of a kind of Balkan Charles Atlas crossed with a ham Hollywood actor, yet his irrepressible energy and optimism are contagious. For Yugoslavs the semiotics, the reading of the film's images, is more complex. For in the spirit of the traditional Marko outlaw mentality, Aleksic embodies the innocence, strengths, illusions, and weaknesses of the Yugoslavs (especially the Serbs) themselves. Makavejev's cross-cutting between history and film forces us all to see this parody in its sociopolitical-historical context as well. And the common realization that the arts in central Europe and the Balkans have become metaphorical and allegorical out of a need to transcend shades of censorship imposed by socialist/communist regimes prompts us to go even further (although clearly Yugoslavia had the most censorship-free culture of these socialist nations).

Innocence Unprotected was released in 1968 at the height of the Yugoslav cultural renaissance that was just as extensive if not more so than the more publicized cultural boom in Czechoslovakia during the same years. By that time Makavejev had already made an international name for himself with his first two features. But *Innocence* is an even more significant film than many realized at the time. In that all important year, 1968, this film by a leading practitioner of the Black Cinema group was a glance backward to the origins of Serbian cinema, a critique of the political and artistic naïveté of those origins as reflected in Aleksic's film, and a comment on the ongoing uneasy relationship between art and ideology. Furthermore, it is Bakhtin who helps us appreciate yet another level—that of festivity and celebration—that such an ironic sense of parody embodies.

In this sense parody embraces the tradition it has spoofed. An ongoing dialogue with the artistic and political/historical tradition has been established. It is this dynamic interaction with a tradition that Bakhtin describes as "the dialogic imagination." Carnival laughter becomes a metatext extending the tradition of Aleksic's original text in new ways. Makavejev, after all, calls his film by the same title as Aleksic's film rather than, let's say, *Innocence Revisited*. If Aleksic is a naive folk hero/fool, Makavejev in his own way is also an ambiguous folk artist, but one who must undo the constrictions of various forms of "logic" in order to become naive again. As in the sanctioned freedom of carnival, Makavejev parodies but does not destroy the object of laughter. Thus, the Yugoslav New Wave builds on a carnivalesque spirit of irreverence, naïveté, and energy, with one important difference: as contemporary artists aware of international politics and art, these filmmakers are self-conscious about the innocence around them. Innocence, like anything else viewed through carnivalesque laughter, becomes both a positive and a negative characteristic.

On a political/ideological level, "innocence" is a double-edged attribute. On the one hand, there is the innocence of the people duped by the politicians, which is often not innocence at all but a lack of courage to speak out. On the other hand, there is the simpleminded political innocence practiced by tyrants/fascists who are self-absorbed and unaware of the subtleties of any complex reality. It is on this last political level that Makavejev's films would have been seen not only as a playful parody with serious implications concerning the occupation but also, by extension, of the more recent Yugoslav political reality. The use of Russian hymns as Aleksic performs his feats of derring-do could not help but imply Joseph Stalin, for instance.

Indeed, the echoes reach out to Marshal Tito himself. Nowhere is such a connection directly made. But simply because of the way in which Makavejev forces us to constantly contrast and compare, critique and celebrate the world of film and of politics, the possibility is there. Those in the Yugoslav audience were aware that Tito was very much a self-made man, and a fine showman at that. As a "strongman," Tito, like Aleksic, was made up of many of the contradictions that a peasant "innocence" bestowed upon him. He was a savior, a lover, and an outlaw (as a communist in the 1930s, he was constantly hiding and running from royalist officials and laws). But obviously even for those in the audience who connect Aleksic with Tito, that leap of association remains within the confines of carnivalesque parody rather than as a direct political critique.

Finally, let me suggest the exhilarating effect on the audience of Makavejev's carnivalesque narrative collages. His seemingly random dialectical cutting appears seems to be a form of spontaneous and whimsical tomfoolery. Such ease deceives. Like the best work in the tradition of parody, *Innocence* is actually carefully and intricately orchestrated and calculated. But the impression is of an almost total sense of freedom seldom seen on the screen anywhere.

Makavejev calls war, repression (political and sexual), and all forms of fascism into question. But he is too subtle and, yes, carnivalesque a director to end his film with, for instance, the "logical" upbeat choice of footage from the liberation of Belgrade at the end of World War II. Instead, we are treated to yet another surprise: Aleksic's film triumphs over a Quisling newsreel. Some of the documentary sequences used are from the "official," compromised newsreels of the time, and so on yet another level of parody, Makavejev proves that time and the liberation of Yugoslavia have not been kind to the orchestrated scenes of hyped-up victories for the Nazis and happy, productive, pro-Nazi Yugoslav factory workers and peasants.

Toward the end of Makavejev's film we see newsreel footage of the funeral of a Quisling official intercut between the wedding celebration of Aleksic and Milica. The funeral is inserted between the dancing of the most popular traditional of all Yugoslav dances, the kolo (circle dance), and shots of the wedding feast in which one girl's dress is colorized by hand to match the blues and whites of the Yugoslav flag. The funeral is, of course, a foreshadowing of the death of the occupation: the official buried was murdered by a partisan. In a significant manner, Makavejev's film holds true to the carnivalesque pattern of parody in "The Wedding of Marko Kraljevic." The traditional and romantic rituals of the marriage ceremony are both celebrated and disrupted by the murder of a threatening force. The overall tone of both poem and film, however, remains one of joyful exuberance.

For better or for worse, individual freedom is championed throughout *Innocence Unprotected*. Like the Balkans themselves, Makavejev emerges as a complicated and curious combination. In his work we can trace Marxist influences (the dialectical structuring of his film owes much to Sergei

Eisenstein and Vertov), Wilhelm Reich's emphasis on personal/sexual liberation, and, as I have begun to document, a rich Serbian tradition as exemplified in the outlaw Marko. All of these forces find a twin focus in carnival parody. But after such knowledge—the destructive power of the occupation and of time—what salvation? The answer is given in carnival laughter. Laughter of the people, by the people, and for the people as individuals emerges as a form of salvation.

As metatext, parody seldom remains pure. The tendency, as in *Don Quixote,* is to spill into something else, and that something else in Miguel de Cervantes and in Makavejev is a bittersweet sympathy for the central character. It is Makavejev's remarkable accomplishment that having celebrated and critiqued so much on so many levels, he is able to leave us with emotion for Aleksic. The contemporary interviews reveal an aging man who is still able to smash boards on his head and bend iron with his teeth. But as the camera pulls back in the closing minutes, we see he is standing on crutches: a sudden admission that he has not only aged but that one of his stunts backfired.

Strongman and clown, Aleksic is nevertheless human. As he hobbles away awkwardly, Makavejev ultimately leaves us beyond comedy itself. Death is the metatext of metatexts and the last, dark laugh. But the joyful laughter that has gone before guarantees we will not take this quiet ending as sentimental. Makavejev shows us that innocence can be protected through knowing laughter.

Holiday Gone Wrong:
Carnivalesque Sacrifice

Movies are always subversive activities.
Makavejev (71)

Even though Bakhtin's theories of carnival have begun to influence a number of disciplines, a critical perspective has nevertheless developed to refine and critique his works. Writing of carnival under difficult circumstances during Stalin's reign, Bakhtin understandably allowed his exuberance for an idealized folk expression of freedom to occasionally outstrip his critical reasoning on the subject. Thus, he has not adequately accounted for gender (read: women) within carnival or for the darker implications of the violence unleashed by carnival, although he often emphasizes that destruction is part of the process of "becoming" (see Le Roy Ladurie).

The greatest challenge to an exuberant theory of carnivalesque laughter has come from René Girard in his studies of violence. Girard views carnival as a festival that is not complete in and of itself, as Bakhtin might suggest. Rather, Girard holds, "the fundamental purpose of the festival is to set the stage for a sacrificial act that marks at once the climax and the termination of the festivities" (1977, 119).

Carnival necessarily leads to a violent sacrifice. In the Christian tradition, the main period of carnival—the weeks before Lent—leads to Christ's "sacrifice" for his believers and to his subsequent victory over death through the resurrection.

Such is Girard's observation. Violence exists within all cultures and must find an outlet either in ritualized sacrifice or in the far more dangerous venue of spontaneous outburst. The breakdown of carnival traditions in the twentieth century, therefore, is part of a threatening pattern of decadence that has developed. According to Girard, "The disintegration of myths and rituals, and indeed of religious thought in general, leads not to genuine demythologizing, but to the outbreak of a new sacrificial crisis" (1977, 125). In analyzing Euripides' powerful final drama, *The Bacchae,* Girard explains that the destruction of ritualized patterns of handling violence leads to a state of dangerous disorientation called "holiday-gone-wrong."[2]

W.R.: Mysteries of the Organism presents a carnival-gone-wrong that begins as a "personal response" to Wilhelm Reich and his theory of orgasm and ends in the sacrifice of the heroine of the film (Yugoslav actress Milena Dravic). Through Girard's emphasis on the role of violence in festivity, we can more clearly understand the workings of Makavejev's final Yugoslav film.

The film remains his most noted and controversial work. Although not officially banned in Yugoslavia, it was not distributed there until 1986. As a psychology major in college before becoming a filmmaker, Makavejev has explained that he was deeply influenced by the writings of Wilhelm Reich, especially his *Dialectical Materialism and Psychoanalysis.* And certainly *W.R.* is a tribute to Reich's theories of the connections between sociopolitical repression and the thwarting of human sexual/personal potential. In short, Reich dreamed of a liberated world in which every day would mirror the freedom Bakhtin describes as carnivalesque. From such a perspective, Makavejev puts us in a holiday spirit from the opening frame as he flashes on the screen the words "ENJOY. FEEL. LAUGH." Yet as Bakhtin notes, carnival laughter is at heart ambiguous as well as festive, and a film that is a homage to Reich also becomes a critique that has an unsettling, darker side.

With *W.R.,* Makavejev takes his carnivalesque collage method of filmmaking even further than in *Innocence Unprotected* and projects beyond Yugoslavia to a global stage bounded by the influence of the super powers: the USSR and the United States. *W.R.* interweaves the following texts, all playing off each other simultaneously:

Milena Dravic in Makavejev's W.R.: Mysteries of the Organism *(1971)*

1. Makavejev's "contemporary" (1969–1971) documentary of Wilhelm Reich's home in Maine with coverage of his American life, including his trial, imprisonment, censorship, and death, as well as a documentation of ongoing orgone therapy being conducted by his disciples

2. Clips from a 1950s patriotic and patriarchal Soviet film praising Stalin

3. Makavejev's footage of various expressions of late 1960s culture in New York, including comic/parodic street theater performances by Tuli Kupferberg, founder of the Revolting Theater, wandering around Manhattan in battle gear with a semiautomatic singing "Kill for Peace" and scenes with transsexual Jackie Curtis, sculptor Nancy Godfrey, and the editor of *Screw* magazine, Jim Buckley

4. Captured Nazi documentaries of "medical experiments" carried out on victims by Nazi doctors

5. A fictional romance following Milena Dravic as she proclaims sexual freedom and women's rights under Marxism and communism and proceeds to fall in love with a champion Soviet ice skater visiting Belgrade, only to be decapitated by him with an ice skate after they have made love

The sound track provides a wider counterpoint than that of *Innocence Unprotected* as Soviet hymns play off images of couples screwing and as Hawaiian versions of German tunes are wedded to images of Stalin (played by a Soviet actor) addressing the masses.

Makavejev's playful but serious line about the mouse who wants to fuck a cow clearly captures what the film explores. Clearly Makavejev, like Reich, calls out for unbridled pleasure in life: the fourth scene of the film has couples screwing happily refracted in kaleidoscopic multiplication as a female voice-over asks us to "Fuck freely, Comrade. . . . Feel free to tremble and cry!"

But what Makavejev shows is that such an ideal state of sexual carnival is undercut by various elephants who become mice through their misuse of power. The harshness of Soviet communism, German Naziism, and American postcapitalism are all exposed as falling far short of a state of personal liberation. Even further, Reich appears as both a victim of a form of puritanical backlash in the United States (persecution/imprisonment/censorship) and a prophet whose theories are either misappropriated by his followers or may themselves work against the liberation they propose. Again, Makavejev's collage montages defy simplistic evaluation. Yet the cross-cutting between Nazi shots of patients being electrocuted and writhing in unspeakable spasms of pain and shots of patients at Reich's orgasm center writhing in "pleasure," but as a group in a clinic rather than as individuals involved in sex with partners in private, call both uses and abuses of power into question.

The violence that is unleashed in *W.R.* is clearly directed toward women, or, rather, women as represented by Milena. The extreme patriarchy and machismo that Makavejev sees "ruling" the world are hilariously displayed in one memorable sequence of cuts as the romance between Milena and the Soviet skater (named Vladimir Ilich, after Lenin) begins. The sequence appears in the last third of the film, long after we have explored Reich's theories and life. Milena has invited Vladimir home but has hidden him in the closet when her attempted seduction of the Virtuous Soviet People's Artist is interrupted. The shots that follow are:

> Milena lets Vladimir out of her closet (in Belgrade).
>
> "Stalin," played by a Soviet actor, appears (black and white), as if carved from marble, smiling above the masses in Red Square in the Soviet film Makavejev "quotes" from.
>
> A huge plaster-of-paris penis is being molded on top of *Screw* magazine editor Jim Buckley's hard-on as sculptor Nancy Godfrey tenderly shapes her phallus-in-progress.
>
> Stalin, again in the Soviet film, speaks of the benefits his reign is bringing to the Soviet people.
>
> A Nazi-run insane asylum appears, with the camera focusing on one pathetic victim.
>
> Tuli Kupferberg in full battle gear in Manhattan is jerking off his rifle with glee before puzzled businessmen as a bright, fast-paced Yugoslav folksong plays on the sound track.
>
> In winter along the Danube in Belgrade, Milena kisses Vladimir and takes him by surprise. They embrace. His innocent reaction is to say, "The air is as fresh as music."
>
> Stalin is standing in the same position in which we last saw Vladimir, thereby suggesting that it is Stalin who is peering at Milena.

I've never seen this sequence without the audience bursting into laughter. The incongruity of the images makes each cut a joke or gag and often both combined. But laughter, while liberating, is also purposeful in Makavejev—hence his belief that movies are subversive and that real movies do something "quite deep."

There is no need to apply a rigid reductive frame to a reading of these images, for it becomes obvious that Makavejev is implying that international politics is imposed on personal relationships and that such politics (Stalin, communism, and capitalistic pornography in the guise of the sexual revolution) is male generated. Two levels of carnival triumph emerge, even within this minisegment, however. First, Nancy Godfrey's laughable penis statues, created by a woman, represent their subject-as-object out of all proportion and thus satirize their supposed "power." Second, Yugoslav folk music signifies a healthy, irreverent expression of pleasure.

The sequence has its darker foreshadowing, however. Clearly Milena is hemmed in by Stalinism and by American pornography. Existing "in between," like Yugoslavia itself, she is in danger as a woman and as a non-Soviet/American. Add to this her liberated behavior in preaching free love to the masses and making advances on a puritanical Soviet artist, and her fate is sealed.

A holiday-gone-wrong necessarily results. There will be no carnival in the traditional sense. The misuse of power, as Reich and Girard suggest, tends to lead to violence. When Milena and Vladimir finally have an orgasm, he decapitates her with his skate. With no rituals, no outlets for his pent-up violence, Milena becomes the sacrifice. In the morgue, her head is placed on the table by the medical inspectors, who state that their examination suggests she had sex four or five times before death.

But once the doctors depart, Milena's head speaks to us (the speaking severed head is also a part of the Serbian oral epic poetry tradition) calmly, clearly. She states that he was unable to bear their love, their sexual experience, and she concludes that he was a "genuine Red fascist." (*The Loves of a Switchboard Operator* similarly treats a liberated woman murdered by her lover.)

What Makavejev slyly implies in these early films is both the desirability of the carnivalesque and yet the violence that such a liberation must necessarily unleash as the twentieth century has come to be constructed. Neither American capitalism nor Soviet communism, the dominant world ideologies, appears adequate to handle a truly liberated (female) perspective. As close as Makavejev can come to carnival is via cinema, a medium that is limited to evoking such a spirit on celluloid rather than creating the real thing in the streets, in which, as Bakhtin notes, there are no observers, only participants (1968, 7).

But *W.R.* is still not finished. Makavejev cuts to a misty, gray morning by the Danube as the distressed Vladimir wanders with Milena's blood on his hands past beggars gathered around a winter fire. He sings a moving Soviet gypsy song with the chorus, "Grant to each one, one little thing, and remember me as well!" The hope for change is there. Although we end on a somber note, it is not impossible, of course, that the Red fascist may learn through sex, love, laughter, and . . . sacrificial violence. A holiday-gone-wrong may yet lead to carnival laughter. At least Makavejev has kept the discourse open. His dialectics points toward the need for what Leon Trotsky calls "perpetual revolution."

And then two closing shots: Milena's severed head smiles at us, directly, without regrets, without blame or sorrow. And her smile fades, like the Cheshire Cat's, into an almost identical smile on the face of Wilhelm Reich. Makavejev's personal response is now complete. Is the smile one of irony or of innocent pleasure?

Bakhtin and Girard suggest that in the festive guise of carnival, the two are inseparable and ambiguous. Yet finally, in Makavejev's hands, even a holiday-gone-wrong can be triumphed over on film as the joyful Yugoslav folk music on the sound track acts as counterpoint to the image of Milena's severed head. Such counterpoint forces the audience to experience wildly divergent emotions simultaneously and to ponder the ambiguity of these clashes. The mysteries of the organisms endure.

"The freedom of risk is paid in blood and enjoyment of life, which is nothing but a healthy nonsense," says Makavejev (75). The ambiguity of Makavejev's ending is itself in tune with the unfinalizedness of carnival. In every sense.

Notes

1. This chapter has grown out of a speech presented at the Society for Cinema Studies conference in New Orleans, April 1986, entitled "Carnivalesque Parody: Bakhtin and Makavejev Considered." Two later forms of that original work are "Carnivalesque Parody: Bakhtin and Makavejev Considered," *Exquisite Corpse* 5, nos. 6–8 (June–August 1987): 14–15, and "Bakhtin, Carnival Triumph and Cinema: Bruno Barreto's *Dona Flor and Her Two Husbands* and Dusan Makavejev's *Innocence Unprotected,*" *Quarterly Review of Film Studies* 12, nos. 1–2 (1990): 49–62.

2. In discussing *The Bacchae*, Girard points to the danger of carnival, especially of a holiday-gone-wrong, by describing Dionysus not as the god of wine or comedy or carnivalesque laughter but rather as "the god of decisive mob action. . . . The god has no proper being outside the realm of violence" (1977, 133).

References and Additional Reading

Armes, Roy. 1976. "Dusan Makavejev: Collage and Complication." In Armes, *The Ambiguous Image: Narrative Style in European Cinema*, pp. 198–207. Bloomington: Indiana University Press.

Bakhtin, Mikhail. 1968. *Rabelais and His World*, trans. Helene Iswolsky. Cambridge, Mass.: MIT Press.

———. 1981. *The Dialogic Imagination*, trans. Caryl Emerson and Michael Holquist. Austin: University of Texas Press.

———. 1984. *Problems of Dostoevsky's Poetics*, ed. and trans. Caryl Emerson. Minneapolis: University of Minnesota Press.

Baxandall, Lee. 1983. "Toward an East European Cinemarxism?" *Politics, Art and Commitment in the East European Cinema*, ed. David W. Paul, pp. 73–99. New York: St. Martin's Press.

Braendlin, Bonnie. 1986, January. "Deconstruction of the Gaze in *Montenegro.*" Paper delivered at the Florida State University Conference on Film and Literature, Tallahassee.

Cavell, Stanley. 1981. *Pursuits of Happiness: The Hollywood Comedy of Remarriage*. Cambridge, Mass.: Harvard University Press.

Coover, Robert. 1988. "He Thinks the Way We Dream" (Review of Milorad Pavic's *Dictionary of the Khazars*). *New York Times Book Review*, November 20, pp. 15–16, 35.

Eagle, Herbert. 1983. "Yugoslav Marxist Humanism and the Films of Dusan Makavejev." *Politics, Art and Commitment in the East European Cinema,* ed. David W. Paul, pp. 131–148. New York: St. Martin's Press.

Girard, René. 1977. *Violence and the Sacred,* trans. Patrick Gregory. Baltimore: Johns Hopkins University Press.

———. 1986. *The Scapegoat,* trans. Yvonne Freccero. Baltimore: Johns Hopkins University Press.

Horton, Andrew. 1987. "Carnivalesque Parody: Bakhtin and Makavejev Considered." *Exquisite Corpse* 5, nos. 6–8 (June–August): 14–15.

Koljevic, Svetozar. 1980. *The Epic in the Making.* Oxford: Clarendon Press.

Ladurie, Emmanuel Le Roy. 1981. *Carnival in Romans.* New York: Penguin.

Makavejev, Dusan. 1980. "Nikola Tesla Radiated Blue Light." *Studies in Visual Communication* 6, no. 3 (Fall): 69–75.

Morson, Gary Saul, ed. 1986. *Bakhtin: Essays and Dialogues on His Work.* Chicago: University of Chicago Press.

Oumano, Ellen. 1985. *Film Forum.* New York: St. Martin's Press.

Pavic, Milorad. 1988. *Dictionary of the Khazars: A Lexicon Novel in 100,000 Words.* New York: Knopf.

Reich, Wilhelm. 1975. *Early Writings,* trans. Philip Schmitz. New York: Farrar and Straus.

Rose, Margaret A. 1979. *Parody // Meta-Fiction: An Analysis of Parody as a Critical Mirror to the Writing and Reception of Fiction.* London: Croom Helm.

Selected Bibliography and Works Cited

Clearly a complete bibliography of comedy would embrace several volumes. What follows is meant to be suggestive of works that have been of particular value in discussing comedy in many mediums, including works on individual comic filmmakers and specialized topics. The reader is also referred to the works cited at the end of each chapter.

Agee, James. n.d. "Comedy's Greatest Era." *Agee on Film,* vol. 1, pp. 1–21. Boston: Beacon Press.

Bakhtin, Mikhail. 1968. *Rabelais and His World,* trans. Helene Iswolsky. Cambridge, Mass.: MIT Press.

Barber, C. L. 1959. *Shakespeare's Festive Comedies*. Princeton: Princeton University Press.

Bazin, André. 1982. *The Cinema of Cruelty,* trans. Saline D'Estrec. New York: Seaver Books.

Bermel, Albert. 1982. *Farce: From Aristophanes to Woody Allen*. New York: Simon and Schuster.

Brunette, Peter, and David Wills. 1989. *Screen/Play: Derrida and Film Theory*. Princeton: Princeton University Press.

Byrge, Duane, and Robert Milton Miller. 1989. *A Critical Study of the Screwball Comedy Film*. Ann Arbor, Mich.: UMI Research Press.

Capra, Frank. 1977. *The Name Above the Title*. New York: Macmillan.

Chambers, E. K. 1903. *The Medieval Stage,* 2 vols. Oxford: Clarendon Press.

Chaplin, Charles. 1964. *My Autobiography*. New York: Simon and Schuster.

Chapman, Anthony J., and Hugh C. Foot, eds. 1977. *It's a Funny Thing, Humour*. Oxford: Pergamon Press.

Clair, René. 1953. *Reflections on the Cinema*. London: William Kimber.

Coen, Joel, and Ethan Coen. 1988. *Raising Arizona: The Screenplay*. New York: St. Martin's Press.

Cook, Albert. 1949. *The Dark Voyage and the Golden Mean: A Philosophy of Comedy*. Cambridge, Mass.: Harvard University Press.

Cook, Jim. 1982. "Narrative, Comedy, Character and Performance." *Television Sitcom*. London: British Film Institute.

Corrigan, Robert W., ed. 1971. *Comedy: A Critical Anthology*. Boston: Houghton Mifflin.

Culler, Jonathan. 1982. *On Deconstruction*. Ithaca, N.Y.: Cornell University Press.

Derrida, Jacques. 1981. *Positions,* trans. Alan Bass. Chicago: University of Chicago Press.

Doane, Mary Ann, Patricia Mellencamp, and Linda Williams, eds. 1984. *Revision: Essays in Feminist Film Criticism*. Los Angeles: American Film Institute.

Durgnat, Raymond. 1970. *The Crazy Mirror: Hollywood Comedy and the American Image*. New York: Horizon Press.

Everson, William K. 1967. *The Films of Laurel and Hardy*. Secaucus, N.J.: Citadel Press.

Franklin, Joe. 1979. *Encyclopedia of Comedians*. Secaucus, N.J.: Citadel Press.

Freud, Sigmund. 1938. *Jokes and Their Relationship to the Unconscious,* trans. A. A. Brill. New York: Random House.

Frye, Northrop. 1968. *Anatomy of Criticism*. New York: Atheneum.

Griffiths, Trevor. 1976. *Comedians*. London: Faber.

Gurewitch, Morton. 1975. *Comedy: The Irrational Vision*. Ithaca, N.Y.: Cornell University Press.

Handleman, Don, and Bruce Kapferer. 1977. "Forms of Joking Activity: A Comparative Approach." *American Anthropologist* 74: 484–517.

Harrison, Jane Ellen. 1963. *Themis: A Study of the Social Origins of Greek Religion,* 2nd ed. London: Merlin Press.

Hartman, Geoffrey H. 1981. *Saving the Text: Literature-Derrida-Philosophy*. Baltimore: Johns Hopkins University Press.

Harvey, James. 1987. *Romantic Comedy in Hollywood from Lubitsch to Sturges*. New York: Knopf.

Haskins, James. 1984. *Richard Pryor, A Man and His Madness*. New York: Beaufort Books.

Horton, Andrew. 1986. "From Satire to Surrealism in Yugoslav Film Comedy." *East European Quarterly* 20, no. 1 (Spring): 91–99.

Huizinga, Johan. 1955. *Homo Ludens: A Study of the Play Element in Culture*. Boston: Beacon Press.

Janco, Richard. 1984. *Aristotle on Comedy*. Berkeley: University of California Press.

Josefsberg, Milt. 1987. *Comedy Writing for Television & Hollywood*. New York: Harper & Row.

Kael, Pauline. 1974. "Raising Kane." *The Citizen Kane Book*. New York: Bantam.

Keaton, Buster. 1967. *My Wonderful World of Slapstick*. London: Allen & Unwin.

Kerr, Walter. 1967. *Tragedy and Comedy*. New York: Simon and Schuster.

————. 1975. *The Silent Clowns*. New York: Knopf.

Koestler, Arthur. 1949. *Insight and Outlook*. Lincoln: University of Nebraska Press.

Kral, Piotr. 1984. *Le burlesque, ou moral de la tarte à la creme*. Paris: Stock.

Ladurie, Emmanuel Le Roy. 1981. *Carnival in Romans: A People's Uprising at Romans, 1579–80*, trans. Mary Feeney. New York: Penguin.

Lang, Candace D. 1987. *Irony/Humor: Critical Paradigms*. Baltimore: Johns Hopkins University Press.

Levin, Harry. 1987. *Playboys + Killjoys: An Essay in the Theory of Comedy*. New York: Oxford University Press.

Lewis, Jerry. 1982. *Jerry Lewis in Person*. New York: Atheneum.

McBride, Joseph. 1982. *Hawks on Hawks*. Berkeley: University of California Press.

McFadden, George. 1982. *Discovering the Comic*. Princeton: Princeton University Press.

McLeish, Kenneth. 1980. *The Theatre of Aristophanes*. New York: Taplinger.

Maland, Charles J. 1977. *American Visions: The Films of Chaplin, Ford, Capra, and Welles*. New York: Arno Press.

————. 1989. *Chaplin and American Culture: The Evolution of a Star Image*. Princeton: Princeton University Press.

Maltin, Leonard. 1978. *The Great Movie Comedians: From Charlie Chaplin to Woody Allen*. New York: Crown.

Marc, David. 1989. *Comic Visions: Television Comedy and American Culture*. Boston: Unwin Hyman.

Mars, François. 1964. *Le gag*. Paris: Editions du Cerf.

Martin, Linda, and Kerry Segrave. 1986. *Women in Comedy*. Secaucus, N.J.: Citadel Press.

Mast, Gerald. 1979. *The Comic Mind: Comedy and the Movies*, 2nd ed. Chicago: University of Chicago Press.

Maurer, John Howard. 1985. *Curly: An Illustrated Biography of a Superstooge*. Secaucus, N.J.: Citadel Press.

Merchant, Moelwyn. 1972. *Comedy: The Critical Idiom*. London: Methuen.

Metz, Christian. 1974. *Film Language: A Semiotics of the Cinema*. New York: Oxford University Press.

Mikhail, E. H. 1972. *Comedy and Tragedy: A Bibliography of Critical Studies*. Troy, N.Y.: Whitson.

Mulkay, Michael. 1988. *On Humor*. Oxford: Basil Blackwell.

Musser, Charles. 1988. "Work, Ideology and Chaplin's Tramp." *Radical History Review*, no. 41 (April): 37–66.

Nathan, David. 1971. *The Laughmakers: A Quest for Comedy*. London: Peter Owen.

Olson, Elder. 1968. *The Theory of Comedy*. Bloomington: Indiana University Press.

Palmer, Jerry. 1988. *The Logic of the Absurd: On Film and Television Comedy*. London: British Film Institute.

Paul, William. 1983. *Ernst Lubitsch's American Comedy*. New York: Columbia University Press.

Reiner, Carl. 1958. *Enter Laughing*. New York: Simon and Schuster.

Robinson, David. 1985. *Chaplin*. London: Collins.

Rosen, Philip, ed. 1986. *Narrative, Apparatus, Ideology*. New York: Columbia University Press.

Schaeffer, Neil. 1981. *The Art of Laughter*. New York: Columbia University Press.

Schultz, C. E. 1976. *Political Humor*. Cranbury, N.J.: Fairleigh Dickinson University Press.

Sennett, Mack. 1954. *King of Comedy*. Garden City, N.Y.: Doubleday.

Swabey, Marie Collins. 1961. *Comic Laughter: A Philosophical Essay*. New Haven: Yale University Press.

Sypher, Wylie, ed. 1956. *Comedy*. Garden City, N.Y.: Doubleday.

Todorov, Tzvetan. 1984. *Mikhail Bakhtin: The Dialogical Principle*, trans. Wlad Godzich. Minneapolis: University of Minnesota Press.

Torrance, Richard. 1978. *The Comic Hero*. Cambridge, Mass.: Harvard University Press.

Truffaut, François. 1967. *Hitchcock*. New York: Simon and Schuster.

Turner, Victor. 1982. *From Ritual to Theatre: The Human Seriousness of Play*. New York: Performing Arts Journal Publications.

Unterbrink, Mary. 1987. *Funny Women: American Comediennes, 1860–1985*. Jefferson, N.C.: McFarland.

Walker, Nancy. 1988. *"A Very Serious Thing": Women's Humor in American Culture*. Minneapolis: University of Minnesota Press.

Wead, George. 1976. *Buster Keaton and the Dynamics of Visual Wit*. New York: Arno Press.

Weales, Gerald. 1985. *Canned Goods as Caviar: American Film Comedy of the 1930's*. Chicago: University of Chicago Press.

Wilk, Max. 1976. *The Golden Age of Television Comedy*. New York: Delacorte.

Wilson, C. P. 1979. *Jokes: Form, Content, Use and Function*. London: Academic Press.

Wittgenstein, Ludwig. 1968. *Philosophical Investigations*. Oxford: Basil Blackwell.

Ziv, A. 1987. *National Styles in Humor*. Westport, Conn.: Greenwood Press.

Contributors

Peter Brunette is a professor of English and Film Studies at George Mason University. He is the author of *Roberto Rossellini* (Oxford University Press, 1987) and, with David Wills, *Screen/play: Derrida and Film Theory* (Princeton University Press, 1989).

Scott Bukatman teaches history and theory at the School of Visual Arts in New York City and was curator of "Jerry Lewis: A Film and Television Retrospective" at the American Museum of the Moving Image in November 1988.

Noël Carroll is an associate professor of philosophy and associate professor of theater at Cornell University. His books include *Philosophical Problems of Classical Film Theory, Mystifying Movies: Fads and Fallacies of Contemporary Film Theory,* and *Paradoxes of the Heart: The Philosophy of Horror*.

Charles Eidsvik is an associate professor of drama and cinema at the University of Georgia in Athens and an independent filmmaker. He has contributed many articles to film journals and wrote *Cineliteracy: Film Among the Arts*.

Lucy Fischer teaches film studies in the English Department at the University of Pittsburgh. Her latest book is *Shot/Countershot: Film Tradition and Women's Cinema* (Princeton University Press, 1989).

Brian Henderson teaches film studies and is acting chair of the Media Studies Department at the State University of New York at Buffalo. He wrote *A Critique of Film Theory* (Dutton, 1980) and is the editor of *Five Screenplays by Preston Sturges* (University of California Press, 1986) and a forthcoming follow-up collection of four more Sturges screenplays. He is a board member of *Film Quarterly*.

Andrew Horton is a professor of film and literature at Loyola University (New Orleans). He has recently completed *The Zero Hour: Glasnost and Soviet Cinema in Translation* with Soviet critic Michael Brashinsky (Princeton University Press, 1991). His latest feature film (screenplay) is *The Dark Side of the Sun* (1990).

Peter Lehman, professor in the Department of Media Arts at the University of Arizona, is editor of *Close Viewings: An Anthology of New Film Criticism* (Florida State University Press, 1990) and has completed a book on sexuality and the representation of the male body. He co-authored with William Luhr *Authorship and Narrative in the Cinema* (Putnam, 1977), *Blake Edwards* (Ohio University Press, 1981), and *Returning to the Scene: Blake Edwards, Volume 2* (Ohio University Press, 1989).

Stephen Mamber teaches in the Critical Studies Program of the Department of Film and Television at the University of California at Los Angeles.

William Paul is the author of *Ernst Lubitsch's American Comedy* (Columbia University Press, 1983), *Laughing Screaming,* a book about gross-out comedy and horror films, and "It Came from Within the Frame: Hollywood and 3-D" (unpublished). He teaches film at the University of Michigan.

Ruth Perlmutter teaches cinema studies at the University of the Arts (formerly Philadelphia College of Art) and Temple University (Tyler School of Art). She has written widely on film-related topics in such journals as *Wide Angle, Film Quarterly, The Georgia Review, Quarterly Review of Film Studies, Journal of Modern Literature,* and *American Studies.*

Dana Polan teaches film and English at the University of Pittsburgh, edits *Cinema Journal,* and is the author of *Power and Paranoia: History, Narrative, and the American Cinema, 1940–1950* (Columbia University Press, 1986).

Index

247

Text: 10/12 Times Roman
Display: Helvetica, Helvetica Light, Helvetica Bold
Compositor: Interactive Composition Corporation
Printer: BookCrafters
Binder: BookCrafters